RED CREW

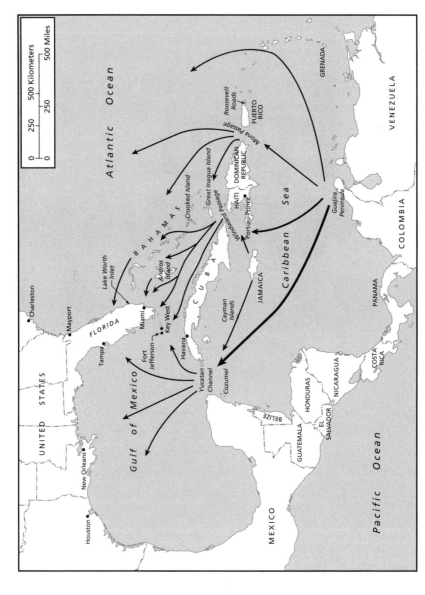

Major maritime drug smuggling routes of the early 1980s

RED CREW

Fighting the War on Drugs with Reagan's Coast Guard

JIM HOWE

Naval Institute Press
Annapolis, Maryland

This book has been brought to publication with the generous assistance of The John and Michele Welch Fund of the Ayco Corporation.

Naval Institute Press
291 Wood Road
Annapolis, MD 21402

Library of Congress Cataloging-in-Publication Data
Names: Howe, Jim, date, author.
Title: Red Crew : fighting the war on drugs with Reagan's coast guard / Jim Howe.
Description: Annapolis : Naval Institute Press, 2018. | Includes index.
Identifiers: LCCN 2017051751 (print) | LCCN 2018013926 (ebook) |
    ISBN 9781682473023 (ePDF) | ISBN 9781682473023 (epub) |
    ISBN 9781682473016 (hardback) | ISBN 9781682473023 (ebook)
Subjects: LCSH: Aeronautics in police work—United States. | Drug
    control—United States. | Smuggling—United States. | United States.
    Coast Guard. | BISAC: HISTORY / Military / Naval.
Classification: LCC HV8080 (ebook) | LCC HV8080 .H69 2018 (print) |
    DDC 363.28/4—dc23
LC record available at https://lccn.loc.gov/2017051751

Maps created by Chris Robinson.

To the late Chief Boatswain's Mate Charles "Chuck" Obenland,
U.S. Coast Guard (Ret.)—may he rest in peace—and to all the
sailors of Red Crew, for their service to our nation.

And to Robert Turner Howe,
a great sailor and an even greater father,
who left a better world in his wake.

Contents

Preface

I t's surprising there aren't more books about the United States Coast Guard. Daring rescues, stealthy patrols, heavy weather, life and death, tragedy and salvation—it's all there for the willing author to snare. There's a big market for action and adventure, and the Coast Guard delivers it in spades.

But that's not why this book came about. It was written as a Christmas present.

My dad was a graduate of Kings Point—the U.S. Merchant Marine Academy—and he sailed on board oil tankers until family called him home. He and Mom raised five kids, and our childhood was full of stories of his life at sea: the sweltering engine rooms, the quirky crews, the rough weather, the exotic ports of call. He had sailed from Buenos Aires to Rotterdam to Houston and all points in between. It often was monotonous duty, but there was high drama, too. One of his ships, loaded with jet fuel, lost propulsion and ran smack into a bridge, and another survived the deadly North Sea storm of 1953, in which dozens of vessels were lost.

Dad could tell a yarn, and his tales cast a spell. His stories were so real that we felt as though we had sailed along with him. And despite being a Naval Reservist, Dad held the Coast Guard in the highest esteem. He was a proud father when I swore an oath on June 27, 1977, a newly minted cadet at the U.S. Coast Guard Academy, Class of 1981. I, too, had chosen a life at sea.

Unlike my dad, however, I kept my sea service quiet. I had served on three cutters before my own five kids started to come along, and I did four more years afloat while they were young. For some reason I held tight to my earlier experiences and didn't share them with the children. It wasn't in my nature to talk too much about what happened in those early days.

But then one morning a switch flipped somewhere inside me, and suddenly I found myself yearning to tell the story as I'd lived it. I'd seen a lot, served with some of the finest crews ever to wear Coast Guard blue, and knew it was time to share that history with my family. So I decided to write of my adventures, self-publish a dozen copies, and hand them out as Christmas gifts. What you're reading began as a stocking-stuffer—the personal journal of a young Coast Guard officer long before he met the woman of his dreams and learned the truest joy, that of being a new father.

To my great pleasure, the manuscript came out better than expected, and the editorial team at the Naval Institute Press—Rick Russell, Paul Merzlak, and Glenn Griffith—agreed to put it in print. I am grateful for their faith and perseverance. Emily Bakely, the production editor, was an absolute pleasure to work with, and Art Pine, who copyedited this book, is a superb professional and a true gentleman. He has a golden touch and offered great improvements to the text.

I am indebted to John Welch, a Navy submariner-turned-corporate-chief-executive-officer, who provided support and encouragement—and showed that generosity can be a lifelong avocation. Jim Dolbow, Todd Hayward, Frank Matulewicz, Mike and Suzie Whatley, and Bill Travis are stalwart friends who pressed me, in their own unique ways, to tell this story. And a million thanks go to my wife and very best friend, Shira, our own five children, and my mom, Alice, for their enthusiasm, without which this project undoubtedly would have withered on the vine.

I wrote the book backwards. Instead of gathering facts and documents and photos and transcripts, I wrote it from scratch, depending on memory and a few dusty fitness reports from my active-duty days. It originally was intended for family reading, not really going into circulation, so why fret over accuracy? Then came the Naval Institute Press, with higher standards—which led to serious research and several rewrites to correct all the misremembered details and mangled facts.

Sincere thanks go to Scott Price, the U.S. Coast Guard historian, who opened his archival treasure chest in Washington for my research effort, and to Chris Siebenschuh and Petty Officer Justin Henderson at Coast Guard Headquarters for helping to track down the ship's logs for the cutters that occupy center stage in this story.

Longstanding friendships and social media helped me connect, or reconnect, with former shipmates to reap the benefit of their experiences. Jerry Lober, Jim Sartucci, Mike Cosenza, Kevin Quigley, Bill Hartsock, Chad Weatherby, Walt Goodrum, and Duane Riopelle generously shared their memories and kept the narrative honest.

Everything in the book happened pretty much as written. To be sure, there probably are some errors in description, and I've presented the dialogue as best as I can remember it. Most of the facts came from official ships' logs, but unfortunately some of the logs could not be found. In those instances, passages derive primarily from my memory, bolstered by situation reports, witness statements, news articles, and the like. Some details regarding intelligence matters and a defector incident have been modified or omitted. Pseudonyms were used for the names of suspects and those detained or arrested. I did make two editorial judgments: first, I deleted most of the salty language—after all, this was originally written for my kids—and second, I called on my imagination to provide the names of a few boats that I recalled having boarded but whose real names were lost to history. All errors are solely my own, and I apologize for any flubs and flaws you may encounter.

There really ought to be more books about the Coast Guard. Until then, I hope you enjoy this one.

Introduction

On Board USCGC *Shearwater*

December 31, 1983

I f we didn't act fast there'd be one hell of a collision. The tugboat *Gulf Express* was wallowing in churning seas, her bow thrashing wildly and her stern held down by a steel tow cable trailing below. From the pilothouse of our Coast Guard cutter, a quarter-mile away, we watched a stream of fifteen-foot waves pass under the tug's hull, sending her bow surging skyward over each crest, hovering briefly and then crashing down, bludgeoning the water, creating plumes of spray that filled the beam of our searchlight with a heavy white mist.

Gulf Express was a powerful oceangoing tug that had been hauling a barge from Houston toward the Chesapeake Bay. Just as she was passing south of the Florida Keys something had gone wrong, and now her engines and generators were dead, leaving no propulsion and only battery power. Sometimes these things happened at sea—just bad luck, probably from a tank of contaminated diesel or a clog in the fuel lines, and in calm weather the tug could have drifted until a salvage vessel arrived. But South Florida was in the grip of an unusually strong storm system that had been building all day and

1

was pounding the region with vicious southerly winds, steady at thirty knots and gusting to forty. The seas were steep, breaking, and relentless.

It was just before midnight. The scene was grim, menacing, with dark, churning rain clouds rushing by, low overhead, and a sliver of moon occasionally visible through breaks in the scud. Lurking behind the tug was the barge, a massive gray rectangle, heavily laden and riding low. Its topside fittings were only three feet above the water, and waves crashed over its broad, flat deck, creating amoebas of foam that meandered through the forest of piping. The barge was sitting perpendicular to the wind and seas, and its sluggish rolling motion was out of sync with the erratic thrusts of the lighter tug; they looked like two people dancing to different beats, one slow and measured, the other wild and frenetic.

Two hours earlier our own ship, the U.S. Coast Guard Cutter *Shearwater* (WSES 3), had been moored at Fort Jefferson in the Dry Tortugas at the westernmost tip of the Florida Keys, the crew enjoying a New Year's Eve romp and waiting out the storm. Then came the call from Coast Guard Group Key West: get under way at best speed. Render assistance. The tugboat and barge were adrift only twenty miles south of the Dry Tortugas reef, a pristine marine sanctuary, and there were no other ships nearby to help. For an hour *Shearwater* pounded through the seas at high speed, her thin aluminum hull shuddering and her crew members holding on to anything they could grab.

When *Shearwater* was four miles away, the master on *Gulf Express* called on a battery-powered radio, his voice calm and professional, but with a clipped sense of urgency. He said he had two big problems. First, the tug and her tow, set by the storm winds, were moving north at almost three knots and would run aground in the shallows by dawn. Second, and more urgent, the tug was drifting down on the barge. The 1,200-foot towing cable that connected them was looped underneath *Gulf Express*, and the two vessels were drawing closer, now only a football field apart. In another hour the wave action would slam them together.

But that wasn't the worst part. The two-hundred-foot barge was fully loaded—with propane. If the two vessels hit, there'd be torn metal, spilled cargo, probably a sinking, and possibly far worse. Metal grating on metal could create a lot of sparks, and that might set off a really big bang.

Our captain surveyed the scene, taking in the chaotic gyrations of the tug, the surging seas, and the fierce wind. He knew that *Shearwater's* sixteen-person crew offered the only hope for heading off a serious maritime calamity and would have to make the save in dangerous and unpredictable seas. Moreover, he knew his team was relatively new and untested. The crew had come together only eight months before and had never faced a challenge like this.

Shearwater was also new, only fourteen months in commission, one of three sister ships operating from Key West. She was a radical design, a 110-foot "surface effect" ship, or SES—a lightweight, high-speed catamaran—and had been pressed into service for the burgeoning war on drugs. The ship was designed for speed, not salvage, and the captain didn't really know whether she could stand up to a mission like this.

I was *Shearwater's* executive officer, second in command, and had three years of seagoing experience, most of it patrolling off New England on my previous ship, USCGC *Active* (WMEC 618), a rugged 210-footer out of New Castle, New Hampshire. We'd rescued a dozen disabled fishing boats on *Active*, and I'd learned the need for crisp teamwork, clear communications, and strict safety protocols. There were immense forces at play in such maneuvers, and one misstep could get someone killed.

Shearwater's crew had towed two vessels before, both of them small, with the operations carried out in mild weather. Here, in the middle of a nighttime storm, hooking a towline to a one-hundred-foot tug and her fully loaded barge would magnify the dangers a thousandfold. The cutter would have to sidle close to *Gulf Express* in order to pass the towing hawser, risking collision. If the line dipped too far into the water it could wrap around *Shearwater's* propellers, disabling the ship. Once rigged, the hawser would come under intense strain. It could snap without warning, almost certainly maiming or killing anyone hit by the recoil. And our crew would have to operate on *Shearwater's* exposed aft deck, slipping and sliding in the rain and spray as the cutter surged and heaved. In these conditions, a man overboard would be a nightmare.

The weather set the battlefield and time was the enemy. In the few minutes that we'd been on scene, the tug and barge had drifted another mile north toward the reef, and the two vessels had drawn closer together, now only two hundred feet apart. The master on *Gulf Express* radioed again, warning that she would be on top of the barge in forty minutes and asking if we could expedite, thank you very much.

On *Shearwater*'s aft deck, our boatswain's mates scrambled to prepare the towline, carefully laying out the hawser to make sure that it didn't snag when it was paid out, all five hundred feet arranged in neat fore-and-aft rows. One of the men cradled a line-throwing gun, which he would use to shoot a thin messenger line to *Gulf Express*, and next to him was a shipmate holding the backup, a coil of quarter-inch heaving line, ready to be thrown by hand if the messenger strayed off course. Our leading boatswain's mate looked up at the pilothouse and gave a thumbs-up. *Shearwater*'s team was in place, primed and ready. There was no time to spare.

The captain gave the order and the conning officer clutched in the engines. *Shearwater* plowed into the breaking waves, headed for a spot just ahead of *Gulf Express*' bow. The next few minutes would tell the tale. Either *Shearwater*'s crew would save the tug and barge from collision and grounding or there'd be a big mess to clean up, and possibly lives lost.

I stole a glance at the captain. His gaze was a laser, eyeing the distance to the tug. We were 150 yards away and closing fast, smashing through white-capped rollers. The captain's decisions would make the difference between success and failure, the burden solely his own, but in the shadows of the darkened bridge he looked calm and confident, even content.

Shearwater slowed to a stop just in front of *Gulf Express*, only fifty feet away, with our aft deck aligned with the tug's bow. The two vessels were surging and falling, the tug corkscrewing crazily, rising ten feet and falling fifteen, then rising again on an immense wave, the seas pounding our hull, spray everywhere, rivulets of foamy water coursing across the cutter's aft deck. Members of the six-person towing detail, almost blinded by the bright deck lights and the haze of salt in the air, crouched against the slashing wind and the spatters of rain, their hair matted, their uniforms soaked, and their bright orange life vests the only hope for survival if the unthinkable happened and one of them fell into the turbulent sea.

The captain pointed to me, and I picked up the microphone for the topside speakers, bellowing orders over the shriek of the wind: "Now, on deck—*pass the towline!*" The boatswain's mates jumped into action. The gunner pressed the line-throwing gun to his shoulder, its long barrel aimed just above the tug's surging bow, and squeezed the trigger. Show time. I looked back at the captain. *Damn*—he was holding back a grin.

Sea duty was 99 percent tedium, interspersed with rare, unscripted moments like this. The captain was in his element, and so was his team. In our few months together we'd had some thrills, chasing smugglers, discovering secret compartments, and steaming through uncharted shallows, and the crew had shown both talent and verve. But this was different. This was worst-case, a major rescue in cruel weather, with lives and property on the line.

For captain and crew, this was the kind of chaos that we worked for, trained for, and lived for—the reason we'd signed up to go to sea in the first place. For Coast Guard cuttermen, this was the heart of our world.

1

Plank-Owner Crew

Nine months earlier—March 1983

Shearwater sat at the Coast Guard pier in Key West, floating idly at the edge of a glassy harbor. The morning sun, cresting the horizon, cast a warm, amber glow. It was my first day on the job, and I'd arrived early, surveying the ship from the foot of the quay, two hundred feet away.

It was impossible not to stare. *Shearwater* was stunning, almost breathtaking—a standout among the other cutters. The product of a revolutionary "surface effect" design, *Shearwater* was built to ride on a cushion of air, to reduce friction and increase speed. Long and wide, the ship sported a one-of-a-kind paint scheme. Where other patrol boats had gleaming white hulls, hers was stealth black, with the words "Coast Guard" and the cutter's hull number, "WSES 3," straddling the red-and-blue stripes on her bow. And while most cutters' decks were painted dull gray, *Shearwater*'s were bright white, to reflect the sun and keep the interior of the aluminum hull cool. The white deck color flowed up onto a two-story superstructure, its bulkheads moist from morning dew. The sharp contrast—of brilliant white over obsidian black—made the ship look new and cutting-edge, solid and intimidating.

At 110 feet, *Shearwater* was bigger than anything else in the Coast Guard's patrol boat fleet. Most unusual was her broad beam—almost 40 feet across, just under three times that of a traditional 95-foot or 82-foot cutter. Sitting atop her catamaran hulls was an expansive main deck, cambered like a highway, a foot higher along the centerline than at the edges. A two-story deckhouse sat forward, with dark-tinted windows and a face that angled sleekly aft. The bottom level of the superstructure held staterooms, and one level up, flanked on both sides by open bridge wings, was the cutter's compact pilothouse. On the aft side of the superstructure, covered by wire mesh, was the plenum chamber, a twenty-foot-wide intake for the air that would be pumped underneath the hull. To starboard was a steep set of stairs—a ladder, in nautical terms—that connected the main deck to the bridge wing.

I scanned the topside deck, picking out anomalies. Forward of the superstructure was twenty feet of open bow, and behind it an even-larger stretch of empty deck space. On other patrol boats, there was little open deck area, with almost every square foot crammed with equipment and fittings. By contrast, *Shearwater* seemed positively roomy. Sitting in a cradle on the port side, behind the superstructure, was the cutter's four-meter RHIB—a rigid-hull inflatable boat—and a thin metal boom used to lower it into the water. Both looked frail, unsuited for rough duty. Further aft, amidships, was a lightweight, three-foot towing bitt, clearly not built for heavy loads. More encouraging, across the width of *Shearwater*'s stern was a six-foot-wide "step deck" that was lower than the rest of the main deck, and only three feet above the waterline. The step deck would come in handy when transferring goods or people to other boats or retrieving debris found floating in the sea.

The sides of *Shearwater*'s hull were flat and her corners were squared off, giving her a bulky, mechanical appearance, devoid of the graceful curves found in most oceangoing ships. Here, graceful wasn't needed. The new cutter wasn't meant to slice through the waves, but rather to skirt above them at high speed. *Shearwater* was built to cruise at thirty knots, far above the sprint speed of any other patrol boat bearing the Coast Guard stripes.

I continued to stare, trying to take it all in. The wake from a passing lobster boat broke the spell, sullying the waters in the turning basin.

Moored behind *Shearwater*, the 95-foot cutter *Cape York* (WPB 95332) began to bob in the ripples, rolling side to side, knurling and pinching the bright orange fenders that had been rigged to keep her from scraping the pier. *Shearwater* didn't budge, moving straight up and down only a few inches, the motion almost imperceptible. Longer, faster, more stable—*Shearwater* was perfect for fighting the war on drugs.

The Coast Guard had just bought three of the surface effect ships. To purists they were awkward-looking and unnatural, but for those of us chosen to take them to sea, the wide, boxy cutters were things of beauty, deserving of their newly coined nickname, "El Tiburon"—The Shark. I was itching to get under way, to give *Shearwater* a full shakedown, to set sail and start putting smugglers out of business.

————

The drive from New Hampshire had taken two days, the vision of my twenty-one good months on board *Active* fading away in the rear-view mirror. New Castle had been an idyllic homeport, a tidy hamlet steeped in history and surrounded by the rugged beauty of the New England sea-coast. Leaving had been hard. The change was just another part of the Coast Guard lifestyle: serve a few years, and then move on.

South Florida offered the adventure I craved. I'd been drawn to the sea early, transfixed by the stories that my dad would tell of his merchant marine days and entranced by our annual trip to Cape Hatteras, North Carolina, where we'd swim in the rough surf and search for hidden treasure in the shipwreck-strewn shallows. Bobbing off Ocracoke Inlet in a small boat, the large sand dunes out of sight, it was easy to get caught up in the thrill of going to sea, man against nature, the perfect environ for explorers and daredevils. I was hooked from the first boat trip beyond the harbor.

Fortune led me to the U.S. Coast Guard Academy. It was a tough school, with a strict military ethos and rigorous academics. I studied history and government and racked up six months of sea time over four summers, training in patrol boats, a 378-foot cutter, and USCGC *Eagle* (WIX 327), the Coast Guard's square-rigged training vessel. Sailing in *Eagle* made you grow up fast. The work was hard and never-ending, and I had to overcome the fear of being perched like a sparrow at the top of a 147-foot mast—just one failed grip from a painful death.

The Academy foreshadowed an exciting future. The more I learned about the storied history of the Coast Guard and the breadth of its day-to-day missions, the more a career as a seagoing officer became a calling. After graduating I reported to *Active*, where I built and honed leadership muscle and operational skills, all while getting bitten by the law enforcement bug. I'd joined the Coast Guard to save lives, but drug interdiction provided another good reason to pursue a career at sea: to put smugglers in jail and keep their poisons off the streets. The transfer to Key West offered a rare opportunity to serve on board a state-of-the-art class of cutter, on the front line in the war on drugs, in an exotic, warm-weather homeport. It didn't get any better than this.

The Coast Guard base sat across the quay from a squadron of high-tech Navy hydrofoils. Key West was home to six of the ultra-high-speed craft. In contrast, berthed at the Coast Guard piers were two ancient, turtle-slow ships, hand-me-downs recently transferred from the Navy—the 205-foot cutters *Ute* (WMEC 76) and *Lipan* (WMEC 85), along with *Cape York*. Unlike the state-of-the-art hydrofoils, the average age of the cutters was thirty-five years.

But that was changing. The three surface effect ships would bring new life to the fleet. In 1982 as drug smuggling became an epidemic, Congress appropriated $14 million to put additional patrol boats into immediate service. The Coast Guard bought three SESs that had been designed as oil-rig crew boats. Two had been operating in the Gulf of Mexico and the third was nearing completion at the Bell Halter shipyard outside of New Orleans. Dubbed the *Seabird* class of cutters, USCGC *Sea Hawk* (WSES 2) and *Shearwater* (WSES 3) sailed to Key West for outfitting in the fall of 1982. The third cutter, USCGC *Petrel* (WSES 4), would be ready for delivery to the Coast Guard in mid-1983.

I'd be serving as executive officer (XO) in *Petrel*—but only part of the time. The Coast Guard needed patrol hours and found a way to get more out of each vessel. It turned to multi-crewing. Rather than assigning a single crew to each ship, it formed 4 teams of 16 sailors each—the Blue, Green, Red, and Gold crews—and rotated them among the three cutters. Each crew would serve on a particular cutter for 6 to 8 weeks at a time, while the one off-duty crew would remain ashore to assist the 20-person

SES Division staff. In theory, this would enable each SES crew to spend 180 days at sea each year, maintaining a reasonable quality of life, while keeping the cutters on patrol for 240 days.

Two of the crews, Green and Blue, had put *Sea Hawk* and *Shearwater* into service. I was assigned as XO of the newly created Red Crew, which would deliver *Petrel* to Key West and place her in commission in July. We'd be *Petrel*'s plank-owners, members of the original crew. Later in the summer Gold Crew would arrive and, once it was fully trained, the rotations would begin. I'd sail on board all three SESs over the next two years. During my time ashore, I'd serve as the assistant engineering officer for the division.

Promotional materials for the new SES Division showed an aerial view of *Sea Hawk* and *Shearwater* cutting a wide swath through sparkling waters, their black hulls and white decks gleaming in the tropical sun. After two years on the slow, top-heavy *Active*, I couldn't wait to skim across the waves and hunt down smugglers at breakneck speed.

At SES Division headquarters, Yeoman First Class Jean Johnson, the office manager, helped me with the check-in paperwork and then took me on a tour, introducing the support staff as she went along. Petty Officer Johnson handled all of the administrative functions for the unit and was perpetually juggling a hundred different tasks, but always with a smile and encouraging words. She was a kind voice of welcome.

The division compound, however, was the type of place that scared away burglars—a dilapidated former barracks that seemed one strong wind away from breaking up into kindling. It was a long, low, white-washed shed perched alongside pier Delta Two, where the SESs moored. Inside, the division's engineers, gunner's mates, boatswain's mates, and electronics technicians toiled in workshops and maintained stockpiles of engine parts, damage control equipment, and a thousand other spares. The administrative team sat in cubicles, and the officers worked in modest offices. The building's ancient wood, shriveled and cracked by decades in the sun, was home to all sorts of vermin, and no doubt the local exterminator put his kids through college fending them off.

Johnson introduced me to the division commander, Lt. Cdr. Bob Council. He was short and stocky, with a moon face and a subdued personality. Lieutenant Commander Council had served afloat as both an enlisted sailor and a junior officer, and his quiet demeanor camouflaged a get-it-done-at-all-costs mindset. He welcomed me to the team, noted that we were the first division of cutters to be formed since the Vietnam War, and asserted that even with the trials of converting civilian ships into functional cutters, the SES Division was the best damned duty station in the Coast Guard, bar none. Lieutenant Commander Council guaranteed that Red Crew would see plenty of action. I hoped he was right.

Petty Officer Johnson led me to my desk. I'd be sharing an office with the division engineer, Lt. Bob Chandler. The walls of Lieutenant Chandler's office were lined with low-rent wood paneling, and a small air conditioner wheezed and rattled in the window. Lieutenant Chandler was nowhere to be found. Petty Officer Johnson said he probably was up to his elbows in oil and grease somewhere on *Shearwater*. "He's former enlisted and loves the hands-on work," she explained. "He can't help himself—it's in his blood."

I sat down and rummaged through the welcome aboard package, pulling out a unit patch. It was four inches round, proclaiming "El Tiburon, SES Division, Key West," and it centered on a cartoon drawing of an SES, the bow morphed into a wide face with red eyes and a menacing set of teeth flashing in its open mouth. The masthead of the SES was bent aft, supposedly from the high speed at which the cartoon cutter was traveling, and just in front of the gaping maw was a bale of marijuana, about to be consumed by The Shark. The drawing had a Matt Groening–like appeal— goofy-looking, but with a serious message: the SES Division was here to give hurt to the cartels.

On the pier, the division support staff was struggling to lower a fifteen-foot slab of thick black rubber into the water off *Shearwater's* bow. The rubber was a low-tech part of the ingenious "lift" system that gave the SES its impressive speed. The basic theory was simple: elevating the cutter partway out of the water would reduce friction and increase velocity. Below the main deck, in a central engine room, two compact diesel engines drove cylindrical fans that pulled air through the plenum chamber to pressurize the ship's underbelly. Thick rubber seals, stretched between the catamaran hulls at the bow and stern, held the air in place. At rest, the SES had a draft of more than nine feet, but when the underhull "wet deck" was fully pressurized, the ship rose up, reducing the draft by half, and allowing two larger propulsion diesels to generate speeds up to thirty knots.

Unlike the stern seal, which was a massive piece of rubber, the bow seal was segmented into eight "fingers," and one of *Shearwater*'s centermost fingers had torn. The division staff had jerry-rigged a series of winches, blocks, and tackle to yank off the damaged rubber and hoist a new finger into position. After an hour of heaving, grunting, and cussing, the seal snapped into place, and members of the Blue Crew made preparations to get *Shearwater* under way so they could test the repair. I ran into Lieutenant Chandler, who was dripping with sweat and cleaning his oily hands on a rag, and introduced myself. He invited me along for the ride.

I stood on the starboard bridge wing, watching the officer of the deck (OOD) maneuver the ship, and quickly realized that handling an SES was unlike anything else in the Coast Guard fleet. With the cutter still moored, the OOD engaged the lift engines at half speed. A modest roar echoed from aft of the pilothouse as the lift fans sucked air into the plenum, and within three or four seconds *Shearwater*'s wet deck pressurized. The cutter rose two feet, and with the reduced drag the OOD easily twisted the ship away from the pier. The ship bounced lightly on the bubble of air, producing an unnatural, rubbery vibration.

Once *Shearwater* was in the harbor, the OOD increased the lift to three-quarters, reducing the cutter's draft by another foot and amplifying the bounce and the volume of the fans. To test the engines, he pivoted the ship by using right full rudder and placing the port engine at clutch speed ahead and the starboard engine at clutch astern. Wobbling on the air cushion, with her widely spaced propellers working in opposite directions, *Shearwater* quickly spun in place, completing a 360-degree circle within her own length. During the pivot, at the edges of the bow and stern seals, the underhull pressure forced out fifty-foot jets of water, in random patterns, misting the air and adding a dramatic visual aura to the muffled roar of the lift fans. Lieutenant Chandler said they called the maneuver the "SES shuffle."

The weather was perfect, with light winds and a slight chop. Once *Shearwater* was clear of the channel, the OOD increased power to what should have been twenty knots. The ship sped up but felt sluggish, as if dragging a large bucket, and the quad turbochargers on the main diesels whined under heavy load. The OOD increased engine rpms. A large curling wake formed behind the cutter and her transom squatted deep into the water, while the bow pointed up at an awkward angle. The OOD added more power. *Shearwater*'s bow fell slightly and the cutter strained forward, hitting twenty-two knots. The OOD nudged the throttles one more time: full speed ahead. The bow fell further, the hull leveled out, and the propellers dug harder into the translucent seas. *Shearwater* was making twenty-eight knots.

It was exhilarating, the fastest I'd ever cruised on a cutter. The warm air whipped past and knocked off my ball cap. Still, something wasn't right, and the engineers wore frowns, muttering "what happened to thirty knots?" and tinkering with the ballast system. Lieutenant Chandler took me aft on the bridge wing, finding a spot where the pilothouse blocked the wind. The strain of the job was evident, the dark circles under his eyes a testimony to the late nights that he was spending to keep the SESs running.

Lieutenant Chandler explained the physics of the surface effect. "These things plow through the water and at about fifteen knots they create a resonant wave that holds the ship back," he said. "We call that hump speed. The ship squats and the bow rises up until the engines power over the wave. There's a second, smaller hump around twenty-two knots. After that the ride flattens out and you start skimming across the water, on plane, all the way up to thirty."

He bit his lip, as if to share a secret. "Since we put so much junk on these boats it weighs them down, and sometimes it's hard to get past the second hump, especially in shallow water like we're in now," he said. "When we got them, brand new, we were zipping around at thirty-plus every day. But these ships are weight-sensitive. With all the food and ammo and spare parts on board, we're lucky to hit the high twenties when there's a full fuel load. That means you have to pay a lot of attention to ballasting and trim to keep the bow down."

He made another confession: the SESs were built to civilian stan dards and weren't as structurally sound or mechanically reliable as vessels that were designed as warships. In their first months in operation both *Sea Hawk* and *Shearwater* had suffered a flurry of engineering breakdowns and minor structural failures, keeping the machinery technicians busy with repairs and the division's only qualified aluminum welder, Damage Controlman First Class (DC1) Bob Holloway, working at a feverish pitch to fix cracks in the hull, water tanks, and pipes.

Lieutenant Chandler's honesty was disconcerting but welcome nevertheless. "I hate to say it, but we're going to see a lot more casualties once we pick up the pace of our patrols," he predicted. "These ships were made for quick jaunts out to the rigs, not for the kind of nonstop punishment that the Coast Guard dishes out."

We walked back into the pilothouse and saw the speed displayed on a digital Doppler readout: 28.7 knots. The engineers might be grumbling, but I was elated. *Shearwater* was the fastest patrol boat in the Coast Guard, with almost twice the speed of my previous cutter. Sure, there were some machinery casualties, and her maximum speed was a few knots short of optimal. But all Red Crew needed was to go out on patrol and get to work.

Test run over, *Shearwater* motored back to Key West. A large crowd was gathered on the pier at Mallory Square, waiting for another trademark sunset, with dancers, jugglers, and street vendors weaving among hundreds of sunburned tourists. As the cutter cruised past the throng, the OOD brought the ship to all stop, increased lift to full, and then split the engines, port forward and starboard aft. *Shearwater* spun in place, bouncing hard and shooting geysers of spray in all directions, leaving rainbows glistening in the misty dome that engulfed the ship. The crowd let out a roar of approval. She might not be as fast or as hardy as advertised, but boy, could *Shearwater* shuffle.

———

If the speed and durability of the SESs were less than perfect, our new crew far exceeded expectations. Coast Guard headquarters had assigned some of the best and brightest to man the new cutters, and Red Crew was the lucky recipient of many stars among them. It started at the top. Red Crew's captain, Lt. Jerry Lober, was six years my senior, solidly built, with a closely cropped brown beard, a wide face, and inquisitive eyes. Lieutenant Lober had a firm military bearing that exuded confidence. He had a rich, mellifluous voice, but he almost never raised it; he listened to his subordinates; and he was precise when issuing orders, always clear and direct—the kind of captain for whom XOs loved to work. Previously he had commanded a 95-footer in California, accumulating a wealth of experience in heavy weather and search-and-rescue (SAR) operations. He also recognized his limited exposure to the Caribbean drug war and told me repeatedly that there was a lot for both of us to learn.

Lieutenant Lober was a playful adventurer. He was endlessly curious about how things worked, loved new tools and tactics, and was continually looking for interesting ports-of-call and the best fishing holes. Most important, he cared for his crew. Lober made sure his shipmates had the training and equipment they needed, and he spent a good deal of time mentoring me in the fine art of command—instruction that I hoped would make me a decent captain someday.

Each SES crew had fourteen enlisted members. Red Crew's chief of the boat was Senior Chief Quartermaster Ivan "Ben" Aiken, who would serve as operations officer and navigator. Senior Chief Aiken was tall and beefy, with a powerful voice tinged with a twang of unknown origin—maybe from Gulf Coast Texas. With more than a dozen years at sea, he was our resident expert on all things nautical, and Lieutenant Lober and I quickly learned to trust his advice. Senior Chief Aiken was gregarious and a forceful personality, never shy in offering his opinion, booming out his thoughts laced with a down-home colloquialism or a creative cussword. He also had a tender side: a good rendition of "The Star-Spangled Banner" would make him misty-eyed. He and Lieutenant Lober had known each other in California and, although they were complete opposites, they had developed a tight bond, constantly sharing sea stories and comparing techniques for landing the biggest fish.

Senior Chief Aiken reveled in self-deprecating humor and loved to mess with people, telling me the first time we met that he was a senior chief and wouldn't be "taking any crap from a wet-behind-the-ears" lieutenant (junior grade). When he saw my shocked expression, he burst into a gale of laughter, wrapped an oversized paw around my bicep, leaned in close, and assured me not to worry—that his job was to make sure I didn't run my fitness report aground.

Red Crew also enjoyed a crop of talented petty officers, led by Boatswain's Mate First Class (BM1) Dan Sanders and Machinery Technician First Class (MK1) Cliff Boldan, who would run the deck and engineering departments. Petty Officer Sanders was of average height and build, bordering on stout, and he hid behind thick glasses and a blond beard. He was soft-spoken and used his words sparingly. But behind his quiet demeanor was a resourceful leader, meticulous and methodical, who set high standards for his team and was the most detail-oriented person I'd ever known. Sanders was an expert coxswain and a natural shiphandler. As an added bonus, he had a cunning sense of humor, pulling stunts when least expected—surprises that helped boost morale when the crew was in the doldrums.

Petty Officer Boldan was shorter and also bearded, his hair thick, like a Viking's. He was a gifted mechanic who didn't shy from the most daunting problems and was quick to get things fixed. He dove right into his work, hands on, often sauntering out of the engine room—or, as he called it, "the hole,"—covered in oil, rumpled and sweaty. Like Petty Officer Sanders, Boldan was a borderline introvert, but with a nonconformist streak. He rode a Harley-Davidson motorcycle and grew his beard as long as he could get away with. Still, he was focused and dedicated, a real engineering pro, and he kept his small team performing at peak efficiency.

Red Crew had five mid-grade petty officers: two boatswain's mates, a machinery technician, an electrician, and a "subsistence specialist"— the latter known in the real world as a cook. Most of the petty officers had previous law enforcement experience. In the lower ranks, our four seamen and two firemen were fresh from boot camp, and training them would consume much of our time. Petty officers Sanders and Boldan had to juggle a never-ending cascade of maintenance, repair, qualification, cleanliness, inspection, safety, and supply functions, all while nurturing and mentoring their subordinates, standing watch, and carrying out law-enforcement boardings and other evolutions. More than anyone else, they held the effectiveness of the crew in their hands. Thankfully, both men proved expert at handling the deluge, while providing solid role models for the younger sailors below them.

As XO, my job was to run the ship, turning the captain's strategic vision into action. He set the standards and made the big decisions, and I'd carry them out; I'd fill in for the captain when he was absent; and I also was the senior OOD, the senior boarding officer, and the unit training officer.

The first task was to mold sixteen strangers into a well-oiled team. In late March, the men and women who'd make up Red Crew began arriving in Key West for three months of indoctrination. We spent our days training, crawling the bilges, and tracing out systems, with the new seamen learning how to handle lines, stand lookout, and man the helm. Our engineers tagged along with their counterparts on the Blue Crew and Green Crew, helping them with maintenance. Everyone studied law enforcement, memorizing relevant statutes and procedures. We blasted away at the range with our .45s, M-16s, and riot shotguns and went through extensive "shoot/don't shoot" training—a prerequisite for boarding personnel—viewing videotaped law enforcement encounters and shooting blanks at the TV screen whenever we thought deadly force was needed. Slowly, Red Crew began to gel into a cohesive unit, its members watching one another's backs during the most intense training and learning the many peculiarities of our unique vessels.

———

Our operating area also was unique, a complex intersection of geography and international boundaries, home to the Coast Guard's most sensitive missions. Key West was the westernmost inhabited island of the Florida Keys, and sat only ninety miles north of Cuba, the hemisphere's enduring Communist dictatorship. With the regime's ruthless leadership, grievous repression, and virulent anti-American saber-rattling, tensions between the United States and Cuba ran high, prompting the Coast Guard to prohibit its cutters from operating within fifteen miles of the Cuban coast, which effectively added a three-mile buffer to the country's twelve-mile territorial sea. The last thing we needed was for a cutter to stray into Cuban waters and spark an international incident.

Beyond Key West, arcing westward, seventy miles of scraggly cays ended at the Dry Tortugas, where Fort Jefferson stood sentinel over

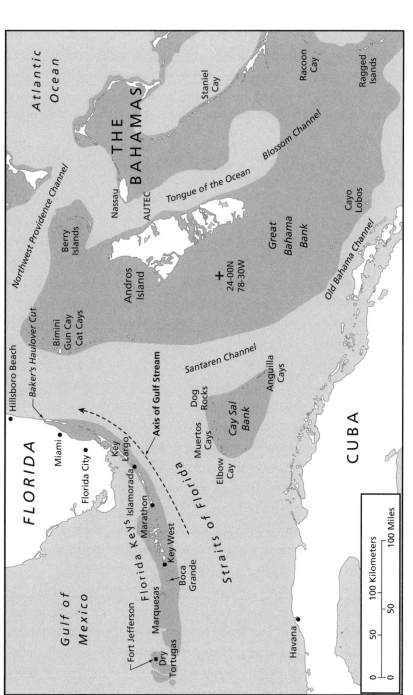

The Straits of Florida and Bahamas, the prime operating area for the Coast Guard's three surface effect ships

the intersection of the Straits of Florida and the Gulf of Mexico. In the opposite direction, one hundred fifty miles to the east, were the Bahamas, a sprawling archipelago of seven hundred islands—some massive, some tiny, and many ungoverned—where drug-trafficking and human smuggling flourished. Tens of thousands of lobster boats, sport-fishing boats, sailboats, cruise ships, and commercial vessels plied these waters.

This was all the province of the Seventh Coast Guard District, the regional command headquartered in Miami, which was responsible for six million square miles of ocean, from South Carolina to South America. The district bordered on twenty-six other nations. Along the U.S. mainland, it was divided into five smaller commands: Groups Charleston, Mayport, Miami, Key West, and St. Petersburg. Each Group oversaw Coast Guard activity along a few hundred miles of coast.

The Seventh District was the busiest operating area in the Coast Guard, with a continual diet of law enforcement, search-and-rescue operations, migrant interdiction, and international intrigue. To the decisionmakers in Washington, and to the men and women that sailed "El Tiburon," it was the ideal locale to employ the high-speed surface effect ships.

———

In late April I got under way on *Shearwater* with the Blue Crew. Its XO, Lt. (jg) Jim Sartucci, was my informal mentor. Tall and lean, Lieutenant Sartucci had graduated from the Academy a year ahead of me and we shared a love for soccer, MTV, and the night life in Key West. We became fast friends, and he spent hours teaching me the ropes of SES operations. Blue Crew was headed out for a ten-day patrol, and I rode along to gain experience.

Leaving Key West, *Shearwater* steamed southwest toward the Yucatan Channel. Intelligence reports estimated that up to half of the marijuana bound for the United States by sea passed through the Yucatan, making it an ideal interdiction choke-point. Typically patrolled by larger cutters, the law enforcement gurus in Miami had decided that the SESs could perform well there, despite their relatively modest range. It was a three-hundred-mile trip from Key West to the patrol area—less than half a day under ideal conditions but a much longer slog when the wind and seas picked up.

With a light easterly breeze behind us, *Shearwater* powered along at full speed. It was my first experience on an SES in the open ocean, and in the mild weather the ride seemed closer to that of a freight train than a ship. *Shearwater* rumbled and shimmied as she clipped along the top of the waves, the fixtures and bulkheads inside the superstructure rattling and chattering with a light, high-frequency vibration, soothing and hypnotic. As the ship approached the Yucatan, the seas built to five feet and the ride became more energetic, with *Shearwater* making unpredictable jerky thrusts every time one of her catamaran hulls bit into a larger swell, requiring a firm grip for anyone who was transiting a passageway or climbing a ladder.

Shearwater arrived in the patrol area a few hours ahead of schedule, and Blue Crew set to work, conducting an east-west barrier patrol across the width of the Yucatan, seeking northbound vessels. Overnight, the weather turned bleak, with a steady twenty-knot wind and gray skies. There were only a few ships in the area, all large freighters and oil tankers steaming toward distant ports, and nothing even remotely suspicious.

The seas swelled to eight feet, making the ship's motion uncomfortable at slow speed and distinctly unpleasant when we were trying to get somewhere in a hurry. Steaming directly into the seas, *Shearwater* would fling herself over the top of a wave and then plummet into the trough, her broad bow bludgeoning the front of the next approaching swell. At low speed this sent a harmless shudder through the ship. When we were traveling at more than twelve knots, though, the acceleration down into the trough became extreme and the slamming severe. The ship couldn't remain on plane and crashed through the larger waves with brute force, subjecting the crew to a punishing, jarring, knee-buckling ride.

There had been a news article about the SESs in which a Coast Guard spokesman lauded their ability to steam faster than thirty knots in calm waters and to maintain full speed, flitting across the top of the waves, in seas up to ten feet. The buoyant optimism of those statements sank to the bottom when it was confronted by the laws of physics. Like every other ship on the sea, the SESs would have to respect the wind and waves.

Blue Crew searched the Yucatan for three days and then headed toward *Shearwater*'s patrol partner, the 205-foot cutter *Lipan,* to replenish fuel and supplies. *Lipan* was a slow but solid ship, designed for heavy salvage work, but effective in cornering the typical motherships that transited the Yucatan. She also had huge fuel tanks and was a trusty gas station for the SESs.

Lipan slowed to three knots and headed directly into the wind, while *Shearwater* closed in behind her, approaching to thirty feet. A boatswain's mate on *Lipan*'s rounded fantail threw a heaving line, lashed to a four-inch towing hawser, to *Shearwater*'s bow. Blue Crew's seamen pulled the hawser on board. Once the line was secure, the OOD shut down *Shearwater*'s engines, and the cutter drifted back on the towline. The deck crew passed a three-inch fuel line tethered to a garden hose—the same kind of hose that you could buy at a hardware store—between the ships. The engineers plugged in the hoses, and *Shearwater* sat behind *Lipan* for two hours, taking on enough fuel and water to finish the patrol. It was a low-tech evolution, almost embarrassingly primitive, but it worked.

Lipan's crew also passed back a box of movies, some fresh vegetables, and a special surprise—a case of beer. Drinking alcohol at sea was *verboten*, but *Shearwater*'s commanding officer, Lt. Ken Bradford, granted an exemption due to the choppy sea-state, noting with a wink that it was essential to maintain morale. Wisely, he limited each sailor to a single bottle. I'd been fighting a persistent headache due to the sloppy weather and was reluctant to take a drink, but I couldn't resist. To my surprise, it turned out to be a healing tonic, and I felt great for the rest of the day. Such was the recuperative effect of a single twelve-ounce beer.

Blue Crew spent the next four days searching for targets to board, but it had no luck. The captain requested air surveillance but there were no C-130s available, and the ship's two commercial-grade radars couldn't see much in the choppy seas. Thankfully, the lackluster radar sets would be replaced in a year with the far more capable AN-SPS-64, the standard radar of the cutter fleet, but until then the SES crews relied mostly on visual sightings during the day. I stood watch with Lieutenant Sartucci, and spent my free time roaming the ship, taking in the unorthodox design and talking with the crew.

On *Shearwater*'s last day in the Yucatan, the bridge team spotted a northbound fishing boat, the fifty-foot *Margaret K*, a bright white vessel with a gaggle of longline floats sitting atop its pilothouse. She was a beautiful boat, motoring slowly toward the Gulf of Mexico. *Shearwater* pulled alongside and the OOD hailed it on the radio and asked a set of preboarding questions. The master on *Margaret K* said they were longlining for tuna. Lieutenant Bradford ordered boarding stations, and I tagged along as part of the boarding party, with Boatswain's Mate First Class Don Kressin leading the team.

Petty Officer Kressin was tall, coolheaded, and steady. He oversaw a thorough inspection of the boat, following standard protocols. First, he directed *Margaret K*'s crew to gather near the fantail, where we could see them, before we climbed over the port rail. Once aboard, BM1 Kressin introduced himself to the master, explained the purpose of the boarding, repeated the preboarding questions for consistency, and examined the crew's IDs. While he reviewed the vessel's registration papers, Kressin dispatched a two-person "sweep team" to conduct an initial safety inspection of all man-sized compartments, to make sure that no one else was on board and to identify unsafe or suspicious conditions. The papers were in order and the sweep team found no irregularities, reporting *Margaret K* to be pristine and shipshape.

Then came the main event. Petty Officer Kressin led a stem-to-stern inspection, checking life jackets, flares, fire extinguishers, and other safety equipment, and shining a flashlight into every bilge. He checked the fishhold—jammed with a dozen gutted tuna and a glacier of chopped ice—as well as the longline gear, but found no discrepancies. In every compartment, Kressin looked for telltale signs of smuggling. He found nothing unusual and completed the inspection in forty minutes. Satisfied, Kressin told the master that everything looked good and thanked him for his cooperation. He wrapped up the paperwork, the boarding party climbed back into the RHIB, and the coxswain whisked us back to *Shearwater*. The boarding was complete.

Jim Sartucci talked with me afterward, his words foreshadowing things to come. "Down here, you have to consider every boat with a level of suspicion," he said. "Everyone. You just never know who's clean and who's a doper. The smugglers know how to hide things and you've got to be thorough. Treat everyone with courtesy, but look for the body language and the little clues. They'll lead to seizures—guaranteed."

The next morning *Shearwater* headed back to port. Unlike the smooth trip out, the voyage back was a horror show. The seas had grown to ten feet and we punched through them, with the engines turning for twenty-five knots, but the ship making far less. The slamming sent shock waves through the cutter, mile after mile. I wondered how the lightweight hulls would hold up over time, and worried about the effect on the crew. Thankfully, the seas moderated as *Shearwater* approached the reef line, and soon we could see the lights of Key West, a glittering tease in the distance. It was good to be home.

––––––––––

For the Florida-based cutter crews, the name of the game was drug seizures, and whoever made the most was king. Competition was intense, and successful crews razzed their peers after hauling in a seized vessel or frog-walking a gang of smugglers into the arms of U.S. Customs.

Drug interdiction was a shiny new mission for the Coast Guard. Before the 1970s, most marijuana smuggled into the United States had come across the southwest land border. Then a massive eradication effort crippled the Mexican supply, and Jamaica, and later Colombia, picked up the slack. The lawless Guajira Peninsula on Colombia's eastern border became home to huge marijuana plantations, and smugglers loaded tons of contraband onto just about any boat able to steam five hundred miles to America. The cartels hired anyone willing to sail the drugs north—fishing-boat captains, college kids, peasant farmers, even retirees seeking one last shot of income. Many were amateurs.

The Coast Guard's first drug seizure was in March 1973, when the cutter *Dauntless* (WMEC 624) nabbed the fishing vessel *Big L*, which was carrying three thousand pounds of marijuana, just off Miami. Quickly the drug war went hot. In 1977 Coast Guard crews seized fifty-four marijuana-laden vessels, and by 1980 it interdicted five times as many, keeping 2.7 million pounds of pot off the streets.

Finding the dopers was the hard part. The Coast Guard was seriously outmatched, with hundreds of smugglers operating across millions of square miles of ocean, faced by a few dozen patrol boats and larger cutters. Bringing them to justice once they were found was simple enough. On most boats, the contraband sat in plain view. But the drug war was changing.

In 1982 the Reagan Administration had established a South Florida Task Force to combat the flood of contraband and stem the escalating drug-related violence. Agents from the Federal Bureau of Investigation (FBI) and Drug Enforcement Administration (DEA) surged into the region to disrupt shoreside networks. The Coast Guard moved cutters to Florida and took on three aged Navy salvage tugs, which became the medium-endurance cutters *Ute*, *Lipan*, and *Escape* (WMEC 6). To expand the fleet even more, the Coast Guard began designing a faster, 125-foot replacement for its 82-foot and 95-foot patrol boats, an effort that was expected to take another four years. Meanwhile, Navy warships were assigned to drug-interdiction missions, carrying Coast Guard Law Enforcement Detachments, or LEDETs, on board to conduct searches and seizures.

The cartels began losing more of their precious cargo. In response, the smugglers adapted, employing new tactics to skirt the law. Secret compartments became commonplace, some deep in the bowels of commercial ships, others on fishing boats or pleasure craft. Many smugglers began using smaller, stealthier, and faster vessels. Some mingled among thousands of innocent boats, hiding in plain sight. Brazen pilots in Cessnas flew waterproof packages of contraband from Colombia into the Bahamas or directly to the coast of Florida, dropping bales to waiting speedboats. Careless amateurs were replaced by steely professionals.

The smuggling networks covered the Caribbean, using Cuba as a shelter and the Bahamas as camouflage. Smugglers wove in and out of the waters surrounding Haiti, Jamaica, the Dominican Republic, the Windward Islands, Puerto Rico, Mexico, Grand Cayman, Tortola, Aruba, St. Maarten, the Turks and Caicos, and Panama. They sailed the open ocean and skirted shallows, moving through darkness and storm. South Florida was the epicenter of the vast smuggling web, home to a bevy of criminal gangs, all waiting for their ships to come in.

At the dawn of this new era, Coast Guard teams faced an increasingly complex challenge. It was no longer as simple as finding a drug-filled boat, jumping on board, and snapping handcuffs on the smugglers. The new breed of dopers had to be outwitted, outmatched, and outperformed.

It was in this environment that the SESs were pressed into service, a placeholder until the new 125-foot patrol boats would arrive in the mid-1980s. The SES Division was established in the summer of 1982 and the first two cutters were commissioned on November 17. It was a big step— a show of resolve from an administration determined to reclaim the rule of law. President Reagan tendered a rare honor, sending a congratulatory message to the cutter crews. The message ended on a personal note, saying "Nancy joins me in sending the officers and crew of the *Sea Hawk* and the *Shearwater* our very best wishes for safe voyages and, again, our congratulations."

Hitting the jackpot didn't take long. Green Crew, on board *Sea Hawk*, made the SES Division's first seizure on January 29, 1983, arresting four persons on the sailboat *Family Affair*, which was stuffed with 8,500 pounds of marijuana. In March, Green Crew scored two more seizures, totaling another 9,240 pounds, while the Blue Crew in *Shearwater* bested them by discovering ten tons of pot on the *Cayman*, a sixty-five-foot shrimp boat. Before Red Crew would commission *Petrel* in July, the Blue and Green crews hauled in five more vessels, mostly small fishing boats moving one-ton loads from the Bahamas. On average, the SES Division was making a drug bust every seventeen days.

The atmosphere at the division was electric. The cutter crews and support staff were flying high on emotion, knowing that their finicky high-tech cutters were setting a hot pace and that each patrol could bring more glory. To herald each seizure, the crew members affixed a six-by-six-inch sticker, depicting a green marijuana leaf under a red X, to their cutter's superstructure. It was a matter of intense pride when Green Crew or Blue Crew pasted its latest trophy to the hull of *Sea Hawk* or *Shearwater*.

Lieutenant Lober understood that Red Crew needed to hit the ground running and join the fight. There were dopers to be busted, and our team was eager to make its first arrests. Watching the other crews return from successful patrols while we muddled through weapons qualifications, training lectures, and routine paperwork only intensified our zeal. By mid-May, Red Crew was ready for sea. We formally relieved the Blue Crew and assumed responsibility for *Shearwater* and set sail for a six-day training cruise.

The training was intense, and for the first time it was carried out with pitch, roll, and salt spray thrown in. *Shearwater* steamed south of the Keys and headed west toward Fort Jefferson, seeking a quiet, low-traffic area where the crew could conduct drills and hold uninterrupted watch-station training.

Red Crew simulated every emergency we could think of, responding as if it were the real thing. For a "fire" at sea, the damage control team energized the fire main and emergency pumps, donned firefighting gear, and dragged charged hoses into the engine room to fight the mock conflagration. Simulated hull ruptures imperiled the cutter and, after battling the faux flood, the crew practiced abandoning ship. Over and over, man overboard drills tested the OODs' maneuvering skills, twisting and turning the ship to recover a life-sized, floatable dummy, nicknamed Oscar, which had been tossed into the water. Every crew member underwent egress training, blindfolded in his or her bunk and forced to feel the way in complete darkness to the safety of the main deck. The gunners blasted holes in fifty-five-gallon drums with *Shearwater*'s .50-caliber and M-60 machine guns, and we conducted our first real boarding—inspecting a small and innocent westbound sailboat.

On the fourth night Lieutenant Lober decided we had done enough training. He wanted real action. *Shearwater* headed toward the westernmost clump of Bahamian territory, a triangular patch of shallows known as Cay Sal Bank. The bank was roughly fifty miles on each side, ringed by craggy, uninhabited islands, and sat one hundred miles directly south of Miami, equidistant from the Florida Keys and the north shore of Cuba. It was a well-known waypoint for smugglers, and although there was some legitimate conch-fishing there, our general view was that any boat found near Cay Sal was suspicious by default.

Real action came fast. The next day, at noon, a Coast Guard helicopter spotted a Florida-registered fishing boat anchored near Elbow Cay, on the northwest corner of the bank, and later saw it heading toward the Keys.

Shearwater chased after her at full speed, aiming for an intercept before the boat could reach the reef line. Low on fuel and in near-calm conditions, *Shearwater* made thirty knots over ground, even while fighting eddies from the Gulf Stream.

A surge of excitement spread through the cutter. This was Red Crew's first intercept and our first potential law enforcement case. If the boat had been fishing in Bahamian territory its crew might have been violating the Lacey Act, which prohibited Americans from poaching in foreign waters. Or better, the boat might be headed home carrying a load of dope, her crew planning for an offload after dark. That'd be a home run—making a seizure on our very first sortie.

The bridge watchstanders, tense and anxious, scanned the horizon for the suspect vessel. Lieutenant Lober stood on the bridge wing, joshing with the lookout and searching with binoculars, while Senior Chief Aiken hovered over the radar, plotting the intercept and looking for a tell-tale blip, humming *Semper Paratus*, the Coast Guard anthem.

In late afternoon the lookout spotted the boat, and within half an hour *Shearwater* pulled alongside the thirty-foot *Flying Deuce*. The *Deuce* was a grubby boat, homeported in Miami, with a cabin forward and an open aft deck. From *Shearwater's* bridge we could see narrow, rectangular boxes sitting on each side of the aft deck. It was a strange arrangement, something we'd never run across before. The OOD used a bullhorn to direct the master to stand by for a boarding.

As Red Crew's senior boarding officer I'd be leading a four-person team. I suited up in the standard law enforcement uniform, stripping down to a T-shirt and strapping on a bulletproof vest. The vest would protect against low-velocity gunshots and could help against knives. Covering the vest was a set of dark blue coveralls with "USCG" stenciled in six-inch letters across the back. Then came a leather weapons belt, with a holster for the .45, two ammo pouches, a ring to hold a foot-long flashlight (useful as a defensive weapon), a can of pepper spray, handcuffs, a handcuff key, a knife, and a radio holder.

Once the weapons belt was in place, I loaded a clip into the .45, secured the gun in my holster, and donned a bright-orange life vest and white-and-blue police helmet, both marked "U.S. Coast Guard." Inside the helmet was a lightweight communications headset, good for discrete talk between the boarding team and cutter, but with limited range, only a few hundred feet.

After a quick trip in *Shearwater*'s small boat, our boarding team climbed onto *Flying Deuce*. There were two persons on board. I inspected their IDs and asked where they were headed. The master, a scrawny man with a weathered face and a permanent sunburn, said the boat was bound for Marathon and that he and his friend had been fishing for the past three days. He couldn't produce any fishing gear, telling us they'd lent it to another boat last night. Right. My suspicions shifted into second gear.

I directed the two men to sit forward of the pilothouse. The sweep team found the boat empty, with nothing in its fishhold. I began the formal compliance inspection, aided by Boatswain's Mate Third Class (BM3) Chad Weatherby. Once we'd checked the safety equipment, we lowered ourselves into the engine room and took a look at the twin fuel tanks, probing the dark, oily corners of the compartment, scanning for marijuana residue or other tell-tales of a smuggling venture. We found nothing amiss.

We climbed back on deck and examined the slim eight-foot-long boxes, which the master said were spare fuel tanks. BM3 Weatherby opened the cap on one of the boxes and sure enough, it was full of diesel. I asked the master why he carried the extra fuel, since there were tanks in the engine room. He gave a vague, nonsensical answer, something about needing it for longer trips. Then he began giving us lip. "Hey, there's nothing here," he said. "You need to finish up—I need to get home before dark."

Petty Officer Weatherby and I walked to the transom. Weatherby was North Carolina–bred and powerfully built, with ham-hock arms and a thick, muscular chest, just the type of guy you wanted at your side when the going got tough. I cupped a hand over my mouth, talking low, like a catcher visiting the mound. "Boats," I said, "their story doesn't add up, and these extra tanks don't make sense. There's got to be something in those lower tanks." Weatherby was staring at the open hatch to the engine room, thinking through the situation. He shook his head side to side. "Yes, sir, but we've looked real hard and there's nothing there—no seeds, no residue, no access plates into the tanks," he said. "I checked the sounding tubes and didn't see anything wrong. We've got to get some evidence or we're out of luck."

By Coast Guard policy, the fuel tanks were off limits to us. The service prohibited intrusive searches unless there were concrete signs that a crime had been committed. That meant our boarding teams couldn't drill into tanks, disassemble pipes or false bulkheads, or cut into inaccessible spaces. Even though more and more smugglers were using hidden compartments, on the *Flying Deuce* our hands were tied. Unless we found marijuana residue or other supporting evidence, we'd have to let the vessel go.

I was frustrated, bordering on being pissed, and felt the same vibe from the boarding team, especially as the master amped up his tirade, taunting us more openly. "You can't find anything here," he said angrily. "I need to get moving. Stop wasting my time. You're acting like a bunch of water-Nazis." The master shimmied around the pilothouse and walked toward me, still spouting off. I warned him to pipe down and back off, or I'd arrest him for impeding a boarding. He shut up and sat, glowering. The sun was setting as I climbed back down into the engine room, inspecting the bilges one more time, tapping the sides of the fuel tanks, looking for anything that could be used as justification for an intrusive search. I found nothing. We were handcuffed by policy.

I conferred with the captain, speaking quietly into the communications headset, describing the fuel tanks and our suspicion there might be contraband hidden inside them. Lieutenant Lober was not going to let lawyerly restrictions stand in the way, and came up with Plan B. He radioed Group Key West, asking that it dispatch a 41-foot boat from Station Marathon to escort the fishing boat to shore for a full border search, where Customs had authority to inspect every inch of *Flying Deuce*, taking her apart piece by piece if necessary. But the Group watchstander reported that all of their 41-footers were tied up on other cases, and Customs had no vessels in the area.

Shearwater couldn't escort *Flying Deuce* ashore, due to the shallow water inside the reef, but the Group suggested that Station Marathon could send out a 25-foot boat as an escort once the fishing boat got closer to the beach. That sounded like a reasonable Plan C. I ordered the master to proceed directly to the pier at Station Marathon and present himself for the Customs search. He agreed, suddenly pleasant. Weatherby and I finished up the paperwork and the boarding team climbed into our small boat for the trip back to our cutter.

For the next hour *Shearwater* crept slowly west, the OOD tracking the fishing vessel on radar as she crossed into the shallows and up the narrow channel. Lieutenant Lober wasn't happy to let loose such a tempting target, but he acknowledged that at least Customs would have a chance to search those tanks.

Then came the bad news. Group Key West said the 25-footer had been diverted to a search-and-rescue case. The *Flying Deuce* was now inside the reef line, well beyond *Shearwater*'s reach, and soon was lost in the radar clutter near shore. Not surprisingly, *Flying Deuce* never stopped at the Coast Guard Station. The boat was gone, undoubtedly hidden in one of the million or so coves that dotted south Florida. To his credit, Lieutenant Lober remained calm in front of the crew, but he ground his teeth as he stood on the bridge wing, staring toward the twinkling lights ashore.

Shearwater continued toward Key West, and Red Crew's first and only training cruise came to a close. The team had exercised the full gamut of emergency procedures, stood its first watches, and carried out two actual boardings. The captain and I were impressed with the professionalism of the crew. They took their jobs seriously. Senior Chief had flexed his navigational skills, our boatswain's mates had performed safely in boat lowering and deck evolutions, and the engineering gang had kept the plant running smoothly. As an added bonus, Subsistence Specialist Second Class (SS2) Walt Goodrum, our cook, had ginned up a steady stream of hearty meals, despite the cramped quarters and minimal equipment in the galley.

Those were the pluses. On the minus side, Red Crew may have blown its first drug bust, but Lober reckoned there'd be plenty of opportunities, and he had no doubt that this crew had a bright future together.

Red Crew's next patrol wasn't for another six weeks. First we had to put *Petrel* into commission. We assigned half of our sailors temporarily to Blue Crew and Green Crew while Lieutenant Lober, Senior Chief Aiken, and I, along with five shipmates, headed to New Orleans to pick up the just-completed SES. Unlike *Sea Hawk* and *Shearwater,* our new cutter had been fashioned specifically for the Coast Guard and had an improved pilothouse, a refined galley area, and upgraded electronics. No doubt, *Petrel* would be the queen of the SES fleet.

———

After a night in New Orleans we drove to the Bell Halter shipyard, arriving before dawn. *Petrel* sat in a shallow, muddy canal. Our streamlined crew inspected the ship stem to stern, documenting every deficiency, while the engineers ran up the engines and auxiliary systems to assure they were working to specification. After twelve hours of scrutiny, Senior Chief, Boldan, and Sanders wrote a report listing the discrepancies for the captain's signature. There were no showstoppers, only minor issues—a loose handrail here, a mislabeled hatch there.

The next morning Bell Halter and the Coast Guard held a formal acceptance and naming ceremony. It was sweltering hot, the June air muggy and oppressive. Representative Bob Livingston and the Eighth District commander, a two-star admiral, were the guests of honor. To protect the crowd from the sun, the shipbuilder had erected a stage inside a tin-roofed fabrication shop, and there, amid piles of aluminum stock and rows of cutting machines, the VIPs made short speeches heralding the cutter's future service in the drug war. The ceremony culminated with a formal signing of the paperwork that transferred *Petrel* to the federal government. Jerry Lober affixed his signature with a flourish. The ship was now part of the Coast Guard fleet—in a special precommissioning status.

There was a brief reception, followed by tours of the ship. *Petrel* was immaculate. Every surface was sparkling clean, her hull freshly painted, the interior decks gleaming, the engine rooms bright and grease-free. The guests wandered about, marveling as we told them of the ship's high speed and unmatched stability. We didn't bring up the pounding that *Petrel* would take when facing a head sea, or the broken welds and split seams that were to be expected when the lightweight hull met the stresses of nonstop Coast Guard operations. Maybe, we thought, just maybe this new ship would suffer fewer of the casualties that were plaguing *Sea Hawk* and *Shearwater.*

After the guests had gone I walked the interior of the cutter, soaking in the ambiance of our new home. Two levels below the pilothouse was the galley, wedged into a compact room on the port side. It opened to a modest mess deck, fifteen feet square. There were two tables with bench seats and a low overhead, just over six feet, making the doorways real head-knockers. A divider ran down the middle of the ship, separating the port mess deck from a similar area on the starboard side, which included a television and entertainment center. This is where crew members would relax, commiserate, and eat their meals. Aft of the mess decks were two- and four-person staterooms. The mid-grade petty officers and non-rates would live there.

A steep metal ladder led to the main deck, emerging directly in the middle of the superstructure. When the ship had been used as an oil-rig transport, the interior of the deckhouse had been an open space, with one hundred forty four passenger seats bolted to the deck, but for the Coast Guard Bell Halter had removed the seats and installed laminated dividers to create five rooms. On the port side, the XO's stateroom sat forward with the captain's cabin directly behind it, next to a ladder to the pilothouse. A wide, longitudinal midships passageway separated these rooms from three compartments on the starboard side. Senior Chief's stateroom sat across from the XO and aft of it were two smaller rooms, an engineering office equipped with a set of gauges and a panoply of alarms, and a two-person stateroom that BM1 Sanders and MK1 Boldan would share.

I stepped into the XO's stateroom, gawking at its size. At twelve feet square, it was bigger than the two-person rooms on *Active*. Against the port bulkhead, underneath a tinted window, was a low-slung bunk, and along the aft wall were a metal desk and a clothing locker. The ship's weapons and ammo were stored in a tidy compartment in the forward bulkhead. What I didn't appreciate was that in bumpy weather, when the cutter was shaking and slamming through the waves, with no handholds to grab or bulkheads to lean against, it would be a game of timing to get from one side of the stateroom to another. Time it wrong, and a strong jolt could fling you to the deck. On a violently pitching cutter, open space often meant trouble.

Aft of the five rooms the central passageway widened, spanning the width of the deckhouse. Nestled at the port and starboard ends of the open area were small bathrooms, or heads. Near the heads, facing aft, were watertight doors that led to the exterior deck. The interior passage was so wide that the shipbuilder must have felt a need to put something in it, and five of the excess passenger seats sat along the aft bulkhead, facing the bow, with four more seats lined up outside the XO's stateroom.

Although the seats most likely were intended for the comfort of the crew, the Green and Blue crews had come up with a better use for them. The seats were where they shackled smugglers they'd arrested. To the SES sailors they were known as the "prisoners' chairs"—and I could hardly wait to get them filled.

Reveille was at daybreak. MK1 Boldan, who had been working since 0500, reported that all engineering systems were go. A swirl of diesel fumes spewed from the side exhaust ports and hovered over the pier, bringing tears to the eye and occasionally setting off the fire alarm inside the main deck passageway. The engineers disconnected the alarm, poised to reconnect it once we got under way, when there was wind across *Petrel*'s deck.

Lieutenant Lober mustered the crew, reviewing the day ahead. "It'll take about three hours to get to the Gulf, and then it's four hundred miles to Tampa Bay," he said. "If everything goes right, we'll get there around midnight and moor at Group St. Pete. It'll be a long run, so keep a good eye out for trouble. Once we're in deep water, get rest when you can." Senior Chief was beaming, thrilled by the moment, his eyes moist. We climbed the ladder to the bridge and Senior Chief tested the engines, then told Lieutenant Lober that we were ready to get under way for *Petrel*'s first sortie as a cutter. The captain replied in classic Coast Guard vernacular: "Make it so."

After threading through a web of canals, the new cutter rumbled and chattered across the open waters of the Gulf, arriving at the entrance of Tampa Bay at midnight. We'd left New Orleans with a partial fuel load and, devoid of equipment and supplies, made impressive speed, registering thirty-two knots on the Doppler speed log in four-foot ocean waves.

Five miles from the sea buoy the captain, senior chief, and I assumed our positions in the pilothouse for the entry into port, with BM1 Sanders and a seaman on the bow, ready to drop the anchor in an emergency. I stood over the radar, measuring the distance to landmarks and calling out buoys as we passed them by, plotting our position on the chart and maintaining the ship's log. Senior Chief manned the helm and throttles, also serving as lookout. The captain assumed the conn, directing course changes and handling the radio. Would we slow down for the transit, Senior Chief asked? "Hell no," Lieutenant Lober said, laughing. "*Petrel*'s going to fly through this harbor faster than any cutter in history."

And so she did. The four-foot waves in the Gulf flattened to a ripple as *Petrel* entered the sheltered mouth of Tampa Bay, and as the ship passed south of Egmont Key the Doppler was reading an even thirty-five knots. *Petrel* rattled and buzzed, the roar of the lift fans meshing with the rush of wind across the deck. It was a dark night, the moon hidden by thick cloud cover, making it impossible for other vessels to see our shape or the Coast Guard stripes on our bow. *Petrel* blasted up the main ship channel, effortlessly passing a cluster of fishing boats operating just outside the buoy line, traveling twice as fast as the typical freighter.

There was chatter on the VHF radio, one fisherman sounding incredulous, asking a compatriot in his deep Tallahassee drawl, "Did you see what just went by? It was crazy loud and really movin'. What the hell *was* that?" Lober couldn't resist. He picked up the radio microphone and pressed the transmit key, speaking slowly and with authority, in a low, clear baritone. "That . . . was . . . *fast.*"

The sprint through the Bay took less than an hour, with *Petrel* passing through the buoy gates at warp speed. Although I'd been nervous about manning the bridge with a three-person team—typically two or three other crew members would be involved—the arrangement worked flawlessly. We were tightly focused with no distractions, constantly double-checking each other's work, leveraging the strength of simple command and control.

"Abeam buoys 23 and 24."

"Buoys 23 and 24, aye."

"Five hundred yards to next turn."

"Roger, five hundred yards."

"Turning to port to zero-six-five in ten seconds."

"Ten seconds, aye."

"Five seconds . . . three, two, one . . . mark turn."

"Left five degrees rudder. Steady on zero-six-five."

"Left five degrees rudder, steady on zero-six-five, aye."

By 0130 *Petrel* was moored at Group St. Petersburg and, after a full night's sleep, we topped off the fuel tanks and headed south for homeport. The winds had died to a whisper and the seas were calm, and *Petrel* sliced effortlessly across the open waters of the Gulf. Even full of fuel we made thirty-one knots, a good sign that our new cutter was superior to her SES brethren. *Petrel* moored at Group Key West in late afternoon, our delivery crew brimming with confidence and eager to showcase Red Crew's worth.

We spent the next three weeks outfitting *Petrel* and preparing for operations. The crew and division support staff loaded food and galley supplies, ammunition, weapons, tools, spare parts, mooring lines, fenders, towlines, bedding, charts, and medical gear. We got under way for weapons testing and saw that the months of training had paid off. The deck force, the engineering gang, the navigation team—all were clicking on all cylinders. Only one thing stood in the way of *Petrel*'s first patrol: tradition.

The commissioning ceremony was held on July 8, on a steamy and unsettled morning, with a line of thunderstorms marching nearby. Our guests of honor were the local congressional representative, Dante Fascell, and the Seventh District commander, Rear Adm. Donald C. "Deese" Thompson. The two made an unlikely pair, the representative short and squat, a rumpled bulldog, and the admiral tall and lean, cutting a distinguished figure. Members of Red Crew, wearing their tropical blue uniforms, manned the ship's rail. The crew saluted the flag, listened to the speeches, and was ready to carry out the most important part of the ceremony—placing the ship into full commission—when the storm blew in. A bolt of lightning struck Christmas Tree Island across the harbor and a sharp thunderclap shattered the still air. The skies opened up in a deluge.

Red Crew took shelter under the tent where the guests were sitting, waiting out the storm. I stood watching the downpour, scowling. A hand settled on my shoulder. Rear Admiral Thompson was behind me, a warm smile on his face, and he spoke like father to son: "Don't worry, lieutenant, these things happen," he said. "It's probably a sign of good luck. Just do your best when you get to sea, and things will work out." He paused, scanning *Petrel*'s lines. "To be honest, I envy you and your crew. I really do. You've got a great ship, an amazing ship here." The look in his eyes showed that he meant it.

He was right. Red Crew was blessed to have the opportunity to take this new cutter to sea. *Petrel* was cutting-edge, with unique and impressive capabilities that gave us a fighting chance against the smuggling kingpins. She marked a transition from the old, traditional Coast Guard into a new and exciting era.

I nodded to the admiral, a strong sense of pride welling inside. The rain ended abruptly, the sun broke through the clouds, and we finished the ceremony only a few minutes late. *Petrel* and her plank-owner crew were now primed for action.

2

On Patrol

July 1983

It was the first day of *Petrel*'s inaugural patrol. We were on the prowl, and Red Crew was eager to make its mark. We steamed northwest into the Gulf of Mexico, boarding shrimpers and looking for smugglers trying to hide in the swarm of boats. We boarded three trawlers but found no trace of drug-running.

The next afternoon Group Key West radioed and directed us to return to port at best speed to receive further orders. *Petrel* slipped home through the Northwest Channel, a narrow cut that bisected swampy shallows and led into the back side of Key West Harbor. We moored at pier Delta Two at sunset. Lieutenant Lober hustled to the Group operations center while I dove into paperwork.

Ten minutes later an animated Jerry Lober hustled into my office. He was bubbling, talking fast. "XO, quick—we have to head over to the Navy command center," he said. "They need to talk to us in a secure room. They want us there in fifteen minutes. Let's go." This sounded promising. A secure room was for classified discussions. I'd never been in one before.

We jumped into Lieutenant Lober's car and sped across town, arriving just as a Navy rear admiral and a flock of junior officers streamed into a dark, tightly guarded operations center, crammed with plotting boards, charts, and television screens. The admiral waved us into a side conference room. An aide picked up a secure telephone and dialed the Seventh Coast Guard District in Miami, putting the call on speakerphone.

The voice from Miami was steady and emotionless. "Gentlemen, this is the chief of law enforcement operations for District Seven. What we're about to discuss is very sensitive." Lieutenant Lober looked at me, curious, one eyebrow raised. "We're working with DOD [the Department of Defense] and other federal agencies, and are tasking you with a mission that may take you to within twelve miles of the Cuban coast," the voice continued. This was the first time I'd heard of a cutter being ordered to enter the fifteen-mile buffer zone off Cuba. Something big must be up.

"A high-ranking Cuban military officer, one of their top generals, will be defecting to the United States tonight," the captain in Miami said. "He'll be leaving the north shore by small boat and arriving at 0300 at a designated point just outside Cuban waters. It's your job to be there to pick him up, without the Cuban authorities knowing what's happened. The general's family might be with him—maybe a half-dozen people. Take whatever actions are necessary to find and recover them. Absolute secrecy and radio silence are essential." I was floored. This was right out of a John Le Carré novel. Lieutenant Lober was trying not to grin.

My euphoria over the cloak-and-dagger mission quickly soured as I considered the dangers. The Communist government in Cuba kept close watch over its borders, both to keep out their enemies and to prevent their own citizens from leaving. Cuba had a brutal and effective border guard, a wing of MiG jet fighters, and its navy, while small, was armed to the teeth with Soviet weapons. The Cubans had a dozen *Osa*-class missile boats, each capable of forty-knot sprints and armed with SS-N-2 Styx anti-ship missiles, which could deliver half a ton of high explosives out to twenty-five miles. In our thin-hulled, lightly armed cutter, we'd be turned into vapor if we got into a shooting match with one of them.

The admiral said that no Navy ships were in the area and that we'd be less conspicuous if we operated alone. *Sea Hawk*, with the Green Crew on board, would provide backup and patrol about forty miles farther north. Lieutenant Lober asked what we should do for guidance if we sighted the defector inside Cuban waters. The admiral hesitated, then replied: "Use your best judgment to make the grab, but whatever you do, don't get caught violating their sovereignty." Don't get caught. There was a twinkle in Lober's eye—he knew that the careful wording amounted to tacit approval for crossing the territorial line, so long as the Cuban authorities didn't see us.

The admiral then introduced a man who had been sitting quietly in the corner. "Gentlemen, this is John, who's running this operation. He's from a civilian agency, but you will do whatever he says. He has full authority over the positioning of your ship so long as it doesn't endanger your crew." The captain in Miami validated the order. John was an everyman, casually dressed, about forty years old with a steely look engraved on plain features. He showed no emotion and barely acknowledged our presence. Whoever John was, we'd be working for him until the Cuban general was in our hands. He'd accompany us on the drive back to the cutter and would be on board *Petrel* during the operation.

Lieutenant Lober was elated. Once we were in his car, he started brainstorming about tactics to keep the Cubans from spotting us. "We won't be able to use the radar full-time, because they can track that from shore. Maybe we could set up a fake distress situation and pretend to be searching for a missing fisherman," he mused. "Wait, that's too risky. We'll have to run darkened ship, but then the general won't be able to see us. No, that's no good. Okay, we'll just flip on the lights every few minutes. Oh, and we'll have to be at battle stations—we don't want to get caught napping." I fed off his energy and began writing notes on a pad, scribbling fast.

"Don't write anything down," John commanded from his perch in the front seat. "This mission never happened—*understood?*" He turned to give me a cold stare. I put the pad away, chagrined.

We didn't tell the crew anything except that our departure had been delayed until midnight. John asked for a private cabin where he could work. I showed him to my stateroom and headed to the bridge, where I quietly studied charts of Cuba's north coast. Four hours later we got under way as quietly as possible, heading south in the main ship channel. There would be no SES shuffles tonight.

Once we were clear of the reef line *Petrel* steamed west, following a course toward Fort Jefferson, in hopes of misleading anyone who was watching our movements. The crew gathered on the mess deck and Lieutenant Lober explained our tasking. "We have to head close to Cuban waters on a sensitive mission," he said. "We have a civilian visitor on board who'll be helping us. Treat him just like you'd treat me. Just to be safe, we'll mount our weapons and set general quarters when we get on scene." The crew stared at him. "I can't get into too much detail on the exact nature of the mission"—the captain gave an exaggerated wink—"but we may be bringing some other visitors on board later this morning, so keep a sharp lookout for small boats." He told the crew members that he trusted them to be alert and to keep *Petrel* safe, and headed to the bridge.

I relieved the OOD. After our westward jaunt we turned south, skimming across the light swells. It was a beautiful night, with a ten-knot breeze and nearly calm seas. Visibility was clear and a quarter-moon shone brightly in the east, occasionally hidden behind passing cumulus clouds. The dry-bulb thermometer read a blissful 82 degrees.

John stepped into the pilothouse. "Go here," he said, handing the quartermaster a slip of paper. The coordinates showed a position twenty miles north of the Cuban shoreline. Maybe we wouldn't arouse the Communist authorities after all.

Petrel approached the rendezvous point at 0230, slowing to ten knots. The quartermaster secured our running lights and radar. Jerry Lober stood just outside the pilothouse, scanning with the night vision scope and directing occasional radar searches. Even with our mediocre civilian radars, we should've been able to detect a skiff two or three miles away in the flat seas. John told the bridge crew what we were looking for, and the quartermaster asked how big the defector's boat might be. "Probably pretty small," John answered tersely.

We cut all radio contact with Group Key West but listened closely in case the general hailed us on a distress frequency. John opened a shoebox-sized satchel and took out a handheld satellite radio, an innovation that the Coast Guard couldn't yet afford, and walked back to the aft deck for privacy. He returned to the bridge ten minutes later. "They should be here on time," he said. Then he stepped out onto the starboard bridge wing and waited.

The captain set general quarters, condition I, and the crew manned all weapons and donned battle helmets and flak jackets. The mood on the bridge was a mixture of high tension and caged excitement, with everyone on edge, waiting for a small boat, or maybe a Cuban gunboat, to emerge from the darkness. *Petrel* came to a stop, unlighted, and drifted. The bridge crew kept the binoculars and night vision scopes in constant use, and the M-60 and .50-caliber gunners served as extra lookouts. The pilothouse was eerily quiet, no one talking except for an occasional scratchy whisper.

It was 0300—rendezvous time—and there still was no sign of the defector. The only contact was a freighter twelve miles to *Petrel*'s northeast, heading toward Miami. The moon was creeping toward its zenith, partially obscured by a thickening cloud cover. Ten minutes crawled by. I energized the radar, letting it rotate for five sweeps and then shut it down, so the Cubans wouldn't be able to track our transmissions. There were no blips. Ten more minutes passed. The quartermaster flashed *Petrel*'s running lights as a signal. There was no response. We shifted from battle stations to condition III steaming. We'd leave the weapons mounted and half the crew on watch for alternating six-hour shifts until the mission was over.

At 0330 John walked aft to make another call on his satellite radio. He hurried back onto the bridge. "Try here," he told the OOD. It was another set of coordinates, farther south. We headed there at full speed and then began a slow barrier patrol, right on the edge of the Cuban territorial sea. Lieutenant Lober switched on the radar again. The mountainous coast was cleanly painted on the screen, only twelve miles away. He turned off the radar set after a half-dozen sweeps.

At 0400 the anxiety mounted. We'd seen or heard nothing from the defector, straining our eyes to cut through the darkness. At 0418 the port-side lookout spotted dim lights between *Petrel* and the Cuban coast. It wasn't our man; in the night-vision scope it looked like a medium-sized fishing trawler, paralleling the coastline. I wondered: where was this guy? Maybe he'd been captured as he tried to leave port. If he'd disclosed the rendezvous point to the authorities, the next thing we saw could be an inbound Styx missile. Our flak jackets and tin-can helmets wouldn't do much good against one of those beasts. With that thought came a jolt of adrenaline, and then more waiting.

Soon it was 0500. A featureless sea surrounded the cutter. The whispers in the pilothouse intensified, with the crew beginning to wonder if the defector had been lost. Half an hour later the captain expanded the barrier patrol and increased *Petrel*'s speed to eighteen knots, still straddling the international boundary. The second set of watchstanders came to the bridge, but no one wanted to leave his or her station.

A dozen sailors scanned the sea. Still there was nothing. By 0630, with the sun tickling the horizon, John showed his first sign of despair, tossing out a string of expletives after another session with his satellite radio. "They got under way, but no one has heard from them in four hours," he said. "They may be lost." It wasn't clear whether "lost" meant they'd strayed wildly off course or had been discovered and killed by the Cuban secret police.

Red Crew continued the hunt, still with weapons mounted, still maintaining radio silence. Our cook, SS2 Goodrum, plied the crew with buckets of coffee and mounds of bacon and eggs. The mood turned grim, with no one speaking, the whispers gone, eyes strained and bleary, faces tense, hoping that one of us would see the skiff and that we could rescue the general.

District Seven ramped up the effort, dispatching a Falcon jet to crisscross a twenty-by-thirty-mile area. The planes were new, fast, and nimble—regular partners when the SESs patrolled the Bahamas. The air crew called on the UHF radio, directed us to join the search for a missing fifteen-foot fishing boat, and assigned us an expanding square pattern to their south. John told us that this was the prearranged cover story in case a search was needed. Jerry Lober had gotten his phony SAR case.

For the next six hours Red Crew scoured the area, with the entire crew helping out—a full-court press. The clouds built into a thick overcast, blotting the sun and limiting the effectiveness of the jet overhead. At noon, a second Falcon joined the search. A civilian yacht, chartered by an unnamed federal agency, showed up and pitched in. John wasn't hiding his satellite calls anymore, standing on the bridge wing and yelling into the radio that we needed more planes and ships to help. *Petrel* finished her second search pattern and headed for the third.

Then suddenly, at 1430, the general was found—but not by us. "United States Coast Guard, United States Coast Guard, this is the motor vessel *Texaco Westminster*. Please come in. Over." The voice had a crisp British accent and was blaring at full power across channel 16, the international short-range distress frequency. Anyone listening within fifty miles of the *Texaco Westminster* could hear the broadcast—including the Cubans.

Group Key West responded, asking the nature of the call. The master on the oil tanker spoke slowly, polite and precise: "Coast Guard, we're at all stop alongside a dinghy with five people on board, and request your assistance. One of them says he's a military official from Cuba and desires transport to the United States. Can you send a ship to pick him up, please?" The Brit then read off his ship's latitude and longitude, eliminating the need for the Cubans to triangulate on the radio signal. They now knew exactly where their missing general was, if they were listening.

Senior Chief scrambled to plot the coordinates. *Texaco Westminster* was thirty miles north of us. The defector's boat had overshot our position badly, or maybe the general had decided to try and make it all the way to Florida on his own. So much for a well-orchestrated rendezvous, I thought. The OOD slammed the throttles forward and *Petrel* headed north at full speed, maintaining radio silence in case a Cuban missile boat was looking for a cutter to blast from the water.

Sea Hawk was closer, and within a half-hour Green Crew picked up the general and his family and headed for Key West, leaving their thirteen-foot skiff adrift. After spending another thirty minutes waiting for a Styx missile that never came, we secured our weapons, our crew red-eyed and stumbling as *Petrel* shimmied toward home port.

John remained aloof at first, but over a late lunch he lightened up and showed his first smile. His eyes sparkled with achievement. "You know, I really like it when the good guys win," he said. He told us more about the Cuban general and his own job with the Central Intelligence Agency, and then detailed the importance of the defection. Even though the rendezvous had gone awry, the agency had gotten its man, and John expected to reap a treasure trove of intelligence from him. Senior Chief asked if we could tell anyone about the defection. "Wait a few years, then blab to whomever you want," John said. "Just don't use my real name. And tell everyone I was tall and handsome, like in the movies."

Red Crew was worn out, staggering like zombies. The lack of sleep and gallons of extra adrenaline coursing through our veins had taken their toll. An hour later, *Petrel* moored in Key West and the captain gave us the rest of the day off. John disappeared in an unmarked car, along with the escaped Cubans. We never saw them again. I lay in bed, wondering how bad things must be for someone to take his or her family to sea in a thirteen-foot boat. Eventually, I fell into a deep sleep, dreaming of a rain of missiles heading toward the ship.

The rest of the patrol was a letdown. We spent a week in the Yucatan, thrashing through choppy seas, boarding a pair of sailboats and towing a disabled fishing boat, the *Don Polo III*, which we turned over to an antiquated Mexican navy ship, the *D15*. The Mexican captain was courteous and professional and thanked us for helping out the fishermen. Then we had some problems with our lift engines; fortunately, of the division's most experienced engineers, Machinery Technician First Class Duane Riopelle was sailing with us, and helped Boldan's team make the repair. After that it was a long, pounding slog back to Key West. *Petrel*'s first patrol was complete, with no drug seizures but one Cuban family to the good. We all knew that the Cubans would find freedom in the United States—and that was a big win.

———

A week later Red Crew headed back on patrol—this time to the east, steaming at full speed toward the Bahamas. In the Straits of Florida business was slow, with only a few lonely merchant vessels painting the horizon. We approached the northern rim of Cay Sal Bank, slowing to look for boats hidden near the rocks, careful to remain outside of Bahamian waters. The bridge crew searched constantly, scanning the jagged islands with the binoculars and "big eyes," our long-range, pedestal-mounted binoculars. In good weather we'd be able to detect a lobster boat eight or nine miles away. We saw nothing but deserted cays.

Petrel continued east through the deep waters of the Santaren Channel, surrounded by an empty sea. The crew ran through emergency drills, practiced boat lowering, trained new coxswains, and, after the work was done, dropped fishing lines in the water in the hope of catching dinner, all while waiting for some real action. One of the engineers snagged an eight-foot hammerhead shark and pulled it alongside the hull, where I shot it through the head with an M-16, repeatedly, until it stopped thrashing. We didn't find any boats to board, but the shark steaks were good on the grill.

We crossed onto the Great Bahama Bank just before dark. The bank was a shallow, sandy, underwater plain that wrapped around the western and southern sides of Andros Island, the largest Bahamian landmass. The bank extended fifty miles from shore and was a prime haven for smugglers, who knew that it was too shallow for larger cutters to patrol. We planned to spend the next five days in these desolate waters, sprinting between potential hot spots and then drifting, conserving fuel, hoping that dopers would pass nearby and that we'd see them before they saw us. Stealth and surprise were key. We didn't want the smugglers to turn and run or dump their loads if they knew the Coast Guard was waiting to pounce.

———

In normal steaming we stood a three-person bridge watch, with an OOD, a quartermaster, and a lookout. A single engineer made rounds of the hole. Each watch was four hours long, just enough time to maximize effectiveness while preventing burnout, and each day at sea was divided into six watch periods, starting at midnight. Everyone stood watch except the captain and Goodrum, who was responsible for turning out three full meals, plus midnight rations, without fail.

The quartermasters fixed *Petrel*'s position using depth soundings, radar ranges, visual bearings, and the electronic Long Range Navigation system, or LORAN, which measured the time differences between pairs of radio signals. Navigation near Cay Sal Island had been a breeze, with a crisp radar picture of the rocks and strong LORAN readings. On much of the bank, however, especially south of Andros, the LORAN signal weakened, and there were no visual or radar landmarks. There, estimating our position was more educated guess than exact science.

At night *Petrel* ran dark, with navigation lights extinguished. I stood the midwatch, between midnight and 0400, my favorite time as OOD. It was the quietest watch, but it had an air of intrigue, knowing that the smugglers operated under cover of night and that we could stumble across one of them at any moment. No land or shipping lanes were visible from the bank and outside the pilothouse was a universe of nothing, inky blackness, the sea and sky melding into a single dark blob. The night-vision scope and radar were indispensable, but so was the human eye. Standing on the bridge wing, scanning the horizon, trying to will a target to appear, straining to see the distant curl of a wake, a glint of water on fiberglass, or a dim white light that might signal the presence of a smuggler—that was the beauty of the midwatch.

Even when there were no sightings, *Petrel* hummed with a sense of anticipation, our crew a tightly wound spring, always on call, prepared to respond without warning to an intercept, a chase, or a rescue. In the meantime, we searched and waited, finding only empty waters, and then searched some more.

———

There's a saying that eternal vigilance is the only guarantee for safety at sea. Red Crew found that out on our last night under way. We were steaming at full speed near the Muertos Cays, on the northern rim of Cay Sal Bank, headed for home. *Petrel* was overtaking a poorly lighted sailboat, its radar return lost in the clutter from the six-foot waves. The sailboat's stern light was burned out, rendering it all but invisible. The lookout, scanning ahead, caught a glimpse of the vessel's sidelight as the sailboat yawed on its axis, and he ran into the pilothouse, shouting, "Green light, close aboard, just off the port bow!" The OOD snatched back the throttles and energized the searchlight. Bobbing in the seas only two hundred yards ahead was a twenty-five-foot ketch. We boarded the boat and found nothing unusual, only a young couple still shaking from almost having gotten speared by a 150-ton cutter.

Eternal vigilance applied to the drug war, too. Even at three in the morning, or after a grueling day, or when the seas were pounding the ship, the OOD and bridge team had to stay fully alert, able to detect the smallest clue—a smudge on the horizon, a sound, or a blip on the radar. Vigilance was the difference between finding the smugglers or letting them pass by, unseen, to deliver their cargo ashore.

———

I'd learned this lesson two years earlier, as a boot ensign on my first patrol on board *Active*. We were on a six-week deployment to the Yucatan, and I was standing watch as the break-in OOD, staring at the sixteen-inch radar screen, hoping to find a northbound vessel for boarding. The screen had been blank for hours.

Suddenly there was a tiny green blip at the edge of the radar display, a solitary splash of phosphorescence. Within a few seconds the faint image had faded away. I stared, hoping for the blip to return, spinning the cursor out to the spot on the screen where the dot had flared. Range: 13.1 miles. Bearing: 305 degrees true. The blip was to our northwest and *Active* was slowly motoring west, toward Cozumel. If the blip represented a northbound ship, then the vessel was moving tangentially away from the cutter. That made it unlikely that there'd be any more radar hits, and the boat would get through the Yucatan without inspection.

I thought we should go after it, but there was probably nothing there. It had only been one blip and then the screen had gone blank. Distant clouds, birds, or a larger-than-normal wave often spoofed the radar and created a return that looked like a target. I wrestled with the decision: should I inform the captain and request to divert north, hoping to find something that might not exist, or wait for another radar hit? The radar screen stayed empty, unhelping, taunting. It would be foolish to divert for a phantom. Still, I thought it was better to chase a possible target than to let it go. I picked up the telephone handset and dialed the captain's cabin. To my relief, he told me to go for it.

We maneuvered to an intercept course and increased speed to full, making turns for eighteen knots. I stood at the radar pedestal with my face crammed into the blackout hood, watching intently as the radial sweep moved clockwise around the display. *Active* gently shuddered with a low-pitched shimmy as she cut through the three-foot swells. The vibration felt good, invigorating, a sign of action. Maybe it signaled good luck.

There—another green dot, twelve miles away and on the same bearing as the first one. This time the radar return was solid, a tiny rectangle, a sure indication of a vessel and not a thunderhead or a flock of birds. Thirty seconds later, the green dot reappeared, this time even brighter. Within five minutes, the target appeared with every sweep of the antenna.

Active was eleven miles away and closing. I plotted the contact's course and speed. It was headed to the north-northeast, toward Florida's west coast, making nine-and-a-half knots.

Fifteen minutes later the lookout spied the target, shouting: "Contact, bearing three-four-zero, range nine miles, appears to be a white-hulled fishing vessel, target angle one-five-zero." The captain, standing beside me, stared through his binoculars and spoke with a lilt of excitement. "Okay, this is looking good," he said. "It might be a western-rig shrimper, definitely headed to the north. Let's get ready for a boarding." One of the other ensigns, a year my senior, gave me a shoulder-punch, smirking. "Nice job, rookie," he said. "Glad you didn't chase a cloud."

When we were two miles astern, the lookout read the name of the vessel using the powerful "big eyes" on the flying bridge: it was *Hopeful*. The vessel was a sixty-five-foot shrimper, pilothouse forward, with a white paint scheme. There was a man on the boat's aft deck, wearing dark shorts and not much else, and he was looking at us. For him, it must have been an unusual sight. Amid the emptiness of the vibrant blue sea, a scattering of cumulus clouds overhead, he'd see our bow profile, the bright white hull with the instantly recognizable red-and-blue Coast Guard stripe. He'd almost certainly know we were coming to board his boat.

The captain told me to station *Active* one hundred yards off the fishing boat's starboard quarter, ready to maneuver quickly if *Hopeful* turned toward us. One tactic used by smugglers was to try and ram the intercepting cutter, which usually ended with the drug boat sinking— taking its cargo and all the evidence with it to the ocean floor. Without any evidence there could be no arrests.

The OOD picked up the VHF-FM marine radio and hailed the boat on channel 16. "Fishing vessel *Hopeful*, fishing vessel *Hopeful*, this is the U.S. Coast Guard cutter off your quarter." The master of the vessel answered, his words thick, as if he'd just awakened from a nap. The OOD ran through the standard preboarding questions. The master said there were three men on board and the boat was empty, heading for St. Petersburg to trawl for shrimp.

Hanging over *Hopeful*'s starboard side were two large tires. Thick black rub marks discolored the side of her hull. The boat's large outriggers were fully extended, and she was riding low in the water, as if full of catch. Best of all, stenciled on the transom beneath her name were three treasured words: Corpus Christi, Texas. *Hopeful* was an American vessel. We could board her with impunity.

The OOD ordered the master to bring the fishing boat to bare steerageway and gather his crew on the fantail, in plain sight, and told him that we'd be sending a boarding party to inspect for compliance with U.S. law. The voice responding was slurred and almost incoherent. "Ah, okay, Coast Guard, uh, we'll, uh, slow down, sure, no problem. Uh, what're you guys comin' over for? Nothing here, really, you know, we're just headed up to go trawlin' in the Gulf. . . ." The voice trailed off.

Watching from *Active*'s bridge provided a bird's-eye view of the boarding, the scene playing out a football field away. The coxswain circled our motor surfboat around *Hopeful* and then nestled along her starboard quarter. The boarding team quickly scaled the side using one of the hanging tires as a foothold. *Active*'s bridge was buzzing, electric with excitement. The quartermaster quietly made a bet with the helmsman: "Five bucks says that boat's loaded with reefer," he said. The helmsman whispered back: "No way. You're on."

They settled the wager two minutes later. *Hopeful*'s crew stood clustered in the middle of the aft deck and our boarding team formed a semi-circle around them. As in a silent movie, we could see the boarding officer talking with *Hopeful*'s master. After a brief back-and-forth, the boat's crew shuffled to the port rail and sat down, one of them stumbling and landing hard. Two members of the boarding team walked over to the main fishhold, fifteen feet forward on the deck. They lifted the large square hatch. One pointed down into the hold, and then waved the boarding officer over to see what they'd found. The boarding officer looked and nodded, then reached for his handheld radio.

"*Active*, boarding team, be advised that the fishhold is full of bales that appear to be marijuana. The hold is packed full. We're detaining the crew and will field-test a sample of the cargo. Over." The boarding officer would take a dime-sized chunk from a bale and test it for tetrahydrocannabinol, or THC, the active ingredient in marijuana. The OOD acknowledged the report and directed the quartermaster to record it in the ship's log. The quartermaster pointed to the helmsman, mouthing "pay up."

On *Hopeful*, the three crew members put their hands on their heads while one of the boarding team stepped down into the hold and muscled up a large package, wrapped in burlap, about three feet by two feet by two feet. It looked like dope, all right. A crowd of our own crew had gathered on *Active*'s flight deck, and when they saw the bale they began to cheer.

"*Active*, boarding party, we've tested the bale and it's positive for THC. I say again, the bale is positive for THC." We now had proof that the fishing boat was carrying drugs, and the captain authorized arrest and seizure. As the boarding party placed *Hopeful*'s crew in cuffs, the crowd on the flight deck began cheering more loudly.

For the next day and a half *Active* escorted the fishing boat to Key West, a custody crew in command. During the transit, the captain dispatched two other ensigns and me to *Hopeful* to take pictures for the evidence package and to see firsthand how smugglers operated. Stepping on board, we were assaulted by a strong organic odor, musky and dank. It was the trademark scent of bulk marijuana. Careful not to disturb the crime scene, we toured the entire boat—or tried to, at least. Much of *Hopeful* was inaccessible, every available spot stuffed with fifty-pound bales. The fishhold was completely full. The forward lazarette was crammed tight. There were bales in every berthing area, in the galley, and partially blocking the passageways. Even the helmsman's chair in the pilothouse had been removed; the person operating the boat sat on a pile of bales instead. On the forward console, next to the ship's wheel, was part of a bale, with a big divot taken out of it, clearly a source of recreation for the crew. Rolling-papers littered the floor. That explained the dopey, slurred responses when the OOD queried the master by radio—*Hopeful*'s skipper had been completely stoned from sampling his own cargo.

Active arrived at Coast Guard Station Key West the next day. It took six hours to offload the marijuana, with Customs officials trucking off the bales for destruction, a representative sample saved for analysis by the intelligence folks. The Customs agents filled a flatbed truck with the bales, then again, and again, and finally a fourth time. The final tally was staggering. *Hopeful* had been carrying 27 tons of marijuana—54,000 pounds' worth, with a street value of almost $21 million. The haul included more than a thousand individual bales. It was *Active*'s biggest seizure yet. And it all came from a single green dot on the radar. Such was the role of vigilance in the war on drugs.

————

Every cutter crew was different, with its own personality, strengths, and quirks. *Active*'s crew had been solid and tough—Boston tough. The men were hardy, thick-skinned, and salty to the core, with a smashmouth mentality, a solid match for the unforgiving waters of the north Atlantic. Heavy weather, persistent cold, a rough-riding ship—none of those got in the way of getting the job done.

If *Active*'s crew was rough and tumble, Red Crew had the persona of a skilled professional, thorough and steady. They had gobs of experience and an adventuresome spirit, well suited for the Wild West Caribbean. Red Crew bonded quickly, sharing a common love for country and disdaining the thugs who were smuggling drugs onto our streets. There were no weak links and no troublemakers. They went the extra mile without complaint, often working around the clock, whether for a boarding, a search-and-rescue case, or an engine repair.

The members of Red Crew had big hearts, and there were a few big personalities to match. Senior Chief was a force of nature, brash and bold. His two quieter sidekicks, Sanders and Boldan, led their men calmly but were equally effective. Together, they were the brains of the team. The mid-grade petty officers provided the heart of the crew. Boatswain's mates Chuck Obenland and Chad Weatherby were polar opposites—the former low-key and professorial, a square-jawed midwestern blond with the gift of leadership, and the latter loud and affable, a southern jokester, with his solid build and wavy black hair. Obenland was filling a second class petty officer's billet, but he had just been promoted, and he'd be reassigned within the next few months. That'd be a big loss, since he was one of our most experienced boarding officers and a great all-around cutterman. Weatherby also was slated for promotion; he would step up into Obenland's spot, and Red Crew would get a new boatswain's mate third class.

Boldan's engineering gang included Machinery Technician Third Class (MK3) Bill Hartsock and Electrician's Mate Third Class (EM3) Chuck Meisner, both highly skilled in law enforcement. Hartsock was a country boy from upstate New York, born with a humble, fun-loving demeanor. He was an intensely hard worker and never gave up on a repair, no matter how intractable. If you wanted something done, you gave it to Hartsock. Meisner, Red Crew's electrician, was more reserved, with a low-key sense of humor, but equally hard-working. Tall and rail-thin, he had jet-black hair, wore dark glasses, and sported a thin mustache—the type of guy you might find in a pool hall. Meisner was an expert technician and had a keen eye for detail, often seeing things the rest of us missed. Weatherby, Hartsock, and Meisner formed a troika and spent their downtime telling sea stories, playing cards, or plotting a practical joke, sometimes with Walt Goodrum's help. Short, thin, and scrappy, Goodrum had a bright personality and a Chicago sense of the world. The care he showed feeding the crew put him in good stead with his shipmates.

Rounding out the team were six non-rates, four seamen who worked for Sanders and two engineers. Of the seamen, Danny Motley stood out, well over six feet tall with a full beard and an ample frame. He was happy-go-lucky, pleasantly dorky, and eager to please. Mark Northen, thin and agile, was mild mannered, extremely bright, and a quick learner. Joan Scott, who was training to become a quartermaster, was slightly built and demure, with a quiet persona, while her roommate, Carrie Corson, was even quieter and tougher than nails. Corson manned the .50-caliber and was an expert shot.

Like Motley, one of the firemen, Stan Elliot, was tall, but with more of a swimmer's physique, and a polite, modest personality bordering on shy. He was instantly likeable, the type of guy you'd want your sister to marry, and as our only Spanish speaker he was a valuable plus for the crew. His fellow fireman, Mike Kassin, was blessed with a wrestler's body, a winning attitude, and a strong work ethic—another big asset.

Red Crew was a pretty diverse bunch along all the traditional lines. We had men and women; whites, a Hispanic, and an African American; city dwellers, country folk, well-to-do and poor; tall and short, quiet and loud, guys who could grow thick beards and others who couldn't; southerners, northerners, and a gaggle from the Midwest; and blonds, brunettes, and a ginger. Some, such as Chuck Meisner, Joan Scott, and me, were all skin-and-bones, and others were a lot beefier. We even had a resident biker. But no one cared about gender, skin tone, size, or accent. What mattered was attitude and devotion to the job at hand. In that sense, Red Crew was monolithic, a tight team of hard-charging, fun-loving sailors, dedicated to the mission and trying their best to make their captain—and the Coast Guard—proud.

In mid-August multi-crewing kicked into gear. Red Crew had just finished its third patrol, still without a seizure, and the newly established Gold Crew was slated to replace us on *Petrel*. Then we'd spend ten days ashore, working with the SES Division support staff. The crew swap required detailed inventories of weapons, ammunition, classified material, and food stores, along with a stem-to-stern inspection. It was six hours of bureaucratic hell but a necessary evil to assure accountability. As plank-owners, the members of Red Crew had an emotional attachment to *Petrel*, and it felt awkward to hand over the keys to another team. We skulked ashore, feeling as though we'd been evicted from our new home.

Multi-crewing wasn't popular, and all of us wanted a cutter to call our own. We knew instinctively that shared responsibility would lead to frictions. It did. Each engineering team stored its tools and spare parts in different spots; every crew had its own standard of cleanliness; each cook had a favorite method for packing food into the freezer; and every senior chief had his preference for what charts went where. As crew swaps became more frequent, standardization went up and tensions died down, but it took a focused effort from all of the SES sailors to refine the change of command process.

Red Crew's unease in leaving *Petrel* was compounded by our frustration for failing to nail our first doper. The Green and Blue crews had continued to find smugglers, with three more seizures between them over the summer, and Gold Crew even scored on its first patrol. It didn't matter that its seizure was for marijuana residue, and not a full load of drugs; it still reinforced Red Crew's growing angst. We were the only SES crew that hadn't landed a bust.

It wasn't for a lack of trying. In our first three patrols Red Crew traveled to all corners of the Bahamas, made a trip to the Yucatan, and searched the eastern Gulf of Mexico. Jerry Lober, ever the adventurer, pushed the boundaries of the operating area, seeking new hunting ground east of Andros Island and sniffing along the Old Bahama Channel as far south as Crooked Island, more than two-thirds of the way to Haiti. All of these were prime trafficking zones, but we never found the dopers.

Red Crew responded to reports of air drops, motherships, offloads, and bales in the water, pulled in one direction and then the next. Hot intelligence from the district operations center in Miami would prove erroneous, or we'd arrive too late, finding empty water, with the smugglers having fled the scene. While patrolling off Bimini, we were tasked to check out suspicious activity near Cay Sal; it turned out to be two Bahamian conch boats. A few hours later, intelligence sources said there was a drug load leaving Bimini. We sped back and spent the night on a barrier patrol off the low-lying island, seeing nothing, too late, having missed the shipment.

Between the intelligence reports, Red Crew boarded everything it could find. On August 2 we intercepted the fishing vessel *El Jesus*, which was suspected of carrying a load of marijuana, near Cay Sal Bank, but we found nothing. The next day we inspected a northbound sailboat, the *Nostalgia*—the boat was clean. On August 12, the 250-foot freighter *Cap de L'ile*, bound from Honduras to Tampa—also nothing. The fishing vessels *Charity*, *Odessa*, *Cynful*—all clean. Near Fort Jefferson, a 40-foot lobster boat named *Jaqueline*; in the Florida Straits, the 60-foot fishing trawler *Rip Tide II*; north of the Yucatan, a 150-foot freighter named *Lisa Elmar*; off Key West, a gorgeous sailboat named *Shira's Song*. The *Polaris*, the *Chaser*, the *Marc Joseph*, the *Mini Lymph*, the *Lone Star*, the *Lucas F*, the *Caribic River*, the *Mary Grace*, the *Excaliber 42*, the *Red Lady*, the *Westwind*, the *Iris C*—we inspected them all with a close eye, pushing to the limit our legal authorities to ensure they weren't carrying contraband. None was.

In August, the Coast Guard instituted a new policy that allowed law enforcement officers to conduct intrusive searches at sea. Red Crew's boarding teams measured compartments and fuel tanks to see if there was unaccountable space between them; when necessary, we drilled a small hole into a bulkhead or tank and inserted a borescope into the void—the thin optical device allowing a view of the empty space. Yet, despite such cutting-edge tactics, our teams still found nothing, nothing, and then even more nothing.

Red Crew knew that its first drug seizure was coming. We just didn't know when or where our luck might change. At the end of August, Red Crew assumed command of *Sea Hawk* and headed toward Cay Sal, itching to score. Three days into the patrol we got a break. Group Key West tasked us to intercept two shrimpers that were traveling from Guyana to St. Petersburg, Florida. They'd been trawling off South America for the past four months and, according to sources, they were loaded with marijuana and possibly cocaine. A Coast Guard C-130 search plane had sighted the boats in the Old Bahama Channel, well to our southeast, around noon. District Seven suspected that the shrimpers would be offloading their contraband to smaller boats as they passed by Cay Sal. At least, that's what the intelligence report said.

The boats were named *Castor* and *Pollux*, sister ships owned by a fly-by-night fishing company suspected of ties to the drug trade. Based on the C-130 sighting, the boats were headed directly for the Anguilla Cays, at the southeastern corner of Cay Sal Bank. Anguilla was a seven-mile-long, narrow, and craggy string of islands, inhabited by armies of iguanas and flocks of sea birds, with low rolling hills, rocky coves, and twisting inlets, the ideal locale for a drug transfer. *Sea Hawk* had to intercept the shrimpers before they dipped into Bahamian waters.

The weather was bad. The barometric pressure had been dropping all day, and blustery winds from the west were setting up against a northeasterly swell, churning the seas into confusion. Once *Sea Hawk* passed south of Anguilla the seas grew to eight feet, slowing our advance to twenty-five knots, the cutter sliding down the faces of the quartering swells. Thirty miles outside of Bahamian waters, the OOD slowed to clutch speed. It was just after sunset. Senior Chief plotted the last known position, course, and speed of the shrimpers and charted an eight-mile-wide barrier patrol across their expected path. Red Crew rested and waited.

Castor and *Pollux* first lit up the radar around 2200. Lieutenant Lober, BM1 Obenland, Seaman Motley, and Seaman Scott were on the bridge when I sneaked up the metal ladder, my eyes not adjusted for night vision, walking in baby steps so as not to jam into anyone. All that was visible in the pilothouse was a dim red light over the chart desk; outside the windows was a curtain of black. Painting cleanly on the radar were two distinct blips, eight miles to the southeast, a few hundred yards apart and traveling to the northwest at eight knots. The shrimpers were making good speed in the sloppy weather. The captain spoke in a whisper: "XO, these have to be our guys—traveling together, right on schedule—let's get the boarding team ready to go." Even though I couldn't see his face, it was easy to imagine the captain's look of anticipation over what could be our first seizure—or seizures.

The seas were trouble, so we put our best heavy-weather coxswain on the case. Chad Weatherby had grown up on the Outer Banks, saltwater in his veins, and at his previous duty station he'd spent a lot of time navigating breaking surf. The captain decided that we'd send a single team to board the closest shrimper and then move to the second boat, rather than deploy two teams at once. Obenland, who had the most experience on shrimpers, would lead the four-person boarding party. I'd serve as his assistant, with Seaman Motley and MK3 Hartsock rounding out the team. On the second boarding, Obenland and I would reverse roles. I went below and donned my bulletproof vest and coveralls, then returned to the bridge to witness the intercept.

Lit up in our spotlight, the shrimpers were pounding the seas hard, smashing through the curling waves and launching sheets of spray a hundred feet into the air. They were big boats, pushing eighty feet, with massive outriggers that looked like horizontal construction cranes. Over the radio, the master on *Castor* said he had four crewmembers and that they were in a hurry to get back to St. Pete. Yes, he'd slow to bare steerageway to allow the boarding party on board, and sure, he'd come a few degrees to starboard to provide a lee, but clearly he was irked at the delay. Lieutenant Lober then called *Pollux*, ordering it to remain two hundred yards off its sister ship. The master complied without complaint.

The boarding team was ready, fully suited up. We checked each others' weapons belts, making sure the .45s and other gear were secure, then donned our life vests and police helmets. The helmets were a recent addition to the boarding uniform, and many Coast Guardsmen didn't like them, thinking they presented too severe an image for a lifesaving service. On a night like this, with the wind and seas and a hundred things in motion, we were all glad for the extra protection.

The boarding party walked to the aft deck and clustered around the RHIB. BM1 Sanders ran the boat deck, winching the four-meter boat over the side. *Sea Hawk* was snap-rolling 10 degrees and elevatoring up and down in the seas. The RHIB slammed against the hull as Sanders lowered it, as fast as the winch would allow. Once the boat was in the water, Weatherby scrambled down the Jacob's ladder—a set of wooden steps strung between two ropes—and jumped on board. The RHIB was bouncing wildly, putting a heavy strain on the sea painter and tending lines, rising and falling five feet, six feet, the waves breaking over its side and flooding the open bilge. Weatherby twisted the ignition switch to spark the outboard engine to life. He looked up and yelled: "Let's go, let's go, we're gonna swamp this thing if we don't hustle up!" Obenland led the way, moving as fast as he could down the swaying ladder, followed by the rest of the team. I was last to descend and, in haste, missed the last rung, falling three feet into the boat, sitting in a heap on the deck, my backside soaked by the sloshing water.

"Cast off!" Weatherby gunned the engine as soon as the lines were clear and pointed the RHIB away from the cutter, at speed, allowing the bilge water to drain out the rear vent tube. Once most of the water was gone he closed the vent and slowed, gently surfing over a ten-foot swell.

I looked back. *Sea Hawk* was a dark silhouette, her powerful search-light knifing through the night to illuminate the shrimper. Weatherby steered the small boat directly toward *Castor*, approaching from her star-board beam. Between the RHIB and the shrimper was a nightmarish scene, a forest of frothing, seething waves, ragged row after ragged row, the waves jumping up unpredictably, some six feet high, others twice that size, their dark mounds capped with roiling foam. *Sea Hawk*'s spotlight cast long shadows that grew and shrank with the motion of the waves, adding to the visual confusion. Surrounding *Castor* was a thick halo of sea spray, millions of tiny droplets glistening in the intense spotlight beam and the bright floodlights that illuminated the fishing boat's aft deck.

From *Sea Hawk*'s bridge the waves had looked big. Once we were in the water, they looked deadly. The four-meter RHIB seemed overwhelmed, too frail to carry a half-ton of boarding party through the bedlam. A line from the movie *Jaws* looped in my mind: "We're gonna need a bigger boat."

The RHIB had only two seats, side-by-side, occupied by petty officers Weatherby and Obenland, leaving the rest of us to sit on the pontoons, just aft of the console, facing inboard. As the RHIB plugged through the waves, slugs of water smacked us hard on the back. We crouched as low as we could, lowering the center of gravity, my instinct telling me that the RHIB would capsize if Weatherby wasn't careful. After a minute Motley slid down off the pontoon and crouched on deck, the rest of us following, on the balls of our feet—an uncomfortable position, sure, but a necessity to prevent falling overboard, backwards, as the RHIB twisted through the surf.

Weatherby showed his skill, speeding up and slowing in time with the waves, minimizing the RHIB's motions. His sea-sense picked out the most dangerous breakers. Every minute or so his North Carolina accent punctured the howl of the wind: "Hang on guys, big one coming in, port side." Counter-intuitively, he'd punch the throttle, sprinting up the face of the wave, then throttling back at the apex, guiding the RHIB gently down the backside. The man could drive.

Seemingly, it took a lifetime to reach the shrimper. There, the scene was even crazier, the flat, white side of the fishing boat looming over us, a huge vertical slab, the size of a billboard, rolling menacingly toward the RHIB, then away, then toward us again. Weatherby approached slowly, carefully gauging the distance to the outrigger, which extended forty feet out. *Castor* didn't have a Jacob's ladder, and the only way to get on board was to climb the side of the hull, using an open scupper as a foothold. The scupper was six feet above the waterline, meaning we'd each have to step up at exactly the right moment, when the RHIB was on the crest of a wave. The scupper was just five feet aft of the outrigger. Weatherby would have to nestle the RHIB alongside the hull without getting tangled in the massive metal latticework.

Weatherby's gaze fixated on the outrigger. He didn't like what he was seeing.

"Hey guys, here's the deal." Weatherby spoke forcefully, his southern twang replaced with a firm monotone, the voice of a surgeon about to crack open someone's chest. "I'm gonna power up alongside so you can climb up, but you've got to be quick. One surge and we'll hit the outrigger, and someone'll get hurt. So when we get there, step up, jam your foot in the scupper, grab the rail, and get on board. I won't be able to hold position for very long." He looked everyone in the eye, the boarding team nodding in acknowledgment. Just then a ten-foot wave lifted the RHIB so that it was even with *Castor*'s aft deck. An instant later, in the trough, we were looking up at fifty tons of shrimper hovering overhead. This was going to be hairy. Weatherby pushed the throttle forward and moved in.

Normally the boarding officer was the first to step on board a vessel, but Obenland called an audible. "XO, why don't you go first, I'll help Chad here in the boat until the rest of the team's on board." If anyone could help Weatherby guide us safely onto the fishing boat, Obenland was the man. I agreed. "Okay, that makes sense, I'll go first, then Motley and MK3. Let's do it."

Weatherby nudged the RHIB alongside *Castor*, just aft of the scupper. I crawled to the bow, spray soaking my chest, salt water dripping off my face and chin. We were illuminated in *Sea Hawk*'s searchlight, the bright, metallic beam almost blinding, distorting our depth perception and killing whatever night vision we'd had. The RHIB was three feet off the boat's starboard side and too low for me to reach the gunwale. Then, in an instant, a large swell lifted the RHIB straight up as the shrimper rolled toward us. I stood quickly, sliding my foot into the scupper and grabbing *Castor*'s rail, trying to vault onto the deck in a single motion. It worked. I twisted over the gunwale like a wannabe gymnast, safe on deck. The fishing boat's crew was huddled fifteen feet away and I motioned for them to stay put. Getting our team on board was the first priority. Motley was next, then Hartsock, each timing the waves, grabbing the rail, and climbing over the side without trouble. They made it look effortless.

That's when we almost lost Obenland. Weatherby was struggling to maintain the RHIB in position and Obenland was stepping up toward the scupper when a monstrous wave lifted *Castor* skyward. As the wall of water passed under her hull, *Castor* rolled heavily to starboard, hovering over the RHIB like a buzzard over road kill. The fishing boat's hull caught the RHIB's port pontoon and squeezed the small boat forward. Obenland, already in motion, leaped up and got both arms over the gunwale but was offset from the scupper and couldn't find it with his foot. He hung over the side of the boat, his head and shoulders above the rail and the rest of him dangling below, trying to get a grip, legs kicking, body slowly slipping. Motley and Hartsock, closest to the rail, grabbed for his arms.

Castor rolled back to port, yawing violently. Then something snapped. A line on the outrigger parted, and a large block-and-tackle swung down, just missing Motley and hitting Obenland on the head. He let go of the rail, stunned, and fell backward, overboard, toward the sea. Motley crashed to the deck, his arms extended, still grasping for his shipmate. Hartsock and I leaned over the rail. Eight feet below us, Obenland was sprawled in the RHIB's sodden bow, eyes closed, body contorted, one hand on his face and the other arm clutching his side. He'd landed hard but had fallen right into the boat. Weatherby clutched the RHIB into reverse and pulled away from *Castor*.

Obenland didn't move. Then, after our hearts skipped a few beats, he stirred, groggy and disoriented. He'd been hit hard, right on the top of the head, but the helmet had saved him. Slowly, he sat up. He flexed his arms and legs, checking himself for breaks and rotating his torso. Finally, after twisting his head left and right a dozen times, he looked up to the boarding party and gave a thumbs-up. He mouthed one word: ouch. He was all right.

Lieutenant Lober broke protocol, booming over the radio: "What the hell happened?" I filled him in and he asked if we should terminate the boarding. I leaned over the rail, shouting through the wind and spray at Weatherby and Obenland. "You good to go?" Obenland gave another thumbs up. Weatherby made a second approach and a minute later Obenland climbed on board, blushing, a huge, embarrassed grin on his face. The block that struck him was a solid piece of wood, studded with metal rollers and weighing a dozen pounds, and, except for the helmet, easily could have broken his skull. And if he'd fallen into the water, Obenland could have drowned, dragged underneath the shrimper's hull by the swirling wave action.

I walked up close to Obenland, staring at his eyes, looking for signs of concussion. "Boats, are you all right?" I asked. "For sure? No dizziness? Any neck pain?" He stared back and responded matter-of-factly, as if nothing had happened. "No sir," he said, "the fall knocked the wind out of me, but I landed right across the pontoons, so nothing broke, it was like falling onto a big, hard cushion. My head hurts a little, but I'm good to go—really." He hesitated, and then his gaze tightened—the consummate professional ready to dig in. "Let's go find that dope," he said.

We never did. *Castor* was clean, the interior spaces wide open and easy to inspect, the master fully cooperative, opening all of the tanks, even digging out blueprints to show the layout of the bilges. We didn't see a single clue, didn't find a single indication of a smuggling operation. After gaining access to every conceivable space, we jumped back into the RHIB and fought our way through the waves to *Pollux*, with the same end result. Nothing found. After three hours of boardings, our team returned to *Sea Hawk* drenched and exhausted. After putting it all on the line, the only thing we had to show was a large black gouge on Obenland's boarding helmet.

A day-and-a-half later, when the two boats arrived in St. Petersburg, Customs boarded them and carried out a more thorough search, bringing in the sniffer dogs and a team of experts. There were no drugs on board, no residue, no hidden compartments. The intelligence report had been wrong.

———

On August 31 Red Crew found its first contraband. *Sea Hawk* was headed out on a seven-day patrol, when the lookout suddenly shouted: "Bale in the water!" A hundred yards away, bobbing in the light seas, was a brown package, two feet square and one foot thick, wrapped in coarse burlap, floating just at the water's surface. The OOD maneuvered the ship so that we could recover the bale from the step deck.

It wasn't a rarity to find a bale floating in the waters off South Florida, often the remnant of an air drop or at-sea transfer gone bad. The locals in Key West gave them a name: square grouper. Some boaters spent their days hunting the grouper, knowing that finding just a single wayward bale would pay all their bills for a couple of months, pure manna from heaven.

Dan Sanders lugged the bale on board and plopped it on deck behind the superstructure. The marijuana was old and had been in the water a long time. Brown liquid oozed from the package, coursing over the bright white deck. The bale was covered in sea slime and stunk to high heaven, the noxious stench of rotting vegetation mixed with seawater. After searching the area for other bales and finding nothing but empty ocean, we headed back on patrol, convinced it was a good omen and that we'd make a seizure on this trip. It wasn't, and we didn't.

After destroying the bale at sea, Sanders broke out the white paint to cover up the nasty stain that it had left on the deck.

3

Snake-Bit

August 1983

Red Crew might have been cursed for drug busts, but we'd really gotten lucky with our captain. Lieutenant Lober was a sailor's sailor, devoted to the mission, willing to take informed risks to get the job done. He also was a generous man. For me, as a single officer with no prospects of a "significant other" in sight, it was a comfort to be invited into the Lober home, where Jerry and his wife, Donna, extended me a warm hand of friendship. Their two infant boys treated me like a new toy.

The Lobers owned a small outboard, and Jerry spent his weekends zipping around Key West, fishing, water-skiing, and visiting the desolate islands that dotted the area. He called me early one Saturday, with mischief in his voice. He wanted to explore Boca Grande Key, an uninhabited lump that sat a dozen miles to the west. "The chart shows that there's a lake in the middle of the island, and I'd like to get in there to see what it's like," he explained. "It'll be pretty hard to get to because of the mangroves, so probably only a few people have ever seen it." That was typical Lober—always curious to do something out of the ordinary.

Forty-five minutes later we were skimming across the shimmering harbor, bright blue sky overhead and crystal-clear water beneath the keel. Boca Grande was surrounded by shallows, but a narrow channel cut close to shore on the northwest side. We arrived in midmorning and ran the boat onto the beach and dug its anchor into the sand, thirty feet from a thick forest of mangroves. The beach was littered with brightly colored foam fish-floats, broken free from their traps, and we scooped up a pile to bring home for decorations. Then we set out for the center of the island.

We quickly learned that there's nothing harder than fighting through a thicket of mangroves. The trees grow dense and twisted, thick and enveloping, and sit in shallow swamps and soggy muck. In some spots, the branches and roots were so gnarled that we couldn't move ahead, having to crawl around them. Jerry and I wrestled through the trees, sweaty and bug-bit, our feet soaked, struggling to squeeze through the maze of twisted branches. Finally, we bludgeoned our way onto the solid ground of the interior.

The mangroves thinned out and we hiked toward the lake, coming to a broad clearing. We could see the lake a quarter of a mile away, shallow and weed-choked, surrounded by fields of mud. It wasn't exactly paradise. Bugs were swarming, so we headed back toward the boat, looking for an easier path through the mangrove forest.

That's when Lober found it. "Hey, XO, get over here," he said. "Goddam, you're not gonna believe this." He stood on an elevated spot under a canopy of tall mangroves, their leaves completely shading the sun, the copse dark and damp. At his feet was a rectangular hole, freshly dug, six feet long and a third as wide. It looked like an empty grave. The bottom of the hole was soggy with turgid water, and there were footprints in the sand nearby. He looked at me, amazed. "What the hell do you think this is?" he asked.

I shrugged, trying to comprehend why someone would deal with the tussle of the mangroves to dig a hole in such a remote spot, but Lieutenant Lober answered his own question. "It's either for hiding a stash of dope, or someone's going to get buried here real soon," he said. "Let's get the hell out of here. This place is bad news."

By noon we were cracking open beers in his kitchen, and Jerry shared our story with Donna. She laughed, told us we were idiots for going there in the first place, and said we were lucky that the smugglers didn't show up and bury us in the hole. Jerry called Group Key West, but no one seemed to care. The Florida Keys were home to dozens of smuggling organizations and weird happenings were part of the landscape. We never learned who dug the hole and never went back to Boca Grande, either.

Lober loved excitement, exploring new worlds, and the thrill of steaming full speed ahead. He and his crew were about to get their fill.

––––––––

The tension between the Communist world and the United States had been growing for years, with the Reagan administration ratcheting up the pressure on the Soviet Union. Then came a horrific act: on September 1, 1983, a Soviet jet fighter shot down Korean Air Lines flight 007 as the civilian airliner was flying over the Sea of Japan. The attack, which killed all 269 passengers and crew members on the South Korean plane, was unprovoked and unprecedented. The simmering tensions blew through the roof and anti-Communist sentiment ran strong throughout the United States.

Red Crew was under way in *Sea Hawk* when we heard about the attack. It was a bright, sun-drenched day, and the captain and I stood on the port bridge wing, looking south toward Cuba, fifty miles away, invisible over the horizon but a lurking presence, nonetheless. We were stunned by the news and tried to predict what it meant for the nation.

Lober was never more prophetic. "Mark my words, XO, the Kremlin has crossed a line and Reagan won't stand for it," he said. "Our Cuban friends have got to be panicked that the president will take it out on them. He'll do something to turn the tables." He scanned the passing waves. "I just hope that whatever happens, Red Crew can be part of it," he said. "I'd do anything to be there when the fun begins."

Seven weeks later the United States, with the support of six Caribbean nations, launched Operation Urgent Fury, the invasion of Grenada, which was then under the control of Cuban-backed Marxists. Chaos in the island nation endangered both the civil population and a phalanx of American university students, prompting the president to take action.

After friendly forces routed the Communists, the Department of Defense requested Coast Guard support. There were fears that elements of the Cuban military would attempt to retake the island. A squadron of patrol cutters, with expertise in interdiction and law enforcement, was needed—in a hurry. The three SESs were tasked to join the American contingent safeguarding Grenadian sovereignty. Lieutenant Lober's wish had come true. Red Crew was headed for a war zone.

The captains and XOs of the three cutters received a classified briefing at the Navy base and were told to get under way within eight hours. The trip to Grenada would take four days, with refueling stops from a cutter near Haiti and at the U.S. Naval Station at Roosevelt Roads, Puerto Rico. The mission would last at least one month, possibly up to six. After the briefing we rushed back to the division and talked with our crew, giving them as much detail as we were allowed to provide, which wasn't much. Secrecy was essential, so as not to alert the Cubans that a flotilla of cutters would be steaming past their shores to support the invasion of their proxy. No one could know where we were headed—not wives, not friends, not neighbors. We sent the crew home to pack for the stealth deployment.

Lt. (jg) Carl Ditto, one of the junior officers from *Lipan,* strolled in as I was grabbing gear in my office. He was a good friend, and he announced his presence in a loud, booming voice, his syrupy southern drawl bouncing off the walls: "Hey, Howe—what's this about you guys going to Grenada?" he asked. I looked at him, stunned. How did he know? This was a secret mission, and we'd just heard about it ourselves. "Carl, I really can't talk about it," I said, stammering. "We're heading out tonight. We aren't supposed to tell anyone where we're going."

"Okay, fine—be that way," he replied, feigning hurt feelings. He said that he had figured out our secret when one of the SES quartermasters borrowed some Grenadian charts from his cutter. He wished us well and said he'd save a few cold beers for our return.

I rushed home and gathered all my work uniforms. No need for many civilian clothes, but I packed my camera, cassette tapes, snorkeling gear, and a handful of books, just in case there was some leisure time. I checked the cupboards for snacks, finding only a few packs of pretzels. Into the bags they went.

I shared a small house with two other Coast Guard officers, both classmates from the Academy. Lt. (jg) Tim Butler was captain on *Cape York* and was on patrol. The other housemate, Lt. (jg) Mike Sobey, was an exchange officer with the Navy, assigned to one of the futuristic hydrofoils, where he was having the time of this life. Mike arrived home from work, tired but content, and cracked open a beer. "You guys really headed down to Grenada?" he asked. Damn, I thought, who *didn't* know our secret? Mike had heard that the Pentagon brass had considered sending the hydrofoils but wanted a less warlike presence—a role that the Coast Guard, with its roots in civilian law enforcement, fit well. We talked a bit, and then I headed back to the ship, skittish about steaming into an active war zone on board our lightly armed SES.

One final errand: I'd promised a friend that she could borrow my car for a trip to Miami, and needed to drop off the keys. Jessica worked the bar at the Navy Bachelor Officer Quarters. Like the other barmaids, she was young, pretty, and flirtatious, and the local contingent of Coast Guard officers spent a lot of evenings drinking her beer. The room was empty and Jessica was washing shot glasses when I barged in. "Hey, Jim, what's up?" she said. "You're here early." It was late afternoon, and we usually didn't show up for drinks until after dinner.

"We're headed out on patrol sooner than we thought, and I wanted to get the keys to you," I said. "Here—there's plenty of gas. Hope you have fun in Miami."

"Is something going on?" she asked, with a look I'd never seen before, a mixture of playful and concerned.

"Ah, well, we just need to get under way, um, quicker than expected," I said. "You know the Coast Guard—always changing plans." She wished me luck and told me not to worry—that she'd take good care of my car. I gave her a hug and headed for the door.

"Hey Jim, do me one more favor," she said.

"What's that?"

"Be careful in Grenada." Then she smiled and turned away.

The three SESs set sail that evening, many of the crew members waving to their wives and kids on the pier. It seemed that the entire Coast Guard community had heard about the deployment and guessed, correctly, that we were heading to Grenada. *Petrel* left first, followed by *Shearwater* and then *Sea Hawk*, which was manned by Red Crew. Two of the wives were crying, some were laughing nervously, and the last words we heard as

Sea Hawk rounded the turning basin were from a young girl, her voice echoing across the water: "I love you, Daddy!"

Our crew members scurried about nervously, not quite sure what to make of the deployment. Once we were outside the reef line we set general quarters to dust off our warfighting skills. After a successful drill, the captain told everyone to get a good night's sleep. We'd spend the next few days preparing, and he wanted the crew fresh in the morning. *Sea Hawk* fell into convoy with the other SESs, pounding into growing seas as the three cutters steamed at twenty-five knots toward the first refueling rendezvous off Haiti.

Lieutenant Lober's plan to have a well-rested crew was scuttled by the weather. The SESs were sailing directly into a stiff breeze from the southeast. Typically winds in the region were more easterly, and we should have gained a lee when we passed Cay Sal Bank, but the southeasterly flow produced a steep eight-foot head sea for the entire six-hundred-mile transit along Cuba's north coast.

Amid the smashing and crashing, Red Crew carried out weapons training, cleaned the guns, inventoried ammunition, reviewed watch assignments, exercised general quarters over and over, and tried our best to not let the severe pitching send us to the lee rail. We all got battered and bruised. I'd just stepped into my stateroom when *Sea Hawk* mashed into a ten-foot wave, catapulting me into the forward bulkhead, hitting hard enough to see stars. Such were the risks of walking across open spaces in heavy seas.

As the flotilla neared the rendezvous off Haiti, the weather moderated and the wind backed to the northeast. The crew perked up, now anxious to get into the war zone to defend the newly freed country from infiltrators or remnants of the Cuban security forces. Red Crew was, if nothing else, a band of patriots, and if its crew members had to get into a firefight in the service of their country, it would be best waged against the tinhorn despots from Cuba.

We refueled from the 378-foot cutter *Dallas* (WHEC 716) in the Gulf of Gonaives, sixty miles northwest of Port-au-Prince, with each SES taking a turn to top off her tanks. Once the fueling was finished our convoy would head south and then hug the Haitian and Dominican coastline en route to Roosevelt Roads. Hispaniola should provide a lee for most of the voyage, and we looked forward to smoother waters than those through which we'd slammed during the past twenty-four hours.

Red Crew had never been more focused. *Sea Hawk* was headed into danger, and our sailors were pumped up, nerves on fire, ready to take on any wayward Grenadians, the Cuban navy, and perhaps the entire Communist bloc. Jerry Lober sported an air of controlled excitement, as content as I'd ever seen him, poring over a slew of tactical documents. I looked forward to the mission, despite the many long days ahead, and knew this would be a life-changing opportunity. We just had to get into theater and get to work.

As the SESs steamed away from the fueling rendezvous, *Dallas* hailed us on the VHF radio and asked all three ships to switch to a secure channel so that our commanding officers could participate in a joint call. Once the radio network was set up, we were given new orders, relayed from District Seven: return to Key West at economical speed. The mission to Grenada had been cancelled. Our services wouldn't be needed.

The news came like a hammer-blow. Some of our crew members were deflated, others incensed. Having counted on being part of a liberation force, they felt that the rug had been pulled from under them. The captain hid his disappointment well, telling the crew that orders were orders and it was time to head back home. He theorized that the Navy had secured the area more quickly than expected, and it just wasn't worth taking three cutters off patrol to mop up the loose ends of the invasion. *Sea Hawk* set course for Key West.

We later heard another explanation, although it was never confirmed. Grenada had been declared a formal war zone, and, at the time, Department of Defense (DOD) policy only permitted men to engage in combat operations. When DOD realized that the SESs had mixed-gender crews, it pulled the plug on the deployment. There was some evidence to support the theory: it wasn't until a month later, after hostilities had officially ceased, that the Coast Guard sent three 95-footers and a buoy tender to assist. As for Red Crew, we hadn't given a second thought to bringing women into a combat zone. Joan Scott was a talented navigator, and Carrie Corson, on the .50-calibers, was a trusted shipmate who, if provoked, would give the Cubans hell.

———

After a brief pit stop in Key West, *Sea Hawk* headed toward the wide expanse of the Yucatan for a week-long patrol, working for *Ute*. As we were passing the Key West sea buoy, the port main engine shut down, and, after a quick fix, shut down again. *Sea Hawk* limped back to pier Delta Two. The engineers had to replace the entire control system, and eight hours later we were under way—hopefully without any further problems.

MK1 Boldan and MK3 Hartsock stood on the bridge wing, plastered in sweat and grime, cooling off and cursing the temperamental engines. I told them that it had to be a good sign, getting all the bad things out of the way right at the start of the patrol. "This'll be a fun trip, and there's a big win on the horizon for Red Crew," I said. "You can just feel it."

My instincts had never been more wrong. The weather was placid and the trip south was uneventful. *Ute* directed us to patrol the western side of the Yucatan while she covered the eastern half. We headed toward Cancun at fifteen knots. Then, a hot tip: *Ute* passed along intelligence from District Seven that a large load of drugs, probably cocaine, was in transit on board a fishing boat that would pass a few miles to the east of Cozumel, just to our south. It was a perfect operation for an SES: we could sprint to an intercept position and shut down our engines, drifting as the doper came to us.

Senior Chief found the ideal spot twenty miles off Cozumel, where *Sea Hawk* could remain well outside Mexico's twelve-mile territorial sea, monitoring the sea lanes on radar. Relations between the United States and Mexico had always been touchy, so we didn't want to take any chance of drifting into Mexican waters. The weather was serene and once we were at the drift spot the off-duty crew threw over a few fishing lines as *Sea Hawk* bobbed gently in the two-foot chop.

At 1620 the OOD detected a northbound contact on radar, about ten miles to the southwest. Was it the doper? We also saw a Mexican naval vessel eight miles to the north, steaming in our direction. As the warship approached, we pulled in the lines, sending our fishermen below decks. Jerry Lober guessed that the Mexican captain wanted to show off his ship, or maybe even invite us on board for some international sailor-to-sailor camaraderie.

The Mexican gunship was an old corvette, *D01*, sister to the *D15* that we'd encountered at the end of our first patrol. The ship was about 180 feet long, with a dull gray hull. *D01* looked like something from World War II, and we learned later that she was a converted U.S. Navy minesweeper, formerly the USS *Jubilant* (AM 255), built in Lorain, Ohio, in 1943 and later sold to Mexico. *D01* sat low in the water with a boxy pilothouse forward and an assortment of booms, small boats, weapon mounts, and cranes haphazardly crowding her decks. We had no apprehension when the corvette, now a mile off our bow, turned directly toward us.

It was 1700 when *D01* passed close down our port side. Captain Lober and I stood on the bridge wing, ready to render honors with a well-timed salute to our foreign comrades. We were surprised when the officer conning the corvette applied a hard backing bell. The Mexican warship came to a stop directly off our beam. For a moment we sat in silence, awkwardly, one hundred yards apart.

We were even more surprised when, without warning, a shrill whistle blasted and what seemed to be *D01*'s entire crew emerged from hiding and pointed an arsenal of weapons at us. The Mexicans were fully dressed for battle stations. From bow to stern, a wicked assortment of guns aimed directly at *Sea Hawk*. More than twenty Mexican sailors were staring down the barrels of rifles and shotguns, and others trained 20-mm deck guns on our pilothouse. A dual 40-mm anti-aircraft battery pivoted on its mount and joined the smaller weapons aiming directly at the cutter. The 20-mm rounds could rip *Sea Hawk* to shreds; the 40-mms could sink us in a heartbeat.

My jaw dropped. From his station inside the pilothouse, Senior Chief blurted out: "Holy *shit!*" After a few seconds, Lieutenant Lober murmured under his breath: "Well, this doesn't look good."

Someone on the corvette hailed us on channel 16, but he spoke broken English and was hard to understand. Our interpreter, Fireman Elliot, was home tending to a family emergency, and no one else in our crew spoke Spanish—a prime example of Murphy's Law in action. Lieutenant Lober ignored the radio call and another Mexican officer leaned over their bridge wing, bullhorn in hand. His English was adequate, and we could hear him clearly across the gap between our ships.

The nub of his message turned my blood cold. The Mexican officer said that *Sea Hawk* was operating illegally in Mexican territory and they would be sending a boarding party to take control of our vessel to escort us from their waters. It was a mind-bending situation, completely unprecedented, unthinkable. A Third-World naval scow was holding a patrol boat from the world's largest superpower hostage, at gunpoint, in clear contravention of every norm of acceptable behavior at sea, and had stated the intent to commandeer our ship, a threat tantamount to piracy.

One thing was for sure: that wasn't going to happen. Captain Lober gave the Mexicans a casual shrug, thought for a minute, and picked up a bullhorn. He replied clearly and slowly: "Mexican naval vessel *D01*, this is the U.S. Coast Guard Cutter *Sea Hawk*. Be advised—we are a warship of the United States fleet. We are operating in international waters and have no intention of leaving the area. You do not have permission to come on board our vessel." This stumped the Mexicans. We could see a cluster of them conferring in their pilothouse, clearly animated.

I'd never had a live weapon pointed at me, much less dozens, and realized that one itchy trigger finger could send us to our graves. I whispered: "Captain, we've got to buy time. These guys are nuts. What do you think we should do?" Lober paused for a moment, deep in thought. Then he spoke solemnly, looking me directly in the eye. "XO, this cutter is U.S. territory," he said. "They will not—not—come on board without our permission. We'll resolve this peacefully. We'll buy time and eventually they'll get tired and go away. But if not, we won't let them hijack this ship."

Lober glanced over at *D01*. "Their captain must be crazy and might do something really stupid," he said. "Hell, they might start shooting. We need to be ready. Head below and let the crew know what's going on, and break out every weapon. Set 'silent GQ.' Load the machine guns and get them ready for action, but keep them hidden, so that the Mexicans think we're unarmed. Everyone should be packing a piece—*everyone*. If they whack out and attack us, we'll need to fight back to have any chance of getting away."

I scuttled down the ladder and put Obenland to work readying the weapons. Boldan and Hartsock ran into the hole and lit off the engines. Senior Chief got on the high-frequency radio and reported the situation to *Ute*, for relay to District Seven. *Ute* said she'd make best speed en route to our position but was five hours away. Until then we were on our own.

On the bridge, negotiations weren't going well. The tone of the Mexican officer talking through the bullhorn sounded increasingly tense, until he was shouting, repeating their intent to board the cutter. Lieutenant Lober remained calm, replying that *Sea Hawk* was off limits and that the Mexicans could not—repeat, *not*—come on board.

The situation was going downhill, fast. Sailors on *D01*'s deck readied a small boat for launch, a heavily armed boarding party standing nearby. Lober told *D01* that we had reported the situation to our headquarters in Miami and suggested that they contact the Mexican government in order to prevent an international incident. This led to another conference on *D01*'s bridge, with one officer gesturing wildly. After a few minutes the Mexican officer bullhorned that they'd contact their naval headquarters. They kept their guns trained on us.

Obenland approached me on the bridge wing. "XO, we're all set—all the .50s and M-60s are ready, and everyone has at least one small arm," he said. He handed me a white canvas bag. "Here's a couple of .45s for you and the captain. They're loaded, on safe. I put ten extra magazines in the bag. We also sneaked up an M-16 and hid it near the chart table, with five extra clips, for Senior Chief to use." He hesitated. "I hope it's okay, but I also let the guys break out their personal weapons," he said. Some of our sailors stored their own guns on board the cutter, to use during morale shoots at sea. "Hell, yeah," I told him. "If this goes south, we'll need all the firepower we can get." I headed below to update the crew.

In the main deck passageway Walt Goodrum pulled me aside. Walt seemed choked up, shaking slightly. He held out a vicious-looking rifle. "XO, I want you to use this," he said. "It's my personal piece." It was a semiautomatic assault rifle, a variant of the AK-47, with a custom wooden stock. "It's a great little beast. You can rip off rounds real quick, and it's super-accurate. And here's the best part," he added, holding out a long banana clip that he had taped at the top to a second, inverted clip. "Each of these holds a hundred rounds, so you'll have two hundred to shoot up as many of those bastards as possible. When you're done with the first hundred, just eject and turn the clip upside down, slam it in, and you're back in business." He jammed the first clip into the receiver, hit eject, reversed the clip and reinserted it, his hands a blur. I'd had no clue that our cook was a weapons ninja. "If this shit goes down, I really want you to use this," he said. "Please—I've got a shotgun and a .45 for myself." I didn't know whether to laugh or cry. Instead I just took the gun and thanked him. If the Mexicans opened fire, they'd pay, with Goodrum's AK blazing on my hip.

Most of the crew sat on the prisoners' chairs, fully dressed for battle, some looking anxious, others with their game faces on. Ammo cans lined the passageway and the machine guns lay on the deck. The pungent exhaust of the idling main diesels spiced the air. Climbing back to the bridge, I was stunned by the number of barrels trained on us and had a flash of inspiration. "Captain, if one of those guys sneezes, one of us will get a bullet through the head," I said. "Let's just ask them politely to point their guns away." Lober nodded, picked up the bullhorn, and made the suggestion. The Mexicans huddled again. Nothing happened for a few minutes but then we heard something piped in Spanish over their topside speakers. Slowly, with hesitation, the Mexican sailors angled their weapons a few degrees away from *Sea Hawk*, training them toward the water and sky. Finally, there was progress. It was forty minutes since the start of the standoff.

For the next hour and a half we sat, dead in the water, dozens of armed Mexican sailors and a seemingly unarmed Coast Guard cutter facing each other across three hundred feet of tranquil blue ocean. The corvette's crew launched their small boat with a five-man boarding party, and it zipped back and forth along *D01*'s waterline. I stayed on the bridge with the captain and senior chief, watching the Mexicans, and made occasional forays below deck to talk with the crew. *Ute* was now three hours away and reported that the State Department was protesting *D01*'s actions to the Mexican government. Meanwhile, the radar contact we'd noted just before *D01*'s arrival had stopped and extinguished its running lights and was now just under six miles away. Could this be the dopers, and did they know we were here?

We waited. The captain and I stood on the bridge wing, gaming options to react to the Mexicans' next move. It wouldn't be hard for them to board *Sea Hawk*, since they could jump directly from their small boat onto our step deck. Lober decided that if they boarded us, we'd let them onto the ship, and as soon as they were crossing the aft deck, we'd clutch in the engines, sprint forward, and cut underneath *D01*'s bow. He said he doubted that *D01*'s captain would open fire on his own people, and our hidden gunners could quickly corral the Mexican boarding team.

Captain Lober stood silent, staring at the dual 40-mm cannons aimed just a few feet above his head. Unexpectedly, he spoke to the bridge crew, powerful and passionate.

"I'll tell you what this is all about—we're protecting our country," he said. "It's no different than if these guys were trying to steal a piece of Texas or Maryland or Connecticut. The world's gotta have rules, and the rules say you don't mess with other people's territory." He paused and took a deep breath. "I'll do everything possible to resolve this peacefully, but we won't surrender to these outlaws," he said. "If they attack, I'm prepared to take a bullet for my country." I nodded, nothing left to say, praying silently that the Mexicans would back down, but ready to defend the integrity of our nation, regardless of consequence. The situation was insane, unstable, but I found myself surprisingly at peace, poised to fight back if the Mexicans shot first. The stalemate dragged on, the minutes crawling by, neither side blinking, *Sea Hawk* still drifting, *D01*'s weapons fully manned and her small boat coursing nearby.

Then came salvation. The Mexican with the bullhorn leaned over their bridge railing, shrugging and smiling. He said that they'd decided to allow *Sea Hawk* to remain in the area. His voice had lightened and he sounded jovial, as if the entire escapade had been a big misunderstanding. The Mexican sailors on deck began securing their weapons and removing their battle gear. A few waved at us; others lit cigarettes. Most shuffled below deck. Just like that, the standoff was over.

I stepped below to brief the crew, relaxing battle stations but asking them to keep the weapons at the ready until the Mexican warship had moved on. High anxiety became elation, laced with a streak of disgust. Red Crew was deeply insulted that *D01* had placed us in harm's way. A week earlier we'd been steaming toward a real war zone, and here our Mexican neighbors had brandished weapons like a bunch of drunken pirates. Senior Chief said it was the most screwed-up thing he'd ever seen. I handed the AK back to Goodrum, thanking him for looking after me. BM3 Weatherby lightened the mood by singing an impromptu and anatomically explicit ditty about where the Mexicans could stow their weapons.

D01's crew recovered their small boat and the officer on her bridge hailed us again. He said they were going to patrol nearby and would follow *Sea Hawk* as long as we remained within the Mexican Exclusive Economic Zone—which extended halfway across the Yucatan Channel. That was bad news. If *D01* tagged along, there'd be no way that *Sea Hawk* could intercept and board the mystery contact. Captain Lober offered a solution: head east at high speed until we lost sight of the gunboat, and then circle back to reacquire the unknown vessel to our south.

At 2015, as the OOD clutched in the engines, *Ute* changed our plans, directing *Sea Hawk* to head east for a rendezvous at first light. District Seven wanted to debrief us on the standoff. If the unknown contact was a doper, *Sea Hawk* left it in her wake.

Eight hours later, low on fuel and cruising at twelve knots, our lookout spotted navigation lights off the starboard bow. The target was headed north. We intercepted the vessel and lit it up in our spotlight, seeing a seventy-five-foot coastal freighter, *Belize Trader*, belching smoke from a rusty stack. Lieutenant Lober called the freighter on the radio, and the master said he was bound for New Orleans for repairs and had no cargo on board.

This was a profile vessel if we ever saw one. Senior Chief radioed *Ute* with a description of the freighter. *Ute* replied there was no intelligence on the ship on file and that we were clear to conduct a boarding. Twenty minutes later, Cliff Boldan led a four-person team onto *Belize Trader*'s decks.

The boarding was uneventful. The crew on the freighter was coopera- tive, the paperwork in order, and the hold empty, just as the master had said. Boldan and his team saw nothing unusual, and after thirty minutes they radioed that the inspection was complete. It seemed a bit rushed, but MK1 was an experienced boarding officer, so neither the captain nor I questioned his judgment. *Sea Hawk* headed back on an intercept course toward *Ute*.

An hour later *Ute* called with an urgent message. District Seven had just reported that *Belize Trader* was suspected of having departed Colombia two days earlier with a load of marijuana hidden in its peak tank, in the forward section of the freighter's bow. Senior Chief piped Boldan to the bridge. MK1 told us that the boarding team hadn't been able to access the peak because the access plate to the tank was rusted shut. Boldan was furious with himself for not looking for another way to inspect the peak. I was mad at myself for not having prodded the boarding team to take more time in its inspection. The captain was too beat to be upset. He'd had a long night.

Once again, Red Crew might have blown an opportunity to make our first seizure, and this could've been a big one. Our report to *Ute*—that we had completed the boarding, had not accessed the peak tank, and did not have enough fuel left to hunt down *Belize Trader* for a reboarding—was met with frosty silence.

We rendezvoused with *Ute* at 0830. The seas were calm enough for *Sea Hawk* to moor alongside the larger cutter, which would speed up the refueling. We approached to thirty feet and waited for them to pass a sea painter, but their boatswain had a hard time heaving the line, missing our bow on two attempts. *Ute*'s captain, Cdr. John Hearn, a crusty, lifelong sailor reputed to have a nuclear-tipped temper, stormed from *Ute*'s bridge and headed for the fantail, blasting curses all the way. He picked up the heaving line, telling his crew, "Dammit, watch me, this is how you throw the goddamn thing." By then *Sea Hawk* had drifted away, the gap forty feet and growing. But throw it he did, placing the monkey's fist smack in the middle of our forecastle. Lober leaned toward me and whispered: "He's going to take me to the woodshed for shanking that boarding."

Fortunately, Commander Hearn was as good a leader as he was a sailor. Lieutenant Lober stepped across the gap between the cutters and headed for *Ute*'s cabin, ready for a tongue-lashing. Instead, the two captains had a frank and pleasant talk. Lober described the Mexican standoff, detailing Red Crew's actions. Commander Hearn thanked him for exercising sound judgment. "Dammit, you did everything right with the Mexicans, absolutely right," he said. "Make sure you tell your crew that they should be proud for standing up for our flag." Commander Hearn also brushed off the *Belize Trader*. "The damned intel on that freighter was probably wrong anyway," he said. "It's only good about half the goddam time, maybe less.

You'll get a seizure soon enough—just be patient. Now get back to your ship and get back on patrol." With that, our captain returned to his crew.

Red Crew spent the next two days on a port call to Grand Cayman. It was paradise, with stunning white beaches, crystal-clear water, and glamorous hotels—a quiet, clean tourist haven. We drank and swam and tried our best to relax, but the incident with the Mexicans and the specter of *Belize Trader* haunted us. We steamed back to the Yucatan with egos deflated and in a serious funk.

The next morning we intercepted a northbound sailboat, U.S.-flagged, forty-two feet long, and in great shape. The winds were light and the boat had only her mainsail raised, and as *Sea Hawk* approached her crew dropped the sail, coming dead in the water. There was a family of four on board, from North Carolina, and they'd chartered the boat to spend two months exploring the Caribbean. The father was a just-retired Marine colonel, and as the sweep team inspected the interior of the vessel, he and I talked in the open cockpit, his wife sitting next to him, and his daughter and son, both in their late teens, sitting further aft. The girl was thin and pretty and the boy was delicately built, a bit wispy, the complete opposite of his thick-necked, burly father.

As I inspected the boat's papers, the colonel started to gripe. He said it was an intrusion, indeed a violation of his rights, that we could come on board and search his vessel without a warrant. He quoted the U.S. Constitution. I explained our legal authority. He became increasingly agitated and when his wife tried to soothe him, he amped up the volume, cheeks reddening. I handed him a laminated copy of 14 U.S. Code §89, the legal source of Coast Guard law enforcement authority. He scanned the card, grunting, a red blush spreading across his face, angrily spitting out: "I'll look into this when I get back home. My lawyer friends at [Camp] Lejeune will know the truth."

His son broke the tension. He jumped to his feet and yelled out, "Well, if you Coast Guard men can look anywhere you want, come and search me! But first, you have to catch me!" With that, he dropped his bathing suit to the deck and jumped overboard, into the sparkling sea, stark naked.

We all stared as the teenager pirouetted and posed, splashing water at us and singing show tunes in a rich alto voice. For a few seconds no one said a word. Then, simultaneously, the colonel, his wife, and I burst into laughter, with the daughter and the rest of the boarding team chiming in. By the time we wrapped up the inspection, we were all best friends, the colonel thanking us for our diligence and apologizing for his boorish behavior. Our boarding team climbed back on board *Sea Hawk*, trying hard to keep straight faces, and for the rest of the night the crew ribbed and joked and carried on about the unlikely scene.

Like releasing a pressure valve, the boarding was a catharsis, the stress and angst and failure of the past two weeks washing away, our crew revitalized. Twelve hours later, when our patrol time was up, we set sail for Key West knowing that better days lay ahead and that Red Crew just needed to stay in the fight.

We never heard a rational explanation why *D01* had held us at gunpoint, and we received no feedback from the State Department. The prevailing theory was that the Mexicans were trying to make a statement in response to the U.S. invasion of Grenada. There was another theory, based on sketchy rumor: that *D01*'s captain had been in league with the drug cartel moving the load of cocaine up the coast, and when the Mexican naval leadership figured this out, he'd been arrested and shot. It probably was an urban legend, but it was too good a sea story not to make the rounds on the waterfront.

————

Red Crew's next patrol went east, to the shoals, nooks, and crannies of the Bahamas. The Coast Guard had limited presence across much of the archipelago. There were vast stretches of treacherous shallows where larger cutters couldn't operate, and the older 95- and 82-foot patrol boats didn't have the legs to travel to the eastern islands. The SESs had fewer constraints. We could sail in as little as ten feet of water, had the speed to sprint quickly between distant points, and, with our larger crews, had more staying power. The weakness was our modest tank capacities, complicated by the limited number of fueling depots in the eastern Bahamas. Sorties to the far reaches of the islands were crimped by logistics.

Senior Chief found the answer—a sleepy government outpost nestled in a cove on the eastern side of Andros Island, where fuel and supplies were readily available. The U.S. Navy's Atlantic Undersea Test and

Evaluation Center, AUTEC, was a testing facility for submarines, and sat on the western edge of the Tongue of the Ocean, a maritime cul-de-sac where Navy subs could operate unmolested from tankers, freighters, and other large shipping. The Tongue was an L-shaped expanse of deep water, 150 miles long and 30 miles wide, that extended south from New Providence Island. The only deepwater opening to the Tongue was on its northern end, near Nassau; to the west was Andros Island, and the eastern and southern sides were ringed by treacherous shallows. Besides the Navy subs, the only vessels that traveled the area were charter fishing vessels, Bahamian conch fishermen, a smattering of pleasure craft, and an unknown cast of dopers. The scraggly Navy outpost helped open up the eastern Bahamas to the SES fleet.

Getting to AUTEC was the challenge. It was easy from the north, but the SESs spent a lot of time patrolling south of the Tongue, in the Old Bahama Channel and on the Great Bahama Bank. If the SESs could cross into the Tongue from the south, somehow passing through the shoals, it would put AUTEC within easy reach.

In theory, it was possible. Along the Tongue's southern edge the deep water sloped steeply upward to extreme shallows, only a few feet deep, where strong currents carved furrows in the sand. The broadest furrow was named Blossom Channel, which was oriented northwest-southeast and flanked by underwater dunes, known locally as sand bores. Blossom Channel was deep enough—barely—for an SES to pass through. Because of the powerful currents, however, the contours of the channel slowly shifted over time, making charts of the area unreliable and the exact positions of the opening and terminus anyone's guess. No one in the SES Division was aware of a cutter that had transited Blossom Channel. Running aground was a risk that most sailors avoided with a passion.

Enter the Blue Crew. Lt. Ken Bradford and Lt. (jg) Jim Sartucci were born explorers and sailed *Sea Hawk* through Blossom Channel at midday, passing through at a slow bell, watching warily for hazards. The crystal-blue water showcased every detail on the ocean floor—starfish, small rocks, the occasional coral head, and random clumps of vegetation. Blue Crew reported depths no less than five feet under keel for the length of the transit and estimated the channel to be two hundred yards wide, narrowing to one hundred twenty yards in the middle stretch, and guarded on both sides by thick sand bores. Sartucci said it was like threading a needle, but on a clear day it was a safe trip. Blue Crew recorded the LORAN coordinates of the entrance and exit of the channel and passed them along to the Red, Green, and Gold crews. Now there was a documented path from the southern Bahamas into the deep waters of the Tongue of the Ocean, if a captain were willing to take the risk.

A week before Thanksgiving, Red Crew was patrolling in *Shearwater* along the southern leg of the Great Bahama Bank, far to the southeast of Andros, when District Seven passed along urgent news. According to a confidential informant, a major drug transfer at sea would occur in the middle of the Tongue in four hours. *Shearwater* was the only cutter available, but the only way to get there in time was to transit Blossom Channel—at night.

It was already sunset and the cutter was fifty miles south of the Tongue. *Shearwater* would be running blind, threading the needle in the dark. I carefully watched Lieutenant Lober as he mulled his decision, studying the chart. He itched to respond to the offload, but he knew the dangers of hitting bottom in the shallows.

Lober turned to Senior Chief and asked for his best advice. Senior Chief was uncharacteristically silent, his brow crinkled. Then he spoke, slowly and firmly. "I think we can do it, but it's a risk," he said. "I'm old-fashioned, and I don't trust the LORAN down this way, since the signal's weak." He hesitated, glancing at the chart, then looked back at Lober. "I'll be honest, captain. I'm worried about a stray coral head, or getting stuck in the sand. I may be wrong, but I'd hate for you to flame out your career over this. If you do decide to go for it, you have to keep the speed low and some lift in reserve, so we can stay out of trouble if we come up on a shallow spot."

Lober nodded, took one more look at the chart, and then turned to Dan Sanders, the OOD. "Boats, full speed ahead," he said. "Senior Chief will give you the coordinates to aim for. We're headed for the Tongue."

Ninety minutes later I joined the captain, senior chief, Sanders, and the bridge team for Red Crew's first trip through Blossom Channel. Weatherby and Motley stood on the bow, ready to take depth soundings using a lead-line—a weighted cord with depth markings. It'd be a double-check for the fathometer.

The weather was calm, with a glassy sea. Cloud cover reduced available light. I'd hoped that a strong moon would allow us to see the bottom, but instead we were steaming into darkness. According to Blue Crew, Blossom Channel was fourteen miles long, with the most danger at the narrower, shallower middle section. There was a 20-degree dogleg about a mile north of the halfway point. At 2020 we entered what we hoped was the southern opening of the channel, all eyes locked on the fathometer, its red light blinking at the three o'clock position on the circular display.

The depth under keel stayed steady at twenty feet as we steamed northwest, turning for twelve knots. Sanders called out course adjustments to Seaman Corson on the helm. Eighteen feet, sixteen, fifteen. The water was getting shallower, just as Blue Crew had reported, but there were no visual cues to assure us that we weren't about to run into an underwater mountain of sand. I was nervous, Senior Chief was pacing the bridge, and even the captain looked tense. *Shearwater* continued forward.

Fifteen feet, twelve, ten—the depth plateaued, oscillating only a few feet for the next half hour. *Shearwater* glided through the placid water, still at twelve knots, the lift engines set at 50 percent. By 2100 we were halfway through the channel, with seven miles to go, the shallowest spot eight feet under keel. Then it was six miles to deep water, and all remained well. Sanders ordered the turn at the dogleg and the cutter swung 20 degrees to starboard. Nine feet under keel. Five miles to safety.

By 2120, *Shearwater* was four miles from the Tongue, with eight feet of water beneath the keel, then six feet, then back to eight. The captain looked at the chart. Senior Chief reminded him that it couldn't be trusted and that we had to follow the LORAN track line. The depth held steady at eight feet. *Shearwater* began falling off track, to starboard. Senior Chief piped up: "There's a hell of a rip current pushing us east. Boats, you need to correct hard, recommend coming ten degrees to port." Sanders ordered the change.

The cutter was three miles from what should have been deep water, with the shallowest and narrowest stretch of channel behind us. The bridge team began to breathe easier. The depth increased to ten feet, then notched back to nine. Suddenly it fell to five. I ran to the starboard bridge wing and aimed a handheld spotlight at the water. The bottom was clearly visible, close enough to reach down and scoop up a handful of sand.

The captain intervened, his voice firm: "Boats, bring her back to clutch ahead, single shaft, and get ready for full lift." Maxing out the lift engines would buy another two feet, although at low speed it also could drive sand and air into the sea chest and shut down the engines. I shined the spotlight further out, eighty feet off the beam, seeing what looked like a dark wall of sand rising close to the water's surface. I could throw a baseball and hit it. *Shearwater* was paralleling a sand bore, uncomfortably close, now creeping ahead at less than eight knots.

There was only one more mile to the Tongue. The water was shallower than what Blue Crew had reported. We were still offset from their track line, pushed to the east by the current. Sanders came another 10 degrees to port to regain the original track. There was five feet of water beneath the keel—six feet, seven, six. Sanders' eyes darted between the forward window and the depth readout, keeping the big picture, but everyone else was staring at the flashing red dot on the fathometer, blinking steadily at the six-foot mark.

No one spoke. Sweat poured down my back. Five feet under keel. A half mile to deep water. Six feet. The fathometer flashed, monotonous. Five feet. Six. Five. Six. The deep water should be beneath us any time now, at most a quarter-mile away. Seven feet. Six. Four feet. Two. Without warning, *Shearwater*'s hull was less than an arm's length above the ocean floor.

Sanders pulled back the throttles and slammed the lift engines to full. The cutter drifted forward, bouncing on the cushion of air. In the beam of the hand-held light I could see the grainy bottom, up close and personal, tufts of seaweed swaying in the current. The captain yelled "Sounding!" and on the forecastle Weatherby tossed the lead weight into the water, shouting back "And a quarter, one!" He'd measured the depth at seven-and-a-half feet, meaning there was barely three feet beneath the keel—and that was on full lift. Without the lift engines, *Shearwater* would be a beach house.

Then, rapidly, the depth began to increase, the flashing red dot on the fathometer ratcheted clockwise—five feet, eight, twelve, eighteen.

Another sounding. Weatherby yelled "By the deep four"—four fathoms, or twenty-four feet. Sanders throttled back the lift, cautiously, and clutched in both main engines. Within a minute the fathometer couldn't read the bottom. *Shearwater* was in the Tongue of the Ocean, now safe, rolling gently in a light swell from the northeast. Sanders increased speed. Blue Crew's route had worked, and we'd threaded the needle, rattled but unscathed.

In unison, Lober, Sanders, Aiken, and I all wiped our brows. Corson saw us and laughed out loud. "I'm not sure what we ran over there at the end, captain," Senior Chief said, "but I think it was a school of fish. Maybe we should go back and toss over a few lines." Lieutenant Lober smirked, his trust in technology validated, knowing that only a few feet of water had separated him from a very bad day. Such were the risks of command. He'd weighed the odds and made a gutsy call. Sanders summed up the evening in typical dry fashion. "*That* went well," he said.

Onward we steamed, full speed ahead, to the drug offload. And, as was our way, we searched through the night but never found the smugglers—just more frustration for the seizure-starved Red Crew.

4

First Blood

December 1983

ed Crew, now back on board *Petrel*, celebrated Pearl Harbor Day by leaving Key West on a twelve-day patrol. The highlight of the trip would be a two-day port call in Nassau. We'd spent a few hours there in August and wanted more time to explore the casinos, beaches, and bars.

Before the port call we'd scour the western Bahamas. *Petrel* steamed across the Santaren Channel and onto the Great Bahama Bank, and after a quiet day headed north to patrol off Bimini and the Gun Cays. In remote areas such as the Yucatan or Cay Sal it could be hard to find something to board. Sitting off Bimini—the province of cabin cruisers, yachts, and sailboats—we had the opposite problem. Picking the right boat from a flotilla of targets was both an art and a science. We avoided the legitimate charter boats that sought blue marlin and swordfish in the deep waters, but we were drawn to vessels headed for the States—those with tire marks or other visible clues, boats coming from remote areas, and those that gave unusual responses to our preboarding questions.

Over the next forty-eight hours Red Crew boarded five vessels, a fifty-foot sport fisherman, two compact cabin cruisers, and a pair of sailboats, all headed toward Florida. We found nothing out of the ordinary. *Petrel* dipped into Miami for fuel. Then came a SAR case—a sailboat named the *Turtle*, disabled with a broken rudder. We boarded the boat—clean—and rigged her for tow, dragged her to the nearest port, Lake Worth Inlet, and headed back on patrol.

Red Crew ran through collision and abandon-ship drills, all while dodging a steady stream of cruise ships and merchant freighters that were barreling through the Florida Straits. With our port call the next morning, we motored toward Nassau through the Northwest Providence Channel and intercepted two sailboats and a cabin cruiser, ready to board. Each time Captain Lober would say: "Nope, not this one." He was exercising law enforcement triage, waiting for just the right target.

At 2200 Senior Chief was standing the OOD watch when he spotted a faint contact on radar, headed northwest. It was another sailboat, her port and starboard running lights combined in a single lantern, waving slowly side to side at the top of her mast. Running dark, *Petrel* circled behind the sailboat and approached from astern. The captain came up to the bridge just before *Petrel* closed to hailing distance and said: "Light it up, Senior, and give them a shout. Let's see what their story is."

The quartermaster energized *Petrel*'s searchlight. From atop our pilothouse, a thin tunnel of bright halogen knifed through the darkness, reflecting off the sailboat's flat transom. Senior Chief picked up the radio handset: "Sailing vessel *Miss Leslie*, sailing vessel *Miss Leslie*, this is the U.S. Coast Guard cutter shining a spotlight on you. Please respond on channel 22-alpha. Over." We could see a man at the helm of the sailboat fumbling for his microphone. He politely answered Senior Chief's questions.

Miss Leslie was an American vessel, homeported in Lubbock, Texas, with two men on board, returning home after a cruise to Staniel Cay, a secluded island resort. The sailboat looked pristine. She was thirty-five feet long, her paint fresh and bright, and well equipped with radar and top-shelf survival equipment. Everything we saw indicated it was a couple of rich guys enjoying some buddy time in the Bahamas. Our quartermaster passed along the description of the vessel and the names of its crew to Group Miami, which quickly reported that there were no intelligence lookouts on either the sailboat or the men. Everything seemed legitimate.

Red Crew was beat, we had an early wakeup staring us in the face, and nothing about the sailboat set off a warning. The captain asked what we thought, and Senior Chief opined that we should go on board. "I know we've all had a long day, but we're going to spend the next couple sitting in the sun and blowing our money on the slots and blackjack," he said. "What the hell, we can be done in half an hour if the boat's as clean as it looks." Lober agreed. "Okay, set boarding stations," he said, smirking, "but don't stay long. This'll be our last one before Nassau, and we all need our beauty sleep."

At 2242 Chuck Obenland, Walt Goodrum, and I climbed over the sailboat's lee rail. The master was a scruffy-looking forty-something, white and saggy, a B-grade version of the dad next door. His crew member was younger, a thin Hispanic man who didn't say anything and gave us a vacant stare. I thought it was strange—I had expected to see two guys from the country-club set—and my law enforcement antennae began to quiver. Once we were on board, we found that the sailboat wasn't as clean as she had appeared in the spotlight. Trash and food scraps were littered around the open cockpit, and there were empty beer bottles rolling on deck. I glanced at Obenland. The slight downturn in his otherwise expressionless face said he felt something wasn't right.

It was Obenland's turn as boarding officer. He introduced himself and explained to the master that, for his safety and ours, we'd make a quick sweep through the interior of his vessel, and that he and his partner needed to sit on deck and keep their hands in plain view. The master acted casual, maybe too casual, and replied in a smug tone: "Sure, go ahead, look around, there's nothing to see here." I wondered: was that a tiny quiver in his voice?

Petrel crept up, close aboard, a sharpshooter on the bridge wing with an M-16 ready if trouble broke out. Goodrum stayed topside while Obenland and I crept down the three steps into the main salon. The room was dark, measuring twenty feet fore to aft and spanning the width of the boat. We probed the corners with our flashlights and were surprised to find the salon completely empty. The only signs of life were a sleeping bag stretched out on the starboard-side bunk and a crumpled wrapper from a pack of crackers lying on deck. Hadn't the master said they'd been sailing for five days? Where was their food, their clothing, their spit-kits? I looked back over my shoulder, giving Goodrum a nod. He squinted, almost imperceptibly, signaling that there were no problems on deck.

The sailboat, creeping ahead at a knot or two, rolled lazily, in gentle harmony with the sea. It was unnaturally quiet inside. The salon served as a cocoon, protecting us from the wind. Our every movement cast echoes, the three-foot chop slapping the hull like a bongo drum, the sound of our breathing amplified by the contours of the room. The thumping of my heart rang in my ears. Reflections from *Petrel*'s rotating blue light pierced the dark through a twelve-inch port above the compact galley area.

Obenland and I stopped in the middle of the salon, all of our senses on high alert. There was a distant, dank smell, like wet plastic. We stood immobile, listening—for five seconds, then ten. The stillness was unnerving. I surveyed the room. Behind us, underneath the three steps leading to the cockpit, was a tiny opening into the engine space, too small to hold a person. At the other end of the salon was a whitewashed wooden door, which led to a berthing area in the bow. We walked forward, the deck planks creaking loudly, trumpeting our presence. Could someone be hiding in the berthing area? I stood by the thin door, hand on my .45, ready to draw the weapon if there was trouble on the other side. Obenland looked at me and nodded, and then yanked the door open, just as I began to sense a familiar musty odor. Obenland shined his flashlight forward. There, on the bunk, were dozens of bales, each a foot wide and two feet long, triple-wrapped in burlap and plastic. Red Crew had found its first doper.

Obenland and I stared at the jumble of bales, then looked at each other, then back at the bales. Neither of us spoke. After a long pause I just tilted my head toward the cockpit. It was time to make our first arrests.

Obenland led the way back to the main deck, where he stood before the two men, one hand on his hip, above his .45, the other pointing toward the master. "Sir, I am detaining you and your crew for suspicion of smuggling," he said. "Place your hands on top of your heads." Both men looked crestfallen, gut-punched, the master's smugness washed away.

I broke out the secure hand-held radio and called the ship, knowing that Red Crew would be ecstatic with the news.

"*Petrel*, this is XO," I said. "We've located a number of bales that appear to be contraband and have detained the crew for officer safety." We heard a single whoop echo across the water, and then Senior Chief's deep voice belting out "Hot *damn!*" I finished the call: "We're testing the bales and will report back. Over."

Obenland and I reentered the salon, and he cut open the closest bale, using his knife to pry out a fingernail-sized clump of matted leafy material. He inserted it into a drug-test kit, a small plastic pouch with two reagent-filled ampules inside, and squeezed the pouch, breaking the ampules and mixing the chemicals in them with the organic material. Within thirty seconds, the liquid turned a deep shade of purple—proof-positive that the sample was rich in THC. The bales were stuffed with pot. We now had the evidence needed to place the two men—the two smugglers—under arrest.

We stepped up into the open cockpit. Obenland faced the men, speaking slowly and clearly. "You're under arrest for suspicion of smuggling marijuana," he said. "You'll be turned over to authorities in the United States. I'm seizing this vessel, and you'll be transported to our cutter for the trip to shore." I cuffed the master and then his compatriot, securing their hands behind their backs and patting them down to make sure that they weren't armed. Obenland read them their Miranda warnings. The master uttered only a single word: "Whatever."

Goodrum unlaced two life jackets and relaced them onto the prisoners, around the handcuffs, and then guided both men into our small boat for the short trip to *Petrel*. They'd be spending the rest of their voyage in the interior main deck, in the prisoners' chairs, where we'd guard them until they were turned over to U.S. Customs.

To ensure a successful prosecution, we needed to get the paperwork right. Tag and preserve one bale for evidence—check. Search the vessel for weapons, additional evidence, and other contraband—finished in an hour. Sketch the location of the crime scene—done. Take photos of tagged evidence—complete, but we'd need to photograph the prisoners in the morning. My job for the next day would be to collect witness statements and assemble the seizure package for use by the U.S. attorney. Obenland, Bill Hartsock, and Danny Motley would man *Miss Leslie* and remain on board until we made the handoff to Customs.

I headed back to *Petrel*, now exhausted, seeing that it was 0400. I hadn't had time to let the impact of the day's action sink in, but suddenly it dawned on me that our curse was broken: Red Crew had made a real seizure, not some cheap residue bust or action as part of a multi-ship takedown, not even the result of hot intelligence, but a bust completely on our own. We'd found the sailboat, made the boarding, and nailed two smugglers. *Miss Leslie*'s crew had been trying to blend in with the legitimate traffic around Nassau, and we could've easily let them slip by, given their outwardly innocent appearance. But we hadn't. And it was a decent haul, too. By quick count, Obenland estimated there was a ton of marijuana in the forward cabin. We found out later that the grand total topped out at 2,340 pounds—not bad for a bunch of rookies.

District Seven offered another treat. It diverted a 210-foot cutter, the *Vigilant* (WMEC 617), which was four hours away, and directed us to transfer custody of *Miss Leslie* and the prisoners to them. Not only would *Petrel* avoid the day-long trip back to Miami, but we'd make our port call in Nassau, arriving just a few hours late. Our crew would be able to celebrate long and loud.

After climbing back on board the cutter I walked up to the bridge, where Captain Lober shook my hand and said two words: "Nice job." Senior Chief nodded, his eyes glinting, a bit moister than normal. I thanked him for having found *Miss Leslie*.

We'd lost our drug-busting virginity and hit the big time, and I'd expected the crew to be riding the adrenaline rocket, with high-fives and celebration. Instead, members of the bridge team were sedate, calm, and collected, as if they had known that we'd get here some day and that it was just a matter of time. Their composure was impressive, the epitome of maturity.

I headed below. About half the crew was on the mess deck, sitting at the low-slung tables and sipping mugs of coffee and bug juice, talking in low voices, a few laughing quietly. Some joker was playing U2's "Surrender" on the stereo. The scene reminded me of the finish line at the Boston Marathon: there wasn't a lot of dancing about—just a bunch of tired runners catching their breath, relieved to have completed a long and worthwhile journey. It was a picture of Coast Guard contentedness.

I walked back up to the main deck and stood in the passageway, taking a final look at the security arrangements for the smugglers before hitting the rack. The master and his silent partner were sitting in the prisoners' chairs, bathed in red light, facing forward, their hands and feet shackled. They looked deflated, sporting thousand-yard stares. Each had a blanket and pillow so he could sleep, and the security watchstander had a ready supply of water in case they got thirsty.

All was good. An engine room alarm sounded, setting off a wailing siren and a flashing blue light in the office of the engineer of the watch, just forward of the prisoners' chairs. *Miss Leslie*'s master didn't know that it was an engine alarm and assumed it was a police siren. He looked at me and spoke, his voice bitter. "I guess you found another one, huh?" he growled. I burst out laughing and stepped into my stateroom. If only it could be so easy, I thought.

———

Putting smugglers in jail and keeping their poison off the street was its own sweet reward, bringing a warm sense of accomplishment. Not everyone felt that way, however, and sometimes the small city in which we lived was just too snug for comfort. A few days after the patrol was over, Jim Sartucci and I were in a pub in downtown Key West, trying to strike up a conversation with the pretty young woman tending bar. The pub was crowded and noisy, and it took a while to get her attention. Once we finally started talking, she looked at our high-and-tight haircuts and asked if we were in the Navy. Before we could answer, she added: "I just hope you're not some of those Coast Guard pukes. They caught my uncle last week on his sailboat with a bunch of pot, and now he's looking at spending five years in jail. Who cares if he's carrying some weed? It's not gonna hurt anybody." She leaned toward us, eyes narrowed, her voice ice cold, and hissed: "I really hate those Coast Guard bastards."

———

On Christmas Eve morning the in-port OOD called me at home, interrupting a sound sleep. "XO, we've been recalled on a law enforcement case," he said. "Captain wants the crew on board by 1000 so we can get under way by 1030." I threw my uniforms in a bag, along with some cassette tapes and a Christmas package from home, and rushed to the ship. We'd just relieved Gold Crew on *Shearwater* and would be starting our patrol two days earlier than expected. Red Crew set sail, heading southeast toward the Old Bahama Channel.

District Seven had received a tip that the 220-foot freighter *Betty K* was en route to Miami from the Dominican Republic with a large load of marijuana in her fuel tanks. But the tipster also said it might be a smaller stash, or maybe cocaine, and could be hidden just about anywhere. A Customs aircraft had spotted the vessel at daybreak, steaming north toward the Santaren Channel. Our job was to intercept *Betty K*, search for the drugs, and escort the vessel to port. We were still pumped up from the *Miss Leslie* bust and, despite having been dragged away on Christmas Eve, the crew was in good spirits, ready to take on the world.

Once south of Marathon the seas picked up to six feet. *Shearwater* skimmed across the tops of the waves, making thirty-one knots over ground with the boost from the Gulf Stream—better speed than expected with a full load of fuel and marginal seas.

We sailed into a mystical scene. The air was unusually brisk, with the temperature in the forties—a combination that created a dense, four-foot layer of sea smoke that obscured the water, except for the peaks of the rolling waves. There were no other vessels or land in sight and all we saw, horizon to horizon, was the thick plateau of smoke and the undulating wave tops, row after row, marching toward the west. It was stunningly beautiful, even unworldly, as if we were flying over the Himalayas, with the valleys between the mountain ranges enshrouded in fog—except here the mountains were moving.

By midafternoon the OOD had picked up a large northbound radar contact, and fifteen minutes later *Shearwater* was approaching *Betty K* from the west. The blue-hulled ship looked weathered but clean. She had a large, white superstructure forward, a cargo crane amidships, and a second, smaller superstructure aft. We contacted *Betty K* by radio and soon I was climbing up a Jacob's ladder on her port side, leading an eight-person boarding party.

Inspecting a larger ship like *Betty K* could take all day and was infinitely more complex than boarding a fishing vessel or a pleasure boat. There were hundreds of nooks to hide small stashes of drugs, and many spaces where larger loads could be hidden. Cargo holds, fuel tanks, water tanks, store rooms, crew's quarters—all were fair game.

Ensuring the safety of the boarding team was paramount, and it was nearly impossible to keep track of a large crew on a working freighter. *Betty K* had a compliment of twelve, with three on watch. The master had the off-duty crew muster on the mess deck, and we checked their IDs for names, citizenship, and dates of birth, which we called back to the cutter. The OOD passed the information to Group Miami, where they ran intelligence checks to see if anyone in the crew was a wanted felon or under suspicion. None was.

Betty K was Bahamian-flagged. We'd asked the master's consent to come on board and inspect the vessel, and he'd agreed. In a few hours the freighter would be crossing into U.S. territory, where we then could exercise customs authority for a detailed search. With a smile, *Betty K*'s master presented the ship's documents and gave us permission to look anywhere and take as long as we wanted. He was a pleasant, sixtyish Bahamian who had spent most of his life on the water and did not seem the least bit concerned to have the Coast Guard poking around his ship. He'd seen this show before.

The boarding party broke into three teams. The first group remained with the freighter's crew. The second team, led by MK1 Boldan, headed forward to inspect the superstructure, where the berthing areas and forward storerooms were located. For the third team, I took MK3 Hartsock and Fireman Kassin aft, inspecting the cargo holds, engine room, and fuel and water tanks.

The main engine space was old but sparkling clean, crammed with a massive diesel engine and a forest of pipes and vents, with dozens of fluorescent lights humming overhead. We walked forward along a catwalk to a wide passageway, the fuel tanks on the outboard sides and an assortment of whirring and clanking auxiliary machinery between them. The tanks were massive, built into the hull, twenty feet long and ten feet high, each accessible through an oval service hatch that was held in place by two dozen thick bolts. We looked closely at the hatches. Like the tanks, they were slathered with thick coats of reddish-brown anti-rust paint, and it was clear that the bolts hadn't been turned in years. Hartsock and Kassin sounded each tank, finding them three-quarters full. We examined the outer surfaces of the tanks, looking for fresh welds or hidden seams. There was nothing.

The water tanks were further aft, crammed into a low-ceilinged room. A fifteen-inch-diameter drive-shaft ran through the center of the compartment, angled slightly down, toward the propeller. We crawled on hands and knees, tapping on the tanks, looking closely for alterations, while carefully avoiding the rotating shaft. Again, we found nothing. The cargo spaces also were in order, neatly stowed, with a detailed manifest for all of the pallets and containers.

We'd been searching for three hours, and now *Betty K* was twenty miles from Miami. The boarding team regrouped on the mess deck. Boldan reported that he had accessed all of the forward holds and staterooms, with the crew members voluntarily opening up their personal lockers, closets, and drawers, and he hadn't seen anything unusual. There was no doubt that *Betty K*'s crew was trying to be as cooperative as possible.

I asked Boldan to head below with Kassin to reinspect the tanks, just to make sure we hadn't missed anything. MK1's engineering expertise might make the difference. Hartsock and I headed to the aft superstructure, which sat one deck above the engine room. It was the last area to check.

Inside the superstructure, on the port side, was a longitudinal passageway, and to starboard of it were two compartments, a large workshop forward and a midsize machinery room aft. We searched the spaces, probing into every corner, looking for any signs of smuggling. Everything looked shipshape. To complete the inspection Hartsock broke out a fifty-foot tape measure. First we measured the passageway and found it was thirty-five feet, six inches long. Then, the workshop. It was exactly twenty feet, fore to aft. The machinery room was fourteen feet, two inches.

Hartsock looked at me, puzzled. It didn't add up. The passageway was thirty-five feet, six inches end-to-end, and the two rooms next to it totaled only thirty-four feet, two inches. This meant that the bulkhead separating the rooms was sixteen inches thick. Typically, a metal bulkhead would take up less than an inch. We remeasured, with the same result. A shot of adrenaline jolted me into a state of hyper-awareness. There was plenty of room in a sixteen-inch-thick bulkhead for a secret compartment, which could be crammed with dozens of kilos of cocaine, pot, or heroin. Hartsock also perked up, now fidgeting, eager to account for the hidden space.

We stepped inside the machinery room, scanning its forward bulkhead. It looked perfectly normal. Two air compressors and a wiring run were mounted on the wall, and our inch-by-inch inspection found no secret access points or hidden hatches. We tapped the bulkhead along its entire length and height and found it solid throughout.

We headed forward to the workshop. The room was filled with wire rope, storage bins, and spools of manila line. On the compartment's aft bulkhead was a four-by-eight-foot pegboard rack, festooned with an assortment of hammers, caulking guns, and wrenches. Hartsock walked over and gave the pegboard a closer look, scratching his chin. The pegboard was held to the bulkhead by a dozen metal screws. Hartsock studied one of the screw heads in the beam of his flashlight. "Hey XO, I'm gonna try and take this out and see what happens," he said.

He removed the screw with only modest effort. Then he grinned, chortling: "Yep, that was too easy, there's something behind this board, for sure." We took the tools off the pegboard, piling them on a bench nearby, knowing that if we didn't find anything we'd be putting them right back in place. Then we set to work removing the other screws. Ten minutes later we were manhandling the pegboard off the wall. Behind it, in the middle of the bulkhead, was a hatch. I'll be damned, I thought—we'd found a hidden compartment.

The hatch was four feet tall and three feet wide and had a simple brass clasp securing the door in place. My heart rate rose. There was plenty of room behind the hatch for a few dozen kilos, enough to make someone on *Betty K* a tidy profit. I stepped forward, undid the clasp, and swung the hatch open, imagining the rush of excitement on *Shearwater* when we reported we'd found a stash of cocaine. It was empty.

Hartsock and I looked at each other, and he exhaled loudly, kicking the deck with his steel-toed boot. "Damn, XO," he said, "we find a tiny secret compartment on a huge ship like this, and it's goddamned empty?

Are you freakin' kidding me?" He kicked the deck again, harder, his freckled face now beet-red. "I guarantee this hole'll be full of dope next time they make port. This is un-goddam-believable."

We searched inside the hidden compartment, tapping on its walls, and swabbed up dust from the bottom shelf, testing it for marijuana and cocaine, figuring that maybe there was minute residue from a previous drug shipment. Both tests were negative.

Hartsock closed the hatch and leaned the pegboard against the bulkhead, leaving it unsecured so we could show it to the Customs agents in Miami. By then *Betty K* was entering the harbor. We returned to the mess deck and reunited with the rest of the boarding party, letting the ship's crew members man their mooring stations. I walked to the pilothouse and talked with the master. He seemed genuinely shocked to learn there was a hidden compartment on his ship and vowed to have it welded shut.

After *Betty K* moored at a commercial pier a mile up the Miami River, Customs came on board with three inspectors and a dog team. We briefed the agents on our search and showed them what we'd found, spending an hour pointing out areas in the engine room, cargo hold, and tanks that could use closer scrutiny. The lead Customs agent said they'd been on board *Betty K* before but had never measured the inside contours of the aft superstructure. No one in our boarding team was comforted to hear that, as we'd always considered Customs to be the best of the best when it came to finding hidden spaces. Maybe this crop of agents was new.

We left *Betty K* after six hours on board. On the pier, Hartsock took me aside, speaking softly. "You know, XO," he said, "I was pretty pissed that that compartment was empty. I knew for sure that we'd found some dope. But I gotta tell you, I'm really glad we found it—I bet those Customs guys'll be saying good things about us tonight." I just nodded, knowing we'd learned the skills that might help us make other seizures, some day, somehow.

Shearwater spent the night at Base Miami Beach and early on Christmas morning headed back to sea. The crew was disappointed but not gloomy. Senior Chief plotted a track along the reef line. We'd return to Key West for five days, have a delayed Christmas at home, and then resume the patrol. Lieutenant Lober hinted he had a special way to celebrate the New Year; he was a hell of a poker player and a master at keeping secrets, so we'd have to wait a week to find out his plan.

I headed to my stateroom and rummaged through my bags for a fresh uniform, finding the package from my parents, still unopened. There, in solitude, I unwrapped their present. It was a set of books, exactly what I'd wanted. Part of me was thinking that this should've been a bittersweet moment, away from home, working on the hallowed day, and not even having success in our search for drugs. Unexpectedly, though, I felt as content as I'd ever been—blessed to be surrounded by talented, honest, dedicated people, and knowing that our jobs mattered. That made for its own special gift.

———

We got under way again on December 30. *Shearwater* headed west, patrolling slowly to the south of the Marquesas, and the next morning we angled toward the Dry Tortugas. A storm was brewing, with strengthening winds and lumpy seas that were starting to break.

The captain unveiled his big surprise: we'd be overnighting at Fort Jefferson. We had moored there before but had never spent more than a few hours. With an entire night ahead of us, Red Crew would have a chance to decompress and enjoy the fort's exotic beauty before getting back to business in the New Year.

Fort Jefferson was the centerpiece of the Dry Tortugas National Park, under the supervision of federal park rangers who lived on site for weeklong stints. The fort had been built over the span of three decades in the mid-1800s, to guard a strategic anchorage and coaling station. Unfortunately, by the time the structure was complete, new technology in ships and weaponry had rendered it obsolete, its strategic value lost.

The fort was an immense hexagon, built from more than 16 million bricks, and at its widest point the outer walls were an eighth of a mile apart. The architecture was right out of *Pirates of the Caribbean*—dark passageways, sweeping archways, dank chambers, and a complex network of cisterns for capturing rainwater. Two stories high, the structure had ramparts, guard towers, and hundreds of cutouts for cannons, and it was surrounded by a deep, wide moat. Inside its walls was a huge open field, at one time a parade ground but now home to an eclectic assortment of grasses, palms, and scraggly shade trees. A large storage magazine, once filled with rifles and black powder, had been dug into coral rock on the north end of the parade field.

Fort Jefferson sat on an atoll in the midst of a pristine ecosystem, roughly hewn but staggeringly beautiful, home to spiny lobster, coral heads, and a constellation of brightly colored fish. On the eastern side of the fort was a modest wooden pier and next to that was a long, white sand beach, the crystal-blue water of the narrow channel bending around the fort to the west. Far from the crowds of Key West and Miami, and seventy miles from the nearest inhabited island, Fort Jefferson was a gem. Seaplanes from Key West would land nearby and power up onto the beach, dropping off small groups of tourists for day-visits.

The channel was tight, and an SES was about the largest Coast Guard ship that could squeeze its way through the narrow and winding approach. We arrived at midday to find two dozen sailboats and fishing vessels in the harbor, cluttering the compact turning basin, waiting out the storm. At the pier was a forty-foot lobster boat. We moored directly behind her, with *Shearwater*'s stern sticking out awkwardly into the harbor.

Dan Sanders, the in-port OOD, sifted through a suspect vessel "hotlist" published by the El Paso Intelligence Center, or EPIC, a multi-agency law enforcement clearinghouse that provided the Coast Guard with up-to-date intelligence. Standing on the bridge wing, he compared the names of the vessels in the harbor to those on the list. Suddenly he looked up, startled. "XO, you're not gonna believe this," he said. "One of the boats here is on the list for drug smuggling."

I looked around the harbor, wondering which of the vessels was the suspected smuggler. "Really? Which one?" I asked. Sanders just shrugged, his face playful, tempting me to guess. "The red ketch over by the seaplane ramp?" I said. I pointed to a weather-beaten sailboat a hundred yards astern. Of all the boats in the harbor this one seemed the most out of place.

Sanders shook his head. "Nope. Even better. It's the lobster boat right in front of us," he said. He nodded toward the blue-hulled vessel tucked underneath our bow. Talk about being lucky—we'd moored right next to a possible drug-runner.

The lobster boat's stern read *Lesly 1*. We contacted Group Key West on the secure radio, and after conferring with EPIC, Group gave us additional information. The master of *Lesly 1*, Armando Gonzalez, was suspected of being part of a smuggling network that operated in the uninhabited cays between Key West and the Dry Tortugas. EPIC recommended an immediate boarding as their intelligence suggested that the boat could be fully loaded. Group gave us a green light to carry out a full customs search, since the boat already was sitting in federal waters. It didn't make sense that *Lesly 1* would moor at Fort Jefferson if she was carrying a stash, but we speculated that, just maybe, the crew was seeking shelter from the rough weather before delivering the contraband ashore. This would be Red Crew's last boarding of the year. It could end 1983 on a very high note.

I suited up along with Hartsock and three others, while Lieutenant Lober talked with the head park ranger, letting him know our plans. The rangers carried firearms and said they would back us up if trouble broke out. It was the only time that I had ever walked to another vessel to conduct a boarding, and it was my only law enforcement experience in front of an audience. About twenty boaters were loitering on the pier, and they watched our every move as we stepped on board *Lesly 1*, outfitted in our law enforcement finest.

A man was sitting in the boat's cabin and met us as we stepped on board. "Yeah, what can I do for you?" he growled. He had a thick Cuban accent and bloodshot eyes, looking as if he'd just spent a rough weekend in Vegas. He said he was the master, Gonzalez. I explained that we were going to conduct a customs search of his vessel and told him to muster his crew. He looked annoyed. "It's just me and one other guy," Gonzalez said. "He's sleeping. I'm not sure when he'll wake up." I told the master to roust his partner. Gonzalez went below, yelled a bit, and after a minute his shipmate staggered onto deck, zipping up the fly on his cutoff jeans. Hartsock and I checked their ID cards, confirming that the first man was the suspected smuggler.

Hartsock and Kassin conducted a security sweep. There was no sign of contraband. Then came the safety inspection—all good. Time for the measuring tape. I crawled into the engine room and measured the tanks and internal dimensions of the compartment. Hartsock did the same in the forward berthing area and fishhold. After twenty minutes of crawling and scribbling, we compared notes.

Hartsock looked at the numbers and his face flushed. "Jeez, XO, look at this," he said. "There's three feet missing between the fishhold and engine room." I double-checked his math—he was right. There was an inaccessible space that ran the fourteen-foot width of the boat, was three feet thick, and extended vertically from the keel to the main deck. There were no hatches, doors, or other entrances into the walled-off void. I did some quick calculations: there could be twenty-five, maybe thirty bales—up to 1,500 pounds of marijuana—stashed in the compartment, if it were full. My skin prickled. Every instinct said we were about to bust our second "Leslie."

By this time the crowd had started wandering off, but Lieutenant Lober and most of Red Crew stayed on the pier. Hartsock examined the deck above the void. It was solid, and the fiberglass had the same pattern as the rest of the main deck. No suspicions there. But, inside the fishhold, the bulkhead between it and the inaccessible void was painted a lighter color that the rest of the compartment, and the paint looked fresher. This was a solid clue. *Lesly 1*'s crew could have onloaded her cargo, placed the contraband in the void through an opening in the fishhold, and then sealed the opening with fiberglass and paint. My pulse quickened.

I questioned Gonzalez. "Sir, do you know why there's a void between your fishhold and the engine room?" I asked.

He shrugged, pleading ignorance. "The boat's always been like that, ever since I bought it last summer."

"Have you repaired any fiberglass or done any painting in the fishhold since you owned the boat?"

"No—why would I do that?"

"Do you know why there's fresh paint on the aft bulkhead in the fishhold?"

"Beats me. It can't be too fresh. Maybe the guy I bought it from fixed it up. I don't know nothing bout that."

It was time to open the void. I explained to Gonzalez that it was a violation of customs law to have a large inaccessible space, as it constituted "outfitting for smuggling." If there were enough evidence to show that

Lesly 1 was rigged to hide contraband, we could seize the vessel. And regardless of whether we found drugs in the void, the space would have to be made accessible. That was the law.

Hartsock asked one of our engineers on the pier to get a battery-powered drill, a reciprocating saw, and a 150-foot extension cord from *Shearwater*. We planned to tap a few holes and cut open the void for inspection but would have to run a power line back to the cutter to use the saw. One of the park rangers overheard Hartsock and asked us to wait. He scuttled back into the fort and emerged a few minutes later, grinning broadly and carrying a compact chainsaw.

It was the perfect solution. There'd be no need for power cords, and the chainsaw would make quick work of the fiberglass. I told Gonzalez what we were going to do, and he shrugged, resigned to having a hole cut into his boat. To preserve watertight integrity, we'd cut the hole in the main deck, where it could be fashioned into a watertight hatch and wouldn't permit flooding to spread if *Lesly 1* sprang a leak in the fishhold.

Hartsock marked a spot above the void, eighteen inches square, between the structural members holding up the main deck. The ranger lit off the chainsaw and its throaty, high-pitched whine drew the attention of people mingling nearby. The crowd filtered back to watch.

The rotating chain sliced easily through the fiberglass and filled the air with a fine white dust, which settled on our clothes, in our hair, and on our sweaty, exposed skin. Wisely, the ranger was wearing long sleeves, leather gloves, goggles, and a hat, limiting his exposure to the debris being thrown by the saw. The crowd on the pier craned their necks to get a better view. The ranger finished the first cut and moved the blade 90 degrees to make the second. Gonzalez and his partner sat on the gunwale, fidgeting. The ranger finished the second and third cuts, and Hartsock inserted a crowbar into the gap to hold the square in place as the ranger cut the fourth side. I looked over at Gonzalez and then toggled back to the ranger, ready to cuff the smugglers as soon as we we'd uncovered the load of dope.

The fourth cut was complete. Hartsock snatched the square of fiber-glass, tossed it aside and shined his flashlight into the void. He didn't say a word. I stepped up and peered over his shoulder, looking at an open bilge. The void was empty. I poked my head into the hole, not breathing in case there were toxic fumes, quickly shining my flashlight into every corner of the space. Yup, completely empty. Standing up, I noticed that the sawdust and fiberglass particles created by the chainsaw covered my chest, midsection, and legs.

Then, unexpectedly, I started to itch. The fiberglass particles were microscopically sharp, sticking to the skin like a million tiny needles. The dust covered my exposed arms and face. Sweat had streamed the fiberglass fibers down my chest and back. Rubbing didn't help, only driving the tiny barbs deeper under the skin. Hartsock was also scratching himself, a look of disgust on his face. We'd expected to uncover a load of pot and instead looked like we were suffering from scabies.

It was time to call it quits. Group Key West reported that Customs was not interested in pressing outfitting for smuggling charges. Hartsock lodged the fiberglass square back into the deck, holding it in place with wedges, while I instructed Gonzalez to install a proper hatch over the newly cut hole, to avoid future trouble. He was calm and courteous, even thanking us for doing our job, despite the fact we'd just ripped a hole in his deck. We wrapped up the boarding by giving Gonzalez a standard claim form, which he could file with the Coast Guard legal office in Miami if he felt the search had caused undue damage to his property. The Coast Guard lawyers never heard from him.

We sulked away from *Lesly 1*, the dwindling crowd staring at us, whispering among themselves. We'd given them a show but with a limp finale. I focused on the promised relief of a warm soapy shower, but even that did little good. The fiberglass dust remained stubbornly imbedded, prickling and itching for days, a constant reminder of the whims of the drug-smuggling gods.

―――――

By sunset Red Crew had made dozens of new friends among the boaters waiting out the storm. One of the stranded sailors was an older, well-dressed gentleman who introduced himself as Harold Sawyer, a U.S. representative from Michigan. Representative Sawyer was filling the seat that Gerald R. Ford had vacated when he became vice president and later president. The representative was fascinated by our cutter, said he had watched the entire *Lesly 1* boarding, and asked a stream of questions about the drug war simmering off South Florida. We found out later that Sawyer was a staunch anti-drug crusader on Capitol Hill. Jerry Lober gave him a tour of *Shearwater* and then discussed the weather forecast, trying to stem the representative's anxiety about missing his flight home to Michigan.

About 1900 Lober gathered the crew and let us in on another New Year's surprise. He had arranged for Red Crew to be the special guests of the park rangers in their quarters within the fort. We knew the rangers had some primitive bunkrooms and a cramped, shabby office but had never heard of anything beyond that. The head ranger walked over, poker-faced, and escorted Red Crew into the interior of the complex, leading us across the parade ground like a pack of Cub Scouts. The wind was starting to howl, buffeting the trees, with dark clouds broiling overhead. We walked deep into the fort, twisting and turning through dark passageways underneath the north wall. Then around a corner, hidden from view, the ranger stopped in front of a bulky wooden door. It had a decrepit "No Admittance" sign nailed to it. This wasn't looking promising. Senior Chief rolled his eyes.

But a few seconds later all of us were beaming as the ranger opened the door and we stepped into a well-lighted room, artfully decorated with a fifteen-foot wooden bar, a pool table, and an arcade game and pinball machine wedged against the far wall. There was an impressive selection of liquor lined up on a shelf behind the bar and an oversized metal tub filled with ice and dozens of cold beers. Two folding tables were covered with finger food. The brick walls and stone floor kept the room perfectly cool, the growing growl of the wind muted and distant, a world away. It was the rangers' secret hideaway, and they told us they'd never shown it to a Coast Guard crew before, but, considering the holiday, they'd made an exception in order to hold a proper New Year's Eve blast. Lieutenant Lober and his ranger friends had really delivered.

The rangers had selectively invited some of the boaters stranded in the harbor to join the party and the room filled with a crush of bodies and loud conversation. A stereo blared beach music. Representative Sawyer and his traveling partners were there, along with a strong contingent of young couples and several gaggles of college girls who'd spent their Christmas break sailing the Keys. For a single guy, it was heaven.

The storm was forgotten and the drinks flowed freely. Four of the college girls started dancing and grabbed some of the guys by the hand, pulling them onto the makeshift dance floor. Working the room, I reminded the crew, one by one, to limit their drinking, considering we were on search and rescue standby. It was hard to be too stern, though, since everyone was having a rousing time, and I didn't want to dampen anyone's spirits. Our men and women had done great work coming together as a crew, and they were letting off steam in a unique and unforgettable setting.

At 2220 our fun turned to rust. One of the in-port watchstanders came running in and escorted the captain from the room. Lieutenant Lober returned ten minutes later, sporting his most serious face. He pulled me aside. "XO, we've got to get under way," he said. "I just talked with Group, and they've got a commercial tug in trouble just a few miles south of here. We need to get on scene ASAP." I corralled the crew, and we ran back to the ship, whipped by the wind and drenched by thick sheets of rain.

Ten minutes later, *Shearwater* was under way. Dan Sanders deftly maneuvered the cutter through the narrow channel that bent around the fort. Negotiating the channel was a challenge by day, and on a rainy, windswept night it was an order of magnitude more frightening. Now I knew why we'd never arrived or left the fort after dark before: it was too hard to pick our way through the shallows when the hazards were so hard to see. Fifteen nerve-wracking minutes later, we'd made it to deeper water and set course for the disabled tugboat *Gulf Express* and her two-hundred-foot, propane-laden barge.

The southerly winds were strong, steady at thirty knots with gusts of more than forty, and pockets of torrential rained pelted the ship. The low cloud cover pressed down, rushing past, dark and confining. The seas were steep and breaking. In the sheltered waters just outside the fort we began plowing through eight-footers, *Shearwater*'s wide bow smashing into each crest, sending a shudder through the hull. As we moved offshore the waves grew, from ten to twelve and then up to fifteen feet. *Shearwater* was slamming harder than I'd ever seen. Despite the vicious pounding, the cutter made good speed, topping twenty-two knots for most of the transit.

Gulf Express and her barge were powerless and adrift, in danger of grinding together, all while they were being pushed north toward the marine sanctuary. If the two vessels collided, each could sink—assuming they weren't destroyed first in a propane-fueled fire. There were six crew members on *Gulf Express,* and they were helpless, the tug totally dark, with her main engines dead and no electricity except for battery power. Six lives were in our hands.

Framed in the beam of our spotlight, *Gulf Express* bucked and heaved, lifting high on the crest of each wave and then slamming hard into the troughs below. The tug was rolling wildly and each time she crashed down it sent a huge sheet of water arcing skyward.

The tug was owned by the Guidry Brothers Towing Company of Galliano, Louisiana, a well-respected firm known throughout the Gulf. Our radio calls with the tug's master found him professional and courteous, despite the dire circumstances. He told it to us straight. "Coast Guard, thanks for being here, but you're going to have to be real quick," he said. "We've got 1,200 feet of wire rope in the water and it's looped underneath us. We're closing on the barge mighty fast. I don't want to cut the barge free, because if I do, there's no way to stop it from going aground. I figure we've got forty minutes, maybe a bit more before we're on top of it." His voice was crisp and even, like a newscaster's. "And we really don't want that to happen."

The captain, BM1 Sanders, Senior Chief, and I huddled on the port bridge wing. Sanders would run the towing detail and Senior Chief would assume the conn. Sanders was confident that he could rig a tow, but it would be dangerous. He warned that our towing bitt might not hold and our four-inch nylon hawser was rated for much lighter loads and would come under immense strain. If it parted, the line would whip back with explosive force. We all remembered a training video that we'd seen about the dangers of synthetic line snap-back. The narrator was a Navy commander who'd lost both legs when he was struck by a recoiling line.

Jerry Lober recapped the plan. "XO, you're the safety monitor, keep your eyes peeled and sound off if you see trouble. Senior Chief, you'll maneuver close ahead of the tug—use the crossing-the-T approach. Try to get about thirty or forty feet off her bow. Boats, pass the line to the tug on XO's signal, and once it's secure we'll move ahead and pay out everything we've got. I wish we had twice as much line, but we'll have to make do. When the tug's under strain we'll turn to the south and head into the wind. I don't know how fast we can go, but we should be able to make a couple of knots. We'll just keep heading into the wind until we get relieved of the tow."

Group Key West had dispatched *Cape York* to assist, and a large ocean-going salvage tug was also en route from Tampa, due within twenty-four hours. "We're probably going to keep this guy on the string for at least half a day, until *Cape York* gets here," Captain Lober said. Then he smiled. "It's gonna be an interesting night."

"Set the towing bill now, set the towing bill." Seaman Scott made the announcement over the ship's topside speakers, her airy voice out of place in the roughneck weather. Sanders and his deck force began laying all five hundred feet of towline in rows on the aft deck. That completed, they manned their stations, ready to pass a thin messenger line to the tug so her crew could haul in and connect the larger four-inch hawser.

It was an hour into the New Year. *Shearwater* and the disabled tug were now only eighteen miles south of the shallows. The tug had closed to within spitting distance of the barge. Senior Chief maneuvered *Shearwater* across the tug's bow. With the seas off her port quarter, *Gulf Express* had a jerky corkscrew motion, and Senior Chief had to judge the distance exactly right. If he crossed too far away, Sanders' team wouldn't be able to pass the towline to the tug. Passing too close risked collision. The captain watched intently as Senior Chief nudged the throttles, *Shearwater* motoring ahead at six knots, now three hundred feet from the tug's surging bow, then two hundred fifty, two hundred. He applied a light backing bell and positioned the cutter directly in front of *Gulf Express*. I barked the order to pass the towline.

Shearwater's aft deck was fifty feet from the tug—too far to throw a line by hand. Chuck Obenland took aim with the .30-caliber line-throwing gun, an ancient Springfield rifle that shot a plastic projectile attached to a spool of thin orange shot line. There was a sharp metallic retort, and the projectile arced toward the tug, the line unspooling behind it. It was a great shot with a not-so-great ending. The projectile passed directly over the tug's bow, disappearing into the night. The orange line draped across the gunwale but then, as the tug rolled 40 degrees, the line slid over the side, gone. The tug's crew hadn't had time to grab it. Obenland would have to retrieve the line and reload the gun.

"Damn!" Senior Chief blurted out. *Shearwater* was drifting away from the tug, seventy-five feet and opening. He pushed the throttles forward, sped ahead, and looped 360 degrees for another pass.

By the time *Shearwater* was making the second approach the tug had crept another thirty feet closer to the barge. We were cutting this one close. Senior Chief made the approach at higher speed, again stopping directly off the tug's flailing bow. Sanders shook his head side to side, signaling "no." *Shearwater* was too far away, and the line-throwing gun wasn't ready for a second shot.

"I've got this," Senior Chief growled. He placed the starboard throttle ahead and the port throttle back, pivoting the ship 90 degrees to port, so that *Shearwater* was pointed in the same direction as the tug. He grabbed the 1MC microphone and yelled: "Stand by on the fantail, you're gonna get wet!" Sanders and his team scrambled forward to find shelter near the deckhouse.

Senior Chief put both engines in reverse and *Shearwater* slammed backwards. The wide, flat transom of the cutter hammered into the oncoming waves, with truckloads of salt water raining over the ship, whipped by the strong winds. Then he snapped the engines back to neutral with *Shearwater* in perfect position, twenty-five feet from the tug—easy throwing distance. Sanders, drenched, gave a toothy smile and a thumbs-up sign.

The view from *Shearwater*'s bridge was surreal, a carnival of motion. Overhead, the thick layer of clouds rushed past, ragged and swirling, low enough to touch. The cutter snapped side to side, rolling 10 degrees, surging vertically as waves passed underneath, plummeting into the troughs, while the tug's movement was unceasingly spastic. One second *Gulf Express* was hovering on the peak of a wave, fifteen feet above *Shearwater*'s aft deck, and the next she was falling into a deep gulley, our sailors looking down at the tugboat's thick bow. I thought that *Shearwater* was too close for comfort. One surge from a rogue wave and *Gulf Express* would come crashing down on our transom.

I gave the command for the second time: "Pass the line!" Chad Weatherby, heaving line in hand, ran three steps toward the fantail and with a deep-throated grunt flung the coil toward the two men waiting on the tug's bow. Weatherby bellowed "Head's up!" at the top of his lungs. As the line flew through the air it uncoiled, the monkey's fist flying fast and straight. It was a perfect strike, low in the zone. *Shearwater* surged down as the tug lifted higher, and the monkey's fist cleared *Gulf Express'* gunwale by inches. One of the tug's crew jumped toward the line, landing on his knees and grabbing the monkey's fist with both hands. He screamed to us, his voice shrill: "Got it!" He and his shipmate began hauling in the line—frantically.

The quarter-inch messenger was attached to one hundred feet of thicker one-inch line, which was shackled onto the bitter end of the four-inch towing hawser. Sanders quickly paid out the one-incher as *Gulf Express'* crew pulled it in, the two ships heaving and falling, close aboard, completely out of step. Senior Chief applied a light forward bell, slowly opening the distance between the two vessels. Thirty feet, forty. The one-inch line completely paid out and Sanders tossed the shackled end of the towing hawser into the water. The tug's crew members cursed and strained as they pulled the heavier four-inch line toward them.

Gulf Express had closed to within ninety feet of the barge. The tug's master leaned out the pilothouse window, and even from distance we could see the tension in his face. He jumped back on the radio, brief but compelling: "Anytime now, Coast Guard, anytime."

Jerry Lober stepped in, speaking curtly. "XO, let's expedite." I ran aft on the bridge wing and yelled down at Sanders. "Boats, we're gonna punch it ahead, and you're gonna have to get that line out in a hurry." He nodded okay. It was risky, paying out line at speed, but we had no choice. As soon as the tug's crew shackled the towline to their bow, Senior Chief clutched in the port engine. Sanders had the four-inch towline looped around the crucifix-shaped towing bitt and as the cutter moved forward he fed out the line, hand-over-fist, moving fast, his arms a blur. One slip and his hand could get caught in the line, pinning him to the towing bitt or even dragging him overboard. Behind Sanders, his team tended the hawser, making sure that it uncoiled cleanly with no twists or kinks.

Two hundred feet of four-inch line at the rail—we were almost halfway there. *Shearwater* moved further forward, with Sanders rapidly paying out the hawser as the gap between the two ships widened. Three hundred, four hundred, four hundred fifty feet—that was all we had. Sanders secured the end of the hawser to the towing bitt, whipping the line in a figure eight, as if lassoing a steer. Senior Chief nudged *Shearwater* farther forward and we saw the strain on the hawser increase, pulling it fully out of the water. Ideally, in a normal tow, the bulk of the line would remain submerged, allowing it to absorb shock, but under these conditions we'd be lucky if any part of the hawser stayed wet.

Gulf Express was perilously close to the barge, offset at a 45-degree angle, with no more than fifty feet separating the two vessels. They would collide within minutes. The tug continued her crazy ride, its bow surging and falling with the waves. Behind her, the barge rolled slowly, ponderously, like a giant whale, broadside to the seas. Then, suddenly, the tug's bow jerked, the tension in the hawser taking hold. *Gulf Express* was under tow. Her bow swept toward *Shearwater* and the gap to the barge began opening, almost imperceptibly at first, then more quickly. Captain Lober looked at Senior Chief and raised an eyebrow. Senior Chief took off his ballcap and wiped his forehead, lacing the air with a spicy slur. Unless the towline parted, there wouldn't be any propane fireworks to ring in the New Year. Collision averted.

Shearwater towed the disabled tug to the northwest, down swell, gradually opening the distance to the barge until the steel towing cable that trailed from *Gulf Express* straightened and came under its own strain. Slowly, surely, the tug's thrashing abated, her bow dampened by our towline and her stern by the wire rope connecting it to the barge. Now under tension, the barge began pivoting toward the tug. Soon both vessels were in line behind the cutter, with *Shearwater*'s four-inch hawser absorbing the full weight of *Gulf Express* and her tow, trailing a quarter-mile astern.

The added load of the barge placed a brutal stress on the towline, which had stretched almost to the breaking point. The nylon hawser was only half its usual diameter, straight as a pipe, completely out of the water, drops of water shimmering off as the load waxed and waned. On *Shearwater*'s bridge, we could hear an unearthly resonant hum coming from the overstretched nylon, fading in and out with the wind. Sanders cleared the aft deck. The hawser was close to parting, and if it let go, there'd be no warning and no time to duck. The recoil could cut a person in half. The tow was set and there was no reason for putting our crew in harm's way any longer. One crisis down, one to go.

During the hour that we'd spent hitching up the tow, *Shearwater* had steamed toward the shallows, which were now less than ten miles away. We had to alter course almost 180 degrees—without putting a fatal strain on the towline—or else we'd end up driving all three vessels onto the coral reefs ahead. If we lost power or the tow parted, with the winds still howling from the south, the tug and its two-hundred-foot companion would be set onto the shallows by daybreak.

Senior Chief applied slight left rudder and, degree by degree, the cutter changed course, first toward the west, then continuing the wide loop until *Shearwater* and the two vessels behind her were heading south, into the churning seas. By the time the maneuver was complete it was 0300. The tug's motion became more pronounced facing the waves head on, and the pull on *Shearwater*'s towing bitt was so strong that you could see the aluminum deck flexing beneath it. But the second crisis was averted. The tug and barge wouldn't run aground on the reef. *Shearwater* could put some distance to the shoal waters in our wake. The broad loop had taken us to within seven miles of the reef line.

I watched as the top of a wave slapped the hawser, soaking it, droplets of water spraying free from the tension in the nylon, glistening in the beam of our spotlight. I marveled at the capabilities of the SES. We'd been able to sprint to the scene at more than twenty knots, and *Shearwater*'s uncrowded decks and relatively steady ride had made setting up the tow possible. There was no patrol craft in the Coast Guard like it. To drive home the point, Group Key West reported that *Cape York* was aborting her mission of relieving *Shearwater* of the tow. In the wicked wind and seas, the smaller cutter could only make two knots' headway and wouldn't have gotten on scene until well after the large commercial tug had arrived from Tampa.

My reverie was shattered by a blast of radio chatter. It was the master on *Gulf Express,* saying that his batteries were just about dead and asking if we could transfer fresh ones. His radio and bilge pumps were jerry-rigged to run off the batteries, and if they died his engine room would slowly fill with water. Boldan and Sanders came to the bridge and said yes, we could spare a few batteries and sure, we could launch the RHIB, but we'd need to alter course to provide a lee. Boldan offered up a hand-held fuel pump and some spare filter material and said that maybe *Gulf Express'* engineers could clean out the gunk from the fuel lines and get their engines restarted.

Weatherby volunteered as coxswain and Hartsock as crew. Both dressed out in survival suits and carried flares, extra flotation, spare radios, and waterproof lights, in case they went for a swim. They loaded three bulky batteries into the RHIB—each about sixty pounds and wrapped in plastic—along with the fuel pump, filters, and a satchel of hot food that Goodrum had whipped up. Gingerly, Senior Chief nudged *Shearwater* 30 degrees to port, to provide a partial lee for launching the boat.

It didn't help. As soon as the RHIB hit the water, a massive wave crashed down, filling it to the gunwales. Weatherby hustled down the Jacob's ladder, bailed a dozen buckets of water, and then started the outboard. Once Hartsock jumped in, they cast off and steered downswell toward the tug. Hartsock bailed furiously. Weatherby said later that being partially swamped provided extra stability that helped them navigate the steepest waves.

The transfer was a circus act. *Gulf Express* was pitching heavily, repeatedly burying her nose. When the tug's bow would thrust skyward, her aft deck would submerge under a rush of whitewater. Our main searchlight couldn't pivot far enough to keep the RHIB in its beam, so we tracked the boat with a weaker, handheld light. Once off *Gulf Express'* port side the RHIB disappeared into a curtain of shadow and spray. All we could see were occasional flashes from the reflective tape on Weatherby's and Hartsock's survival suits, sparkling amidst a confused swirl of froth and foam.

Two minutes passed, then three, four. No one spoke. It looked as though the RHIB was making repeated approaches to the tug, thrashing and smashing. A rain squall let loose, torrential, killing visibility. We waited, on edge, for six minutes, then seven. Then the RHIB emerged from the maelstrom, chugging over the tops of the waves, looking no worse for wear, Weatherby's face plastered with a wry grin. Somehow he'd nudged the RHIB alongside the heaving tug long enough for Hartsock to muscle over the batteries and supplies. Senior Chief cussed again and the captain let out a long sigh of relief, just as *Gulf Express'* master called on the radio.

"Damn, Coast Guard, thanks for the help," he said. "We should have plenty of juice now to keep the pumps running, and the guys really appreciate the food. We haven't had a warm meal since yesterday." He paused, chuckling. Then he added: "And tell your coxswain he did one hell of a job. I could have sworn he drove that boat of yours right up onto our aft deck." He paused again, then said in a more serious tone: "Whatever you're paying those guys, you need to give 'em more."

We set the normal sea watch, posting an extra seaman to monitor the towline from the cocoon of the pilothouse. I relieved Senior Chief as OOD, and he headed below, spent. The quartermaster took radar ranges to Fort Jefferson, which was painting strong on the screen, along with a depth sounding and LORAN readings. I plotted them on the chart, yielding a tight four-line fix. Fifteen minutes later we took more readings, to see how far south we had moved since the last fix. The captain looked over my shoulder.

Something was amiss—I must have measured wrong, since the new fix put us slightly north of our earlier position. I replotted the ranges and LORAN coordinates and got the same result. We waited five minutes and took a third set of radar ranges, which also showed northward movement.

At first, reality didn't sink in. Lieutenant Lober and I just stared at each other, then the chart, then the tow, both of our minds working overtime. Then the truth washed over us, like a breaking wave, drenching me in cold fear. My knees turned to jelly, stomach in my throat. Lober stood aghast, his face drained of color. *Shearwater* was moving *backwards*—toward the shallows—at almost a full knot. The wind and seas were too powerful to overcome, continuing to push the cutter and its tandem tow toward danger, even as we dragged the tug and barge as hard as possible in the opposite direction. Our ship couldn't out-muscle nature's fury. Shoal water was just six miles away.

Quick calculations: at this rate, *Shearwater* would be aground by 1000, and the relief tug was not expected on scene for another eighteen hours after that. The captain and I ran through the options, which ranged from bad to horrible. We could order *Gulf Express* to cut free the barge, saving the tug but guaranteeing a calamity on the reef. Or *Shearwater* could speed up, risking the hawser and potentially losing both the tug and barge to the shallows. Or we could reverse course and angle toward the deepwater channel east of the sanctuary—a desperate dash with the grave likelihood of running all three vessels aground. It was an impossible dilemma. There was no right answer, no silver bullet. Every option carried immense risk.

We took another round of radar ranges and LORAN readings. *Shearwater* continued her northerly drift. The winds were relentless, howling madly, the seas undiminished. The captain and I stared at the lines on the chart, then at each other, helpless in the moment.

Suddenly Captain Lober's face lit up. He dialed in a weather broadcast on the high frequency radio. The transmission was laced with static, fading in and out, but we were able to hear that by late morning the gale force winds would be backing to the west and finally to the north-northeast as the low-pressure system passed over Florida. We only needed to buy a few hours.

The captain made his decision. "XO, we can't reverse course again, and we're not going to give up the barge," he said. "We only need to slow our rate of drift. So let's creep ahead another half-knot." He must have read my mind, thinking about the chaos if the hawser let go, adding: "If we part the line, we'll have enough time to go back and get the crew off the tug before it hits the reef. So bring her up really slow. I mean, painfully slow. Be gentle with the throttles, like you're holding a sleeping baby."

I'd never held a sleeping baby, but I got his point, tenderly nudging the throttles, adding ten rpms to gain a smidgen of a knot. The resonant hum from the towline grew louder, melding into a warped symphony with the shriek of the wind. The diameter of the hawser shrunk another millimeter or two. The deck beneath the towing bitt flexed more ominously. Behind *Shearwater*, streaming directly aft, *Gulf Express* and the barge crashed over fifteen-foot waves. Disaster could strike at any moment if the towline gave way to the massive forces acting on it.

After five minutes, another ten rpms. Five minutes later, ten more. The captain and the quartermaster plotted continually, seeking a sign that

Shearwater's backward slide had slowed. I nursed the engines, adding bit by bit to that extra half-knot, increasing the strain on the grossly over-taxed four-inch line.

"Well, I'll be damned!" Lieutenant Lober said it casually, his voice light and pleasant, as if he'd just found a twenty-dollar bill lying on the ground. He'd just plotted a fix, and looked up from the chart, a sparkle of relief in his eyes. "We've cut the backward drift to almost zero," he said, with obvious satisfaction. "There's a good four-and-a-half miles to the reef. Plenty of room." He sighed. "If nothing else goes wrong we'll get through this okay." I glanced aft, anxious. The towing hawser was pencil-thin, the resonant hum now a mournful wail. No matter—the line stayed intact.

Lieutenant Lober stepped outside the pilothouse, buffeted by the winds, staring at the towline and assuring himself that the situation was stable. I stood watch until 0800, when Obenland provided relief. By then, the winds had relaxed to a steady twenty-five knots and the heaviest seas had abated. *Shearwater* held her position and then slowly began creeping south. Five miles from the shallows, then six. The captain finally stepped below to sleep. As he walked down the ladder he turned and gave a final order: "Keep her so."

Red Crew spent the rest of the day tending the line and transferring more engine parts and warm food back to *Gulf Express*. Just before noon we established communications with the commercial salvage tug, which said it would arrive at 0400 the next day, and watched with relief as the winds finally hauled to the west and then the north.

The rest of the mission was anticlimactic, almost dull. By mid-afternoon on New Year's Day we were twelve miles from the reef line and we'd decreased speed to take some of the pressure off the towline, which was now overstretched beyond repair. Sanders inspected the hawser and rendered his verdict: "XO, I hope we've got a few grand to buy a new four-inch," he said. "This one's ready for the dumpster."

As the winds died down, *Shearwater* and her tandem tow made real progress to the south. By the time the salvage tug showed up the next morning, the seas had flattened to harmless four-footers and the winds were less than fifteen knots, the crescent moon reflecting placidly off the wave tops. The crew on the relief tug must have been curious as to what the emergency was all about. To them, it was just more sultry winter weather off the Florida Keys.

Shearwater headed home to Key West. Lying in the rack, watching ever-changing cumulus clouds float past the stateroom window, I played back the past four weeks. Red Crew had made its first drug bust, found a compact hidden compartment on a massive freighter, chainsawed the deck of a suspect vessel, discovered the ultimate New Year's Eve party, and rescued a tug and tow in rough weather, keeping its crew and cargo out of harm's way, all while pushing the operational limits of the SES. What a life.

A few days later we received a package and letter from the Guidry Brothers Towing Company, thanking us for saving its tug and for giving up our holiday in the process. The package contained a dozen mugs, souvenirs for the crew. A few had broken in the mail, but I handed out the survivors, scratching my neck to try and dislodge the last stubborn bit of fiberglass debris biting into me and wondering what 1984 would bring.

The newly formed Red Crew, plank-owners of the U.S. Coast Guard Cutter *Petrel* (WSES 4), on *Petrel*'s commissioning day, July 8, 1983. Back row, from left: Seaman Carrie Corson, Seaman Danny Motley, Seaman Mark Northen, Fireman Stan Elliot, Electrician's Mate Third Class Chuck Meisner, Lt. (jg) Jim Howe (the author), Boatswain's Mate First Class Dan Sanders, Boatswain's Mate Second Class Chuck Obenland. Front row: Seaman Joan Scott, Fireman Mike Kassin, Machinery Technician Third Class Bill Hartsock, Subsistence Specialist Second Class Walter Goodrum, Machinery Technician First Class Cliff Boldan, and Senior Chief Quartermaster Ben Aiken. Not shown: Lt. Jerry Lober, commanding officer, and Boatswain's Mate Third Class Chad Weatherby. AUTHOR'S COLLECTION

Red Crew's command cadre. From left: Lt. Jerry Lober, commanding officer; Lt. (jg) Jim Howe, executive officer (author); and Senior Chief Quartermaster Ben Aiken, navigator and chief of the boat. The three are standing on *Petrel*'s rain-soaked aft deck immediately after the cutter was placed into commission. AUTHOR'S COLLECTION

Coast Guard cutters *Sea Hawk* (WSES 2) and *Shearwater* (WSES 3)
under way off Key West, late 1982. Just months before, the ships had
been in civilian service, shuttling oil-rig crews to and from shore.
In July 1983 the two cutters were joined by a third surface effect ship,
Petrel (WSES 4). The cutters are steaming at thirty knots on full "lift,"
with their hulls partially raised out of the water by the pressurized air
underneath. The at-rest waterline can be seen at the bottom of the
Coast Guard stripes. U.S. COAST GUARD

Shearwater sits in drydock in Wando, South Carolina, September 1984. The lower sections of the catamaran hulls have been sandblasted clean, and the heavy rubber bow and stern seals have been removed. In normal operation pressurized air would be contained underneath the hull by the catamaran sidewalls and the bow and stern seals. AUTHOR'S COLLECTION

Main deck of the sixty-five-foot fishing vessel *Hopeful*. The three bales of marijuana were pulled out of the cargo hold by a boarding party from USCGC *Active* (WMEC 618). AUTHOR'S COLLECTION

A security team member from USCGC *Active* guards three prisoners on the seized fishing vessel *Hopeful*. AUTHOR'S COLLECTION

A rare crowded moment in Key West. The three surface effect ships are moored next to the SES Division headquarters. Closest to the camera is the 95-foot cutter *Cape York* (WPB 95332), and in the background, from the left, are three medium-endurance cutters, the 210-foot *Dependable* (WMEC 626) and *Courageous* (WMEC 622), and the 205-foot former Navy salvage ship *Ute* (WMEC 76). The four rectangular screens on each SES, just below the pilothouse, cover the plenum chamber, through which air was pulled to pressurize the wet deck underneath the hull. AUTHOR'S COLLECTION

Red Crew, summer 1983, with *Petrel* as a backdrop. Front row, from left: Bill Hartsock, Chuck Meisner, Walt Goodrum, Chuck Obenland, Jerry Lober, the author, Ben Aiken, Dan Sanders, and Chad Weatherby. Standing: Mike Kassin, Stan Elliot, Danny Motley, Mark Northen, and Joan Scott. Not shown: Carrie Corson and Cliff Boldan.

The three surface effect ships steaming at full speed off the coast of Haiti, late October 1983. CAPT. JENNIFER YOUNT, USCG (RET.)

Two seized go-fasts sit alongside the pleasure craft *Moses*, Great Bahama Bank, Friday, January 13, 1984. AUTHOR'S COLLECTION

Cockpit of the red go-fast seized on the Great Bahama Bank, January 13, 1984. The boat was carrying a dozen large bales of marijuana. AUTHOR'S COLLECTION

Entrance to secret compartment on the pleasure craft *Moses*. The floorboard inside the cabinet was removed to reveal an opening into the starboard fuel tank, which held several marijuana bales. The onion was sitting inside the cabinet in an apparent attempt to mask the odor of the bulk contraband. AUTHOR'S COLLECTION

View from *Shearwater*'s rigid-hull inflatable boat as a boarding party approaches a cabin cruiser to conduct a compliance inspection. U.S. Navy

Seized fishing vessel *Mary Jo*. The black garbage bags were filled with loosely packed marijuana. The contraband was located in the forward cabin of the boat and later moved aft by Red Crew's boarding team in preparation for offloading. Author's collection

BM1 Dan Sanders frisking the master of the seized fishing vessel *Mary Jo*. In the background are the other prisoners, handcuffed and awaiting interrogation. AUTHOR'S COLLECTION

MK3 Bill Hartsock at the helm of a seized go-fast, June 1984. Red Crew used the seized vessel to chase another go-fast across the Great Bahama Bank. AUTHOR'S COLLECTION

Executive officers of the four original surface effect ship crews. From left: the author (Red Crew) and three lieutenants (junior grade), Jim Sartucci (Blue Crew), Mark Hoesten (Gold Crew), and Al Bernard (Green Crew). It was the 1980s, and facial hair was all the rage.

The Navy's surface effect ship, *SES 200*. The vessel was an extended version of the Coast Guard's first SES, the USCGC *Dorado* (WSES 1); the Navy moniker *SES 200* refers to the ship's displacement in tons, not its length, as the Coast Guard uses in describing its cutters.
U.S. NAVY

SES 200 (foreground), *Sea Hawk*, *Shearwater*, and *Petrel* steam in formation in the Straits of Florida, February 1985. The Coast Guard conducted a four-month evaluation of *SES 200*'s suitability for maritime law-enforcement operations and found her highly capable.
U.S. COAST GUARD

"Drug bust" stickers adorn *Sea Hawk*'s deck house, February 1985.
Each symbol signifies a vessel seized for smuggling marijuana.
U.S. Coast Guard

The pleasure craft *Tranquil* alongside *SES 200* on the Great Bahama
Bank. A Coast Guard Law Enforcement Detachment working from
SES 200 inspected the boat, finding it clean but with a single mysterious
clue that signaled the possibility of smuggling. Red Crew reboarded
Tranquil the following day, March 9, 1985. Author's collection

Shearwater outbound for patrol, Key West harbor. Three *Pegasus*-class
Navy hydrofoils are moored at the Navy pier.
PH2 (Ac) MARK S. KETTENHOFEN, USN

The second commanding officer of Red Crew, Lt. Wayne Justice
(slightly left of center), is flanked by his shipmates, spring of 1985.
In less than two years most of the plank-owner crew had been
transferred, leaving only six of the original sixteen on board.
Such is the way of the Coast Guard—serve a few years and then
move on. AUTHOR'S COLLECTION

5

Raising the Bar

January 1984

The smugglers were nimble, constantly adjusting to changes in law-enforcement tactics, continually perfecting their craft. They watched the Coast Guard like hawks, knowing when our cutters got under way and trying to predict where we would patrol. But the smugglers had weaknesses, too. Sometimes, unknowingly, they followed set patterns—a flaw that SES crews sought to exploit.

Over the past year the Blue and Green crews had made three drug busts at almost the exact same place—an anonymous patch of shallows on the Great Bahama Bank, twenty-four miles west of Andros Island. To the eye, the spot was indistinguishable from the surrounding sea, the translucent water shimmering over a bright sandy bottom, the nearest landmark well over the horizon. There seemed to be no logical reason for the smugglers to gravitate there.

But the smugglers' strategy became clear when you looked at a nautical chart. Although most of the Great Bahama Bank had no distinguishing characteristics, charts of the area displayed major meridians and parallels, clearly marked. The smuggling hot spot was at the intersection of the only two lines that crossed in that part of the bank, making the smugglers' rendezvous point—24° N. Lat. and 78° 30' W. Long.—a landmark by default.

It was easy to imagine the smugglers planning a drug offload, conspiring to avoid the prying eyes of law enforcement. "Where should we meet?" one of the smugglers would ask. They'd look at the chart and see the point where the horizontal latitude and vertical longitude lines came together, smack dab in the middle of nowhere, the only recognizable feature on the bank. "Here's the place," the other would answer, jabbing the chart. X marks the spot.

Once word of the smugglers' habit spread among the SES crews, we tried our best to visit that intersection whenever time and circumstances permitted. On Thursday, January 12, 1984, Red Crew got under way in *Petrel* on a ten-day Bahamas patrol. We headed straight for the X-spot. After sunset, our bridge team searched for passing vessels, but all they saw were a couple of large freighters in the Santaren Channel.

District Seven had arranged air support, and at 2030 *Petrel* was hailed by Coast Guard 2109, a Falcon jet operating from Air Station Miami. The jet had been sixty miles north of *Petrel* when its crew spotted three small vessels heading to the southeast, all running without lights. A few minutes later, twenty-five miles directly ahead of the three boats, the Falcon crew detected a larger contact, also running dark, moving slowly on a reciprocal course. It looked as though the four vessels were aiming for a rendezvous. This was a classic smuggling scenario.

I had the OOD watch and called the captain and senior chief to the bridge. The quartermaster extrapolated the coordinates and predicted that the four vessels would meet around 2315. At best speed, *Petrel* would arrive on scene thirty minutes later. Most smugglers knew how to transfer drugs in a hurry, and the offload might be complete in only a few minutes. We might not get there in time.

There was another snag. Senior Chief waved Lieutenant Lober to the chart table and tapped the projected rendezvous spot with his thick forefinger. "Shallows, captain," he said. "We're looking at five meters of water, some four, with a few spots down to three. There's not much room for error. This area hasn't been surveyed since before Dubya Dubya Two, so the soundings might be crap." The captain pored over the chart, then made up his mind. "Senior, let me know when we get into four-meter territory," he said. "Let's pay these guys a visit. XO, full speed ahead."

Petrel thundered north, running dark, easily making thirty knots in the flat calm. We rousted the crew and divvied up the work. Senior Chief would relieve me as OOD, assisted by Motley and Scott on the bridge, while Boldan, Sanders, and I would each lead three-person teams to board whatever vessels we could stop. The captain expected the smugglers to run once they saw us. His goal was to snag the larger mothership first and then chase down any of the smaller vessels that were still within range. Having three boarding parties at the ready was a sign of extreme optimism.

The Falcon headed home, its fuel spent. *Petrel* was on her own. At 2330, we began seeing faint radar traces near the rendezvous spot. Fifteen minutes later Senior Chief brought the cutter to a stop, two miles south of the targets. The radar screen showed three small but distinct radar blips sitting close together, with a fourth contact slowly moving away toward the southeast. Red Crew finalized its preparations: an M-60 mounted on the port bridge wing; Obenland serving as sharpshooter with an M-16; Motley assigned to handle the spotlight and loudhailer; Scott managing the chart and the ship's log; the small boat ready to launch; the boarding parties fully dressed out; and the duty engineer monitoring the main diesels and lift engines. Everyone on *Petrel* had a role. Everyone was vital.

The crew was amped up, the excitement contagious. In the darkness, only four thousand yards away, something was happening, almost certainly a drug offload, and *Petrel* was on the cusp of swooping in. Would the smugglers run? Would they shoot? Could we catch any of them, or would they flee into inaccessible shallows? The next few minutes would tell.

Lieutenant Lober stood on the port bridge wing, stroking his bearded chin, staring into the darkness toward the suspected smugglers. I reported that all hands were ready for action. "Go get 'em," the captain ordered. Senior Chief clutched in the engines and *Petrel* sprinted north.

The dopers never saw us coming. The night was coal-mine dark, with cloudy skies hiding the moon. *Petrel* steamed toward the rendezvous spot at thirty knots. A tick before midnight, four hundred yards from the three radar blips, Seaman Scott flicked on the cutter's spotlight, running lights, rotating blue light, stripe light, and masthead light, which illuminated the Coast Guard and national ensigns snapping in the wind. Directly ahead, framed in the tube-like beam of *Petrel's* high-intensity spotlight, was a compact cabin cruiser, sitting dead in the water, with a red-hulled cigarette boat alongside. At the left-hand edge of the searchlight beam was a white go-fast, adrift. A man on the stern of the cabin cruiser was bent over the side as if he were picking up a bulky object from the red boat, frozen in place as he stared directly into the bright glare of the spotlight, his mouth agape.

The captain hit the police siren, blasted the ship's horn, and then commanded over the loudhailer: "Vessels in my spotlight, vessels in my spotlight, this is the United States Coast Guard, remain in your location and stand by for a boarding." Lober's rich voice reverberated across the still waters. *Petrel* was now only 150 yards from the 3 boats, and Senior Chief pulled back the throttles to avoid running them over. The SES settled into the water, decelerating quickly, twenty, fifteen, ten knots, and closing to fifty yards. For about five seconds, none of the vessels moved. Then, suddenly, as if on cue, the two cigarette boats sprinted away, each in a different direction, twisting and swerving wildly, foam from their propellers spraying high into the air. It looked like a chase scene from a 1920s comedy.

The captain glanced at the cabin cruiser—she was sitting still—and made a snap decision. "Forget the cruiser, go after that one," he said, pointing to the red-hulled, twenty-five-foot go-fast speeding away to the north. At least, the boat was *trying* to speed away. She seemed incapable of coming up on plane and was throwing a tremendous wake, her bow high in the air and her stern squatting deep into the water. Senior Chief jammed *Petrel's* throttles forward and increased lift to full, and the cutter bolted ahead.

The red-hulled boat had gotten a head start, and by the time *Petrel* was back up to speed we had fallen three hundred yards behind her. On the bridge, our universe shrank, a world of velvety black surrounding a single cone of intense light, projecting forward from atop our pilothouse. All eyes were on the red go-fast as she struggled to come up to speed, framed in the beam of our million-watt spotlight, a blinding glare dancing off her chrome deck fittings.

The roar of the lift fans and the rush of wind made it hard to hear, and the midnight air was refreshingly cool, tussling our hair and buffeting our faces. On the port bridge wing, the captain leaned into the wind, his eyes locked on the fleeing smuggler, with Obenland next to him, cradling his M-16, left hand on his head, holding down his ball cap. The lookout struggled with the "big eyes," shaking in the wind stream, trying to read the fleeing boat's name.

Petrel closed to two hundred fifty yards, two hundred, one hundred fifty. The red boat was still cocked at an ungainly angle, bow up and transom far too low. It was rushing through calm black water, throwing a frothy white wake. We could see one man on the boat, surrounded by large rectangular packages. Reflections from *Petrel*'s flashing blue police light sparkled off the boat's outboard engines. The lookout tamed the "big eyes" and read the name on the speedboat's stern: *Dino*.

We now were one hundred yards from the go-fast. *Petrel* was still closing, siren blaring, the red boat centered in the spotlight's beam. The quartermaster kept blasting the ship's horn, its deep bass note rattling the windows. Senior Chief looked at the chart, measured with a pair of dividers, then yelled out: "Captain, one mile to shoal water—two minutes." Lober nodded, acknowledging the danger, and pointed his index finger forward.

The man in the red boat leaned into the throttles. He looked over his shoulder, and from seventy-five yards away we could see his eyes widen in fright. He didn't know what was chasing him, but it was big, wide, making a hell of a racket, spraying water in all directions, and getting closer.

Petrel was only thirty yards away, the smuggler at arm's length, when the man pulled back the throttles and threw his hands in the air. Almost instantly, the red boat stopped, her bow slamming into the water. *Petrel* skidded to a halt, fifteen feet away, and from the bridge wing we stared down into the boat's open cabin. It was stuffed with bales. They were big ones, too; each looked to be about fifty or sixty pounds. The man, tall and bulky, with scraggly brown hair, looked dressed for a backyard barbeque.

Senior Chief twisted *Petrel* closer to the boat until the two vessels were touching, while Sanders ran to the main deck, waving a shotgun at the man and ordering him to climb our Jacob's ladder. The man clambered up the ladder and BM1 snapped on the cuffs. Seaman Northen scrambled down the ladder, jumped into *Dino*, threw her anchor into the water, and then scampered back onto *Petrel*.

One vessel seized; one smuggler in custody. It was 0005. The captain noted the time and then, his eyes twinkling, shouted: "Hey XO, we just nailed this guy five minutes after midnight—on Friday the 13th. How's that for luck?"

Senior Chief pivoted *Petrel* south, full speed ahead, to intercept the unseen fourth vessel, the one that had left the pack early. Lober thought it might be the mothership. The contact was pinging brightly on radar, inching to the southeast, four miles away. At 0015 *Petrel* pulled alongside a thirty-eight-foot cabin cruiser named *Moses*, displaying Florida registration number FL-1408-EM. The engine room hatch was open, and *Moses* appeared to be drifting with the current. Lieutenant Lober asked if there were any of the other vessels still on radar. "Two, both within three miles," Senior Chief told him. Lober made another quick decision: *Moses* could wait. Senior Chief picked up the loudhailer and ordered the two men visible on deck to anchor *Moses*, and we sped off into the darkness, the buzz of the lift engines shattering the still of the night.

Seven minutes later *Petrel* was alongside a forty-foot cabin cruiser, the *Union*, the largest of the vessels that we had seen in the original group. Senior Chief hailed the vessel on channel 16 and ran through the standard preboarding questions. The master said there were six persons on board and that they were on a pleasure cruise to Bimini. Senior Chief looked at me and mouthed "bullshit." He directed the master to muster his crew on deck. They shuffled out of the cabin, three men and three women, shielding their eyes from *Petrel*'s spotlight, the glare of the beam glistening off the gold chains around their necks and the thick watches circling their wrists.

My three-person boarding party was up first, but since there were half a dozen people on *Union*, we added Dan Sanders for safety. The four of us climbed on board and corralled *Union*'s crew. Sanders and I stayed topside, checking IDs, as Bill Hartsock and Stan Elliot conducted the security sweep, hoping they would come across a load of bales. No luck—the boat was empty. I radioed the cutter: "*Petrel*, boarding officer, we've completed the security sweep with no signs of contraband. Situation is under control. We're taking a deeper look. Over." The captain rogered the report and Senior Chief turned *Petrel* to the northwest, to investigate a fourth radar contact, loitering two miles away.

The cutter was on scene within minutes. Framed in *Petrel*'s spotlight was the other speedboat from the rendezvous, a white-hulled twenty-five-footer similar to *Dino*. A man was crouched in the open cockpit, washing down the deck with a bucket of water. *Petrel* pulled alongside, and Chuck Obenland ordered the man on board the cutter. Chad Weatherby and Mark Northen jumped into the boat and found clumps of residue that tested positive for THC. From *Petrel*'s bridge, Joan Scott pointed out a handful of bales floating nearby. It looked as though the man had ditched the drugs. Lober authorized the seizure of the vessel and the arrest of its operator, and asked Weatherby to use the speedboat to retrieve the bales from the water. Eventually he would pull eleven bales onto the white speedboat's deck. Red Crew had its second bust of the young morning.

Senior Chief gunned *Petrel* back to the *Union*. At this point, Red Crew was stretched thin and juggling hard. We had boarding teams embarked on *Union* and on the white speedboat, miles apart in a remote stretch of water; a third, drug-laden speedboat anchored two miles to the north; and a fourth vessel, likely the mothership, sitting a few miles distant, yet to be boarded. We had no extra crew to spare and couldn't afford for anything to go wrong.

So something did. At 0200, *Petrel*'s port lift engine shut down, unexpectedly, a bad omen in the Bahamian shallows. Boldan got to work on the repair as I was wrapping up the *Union* boarding. We'd searched the boat from stem to stern without finding a shred of contraband, but we knew that they'd been part of the offload, considering that *Dino* had been sitting alongside when we'd pounced two hours earlier. Captain Lober made another command decision: he ordered *Union* to remain at anchor, while *Petrel* retrieved our boarding party and headed back to *Moses*, before it slipped away. We'd reboard *Union* after dealing with the suspected mothership.

It was 0300 when we pulled back alongside *Moses*. The boat was twenty years old but in decent repair, broad-beamed, built as a shrimper but recently converted to a pleasure craft. We lowered our small boat, and Sanders, Hartsock, Elliot, and I jumped in, clambering over *Moses'* gunwale a minute later. I directed the master to muster his crew on the open aft deck and was surprised to see two women step out from the shadows of the cabin. Both were young and dressed in tight jeans and flowing blouses. That made four persons on board, with only the men speaking even marginal English. Both the master and the other middle-aged man were Cuban nationals. The master said the two young women were from Nicaragua.

Once our team was safely on board *Moses*, Senior Chief pointed the cutter back to *Dino* to take her in tow. Sanders and I conducted a quick security sweep and then began a more thorough inspection. We started forward, probing the bilges, crew quarters, and bridge. There was a jumble of charts sitting in plain view in the pilothouse and one of them showed a trackline heading north from an island off Cuba, with a large cross marked at the position where we had interrupted the offload minutes before. There were no signs of bales or residue, and it didn't look like *Moses'* crew had washed down her decks. If there was contraband on board, the only hiding spot was in the fuel tanks. I climbed down into the engine room through the hatch in the main deck, while Sanders stayed topside.

The engine room was claustrophobic, oil spattered and poorly lighted, four feet high and crammed with wire runs and exhaust piping. It reminded me of the mangroves on Boca Grande, and I had to duck and twist to wiggle through the maze. The two metal fuel tanks sat on the outboard sides of the compartment. Each was ten feet long, three feet wide, and four feet tall, large enough to hold a dozen bales, maybe more. I could see the entire inboard side of each tank, and, crawling on hands and knees, inspected their forward and aft ends, finding nothing abnormal. The top of each tank butted up against the main deck. From the engine room, there was no way to see whether there were any holes cut into the top surfaces of the tanks.

I climbed back onto the main deck and stretched my back, sore from the contortions of the cramped space. Elliot waved me over and pointed to what looked like a bud of marijuana on the deck, sitting in a shadow underneath a bench, just outside the cabin. Good eyes. Sanders scooped up the bud and put it in a plastic bag as evidence.

I looked at the deck directly above the fuel tanks, imagining where and how a smuggler could load marijuana bales. Two-thirds of each tank sat underneath the open aft deck, with the forward ends of the tanks extending below the cabin interior. Sanders squatted low, tapping the aft deck with his flashlight, searching for a patched-over hatch. *Moses'* crew sat on the transom, silently watching our inspection, frozen by Hartsock's laser-like glare. I stepped into the cabin.

Directly above the front ends of the tanks were wooden two-door cabinets, painted white with teak trim. I opened the doors on the starboard cabinet and was surprised to find it empty. The only thing inside was a rotten onion. That had to be a sign. I crouched down, rapping the deck inside the cabinet with my knuckles, producing a hollow echo—too hollow. Unfolding my knife, I leaned into the opening and wedged the blade into the deck where it met the near side of the cabinet. There was a slight gap and the blade sank in a half inch. I tried to pry up the decking, but the floorboard didn't budge.

It was time for the heavy artillery. I took a thick flathead screwdriver from the boarding kit and jammed its tip into the gap, just inside the opening of the cabinet. I pulled the screwdriver handle toward me, creating a lot more leverage than the knife could provide. At first nothing happened. Then, with a screech, the floorboard popped up, revealing a dark void underneath. I grabbed the floorboard and pulled it out of the cabinet, tossing it onto the deck. It landed with a loud thwack. *Moses'* master saw what was happening, blanched, and looked down at his shoes.

Leaning forward I was assaulted by the pungent smell of bulk marijuana. I clicked on my flashlight and shined the beam into the rectangular hole in the floor of the cabinet. Illuminated below was an opening cut through the top of the fuel tank, and in the tank were bulky, rectangular packages. The tank was half-full and I could count at least three bales, with more likely stacked behind them. They matched those that we'd seen on board *Dino.*

I whispered into the communications headset. "Hey, we've got bales in the tank. Looks like this was the mothership. Go ahead and detain the crew, I'm gonna grab a sample for the test kit." Leaning into the opening, I cut a small hole in the burlap covering the nearest bale and removed a nub of the green, leafy material. Sanders ordered *Moses'* crew members to sit on the deck with their hands on their heads, and then walked forward to witness the drug test. With the test results positive, I seized *Moses* and arrested her crew. We'd made our third bust of the new day. *Petrel* had scored a hat trick.

After frisking the prisoners and placing them in cuffs, Sanders weighed *Moses'* anchor and set the boat adrift. *Petrel* had returned with *Dino* in tow, and nestled alongside *Moses* so our boarding team could guide the prisoners up the Jacob's ladder to the cutter's aft deck. I felt bad for the women: both were only twenty years old, and they seemed confused as to what was happening. The taller of the two was sobbing and the other had a my-mother-is-going-to-kill-me look etched on her young face. All things aside, they seemed like ordinary young women, polite and demure. I was taken aback when *Moses'* master told us they were hookers he'd picked up in Miami.

Sanders and I tied up loose ends, cataloging evidence and assembling the seizure package. Prying open the hatch over *Moses'* port fuel tank showed that it, too, was crammed with bales. That begged the question: if the cabin cruiser's tanks were full of dope, where did they get their fuel?

Weatherby and his team arrived in the white go-fast, stacked with bales, and Red Crew gathered its flock, the three seized vessels bobbing in the slight swell. There were two surprises. At 0500 a forty-foot sailboat called *Sweet Dream*, operating under diesel power in the light airs, came chugging past, headed northwest. We quickly scrambled a team and boarded the boat, finding an American family that was gunkholing in the Bahamas, scared to death by the law enforcement activity. The boarding officer, Obenland, assessed that their voyage was legitimate and they had just stumbled across the scene. He sent them on their way.

The bigger surprise was losing *Union*. At first light, *Petrel* steamed back to where the boat had been anchored and found that she had slipped away during the night. By then Coast Guard helicopter 1371 had arrived on scene and began to search, aided by a second aircraft that arrived an hour later. Neither was able to locate the boat, but they spotted a number of small blue barrels floating in the water near where we had seized *Moses*. Our coxswain retrieved the barrels and found them full of diesel fuel, answering the question of how the mothership could feed its engines with her fuel tanks full of pot. Our engineers hooked up one of the barrels to *Moses'* fuel intakes to ensure that she had enough diesel to reach Florida. They judged the rig to be safe for the hundred-mile jaunt.

The trip to Miami took eight hours. *Petrel* took the two speedboats in tow, one from each quarter, while Hartsock and I conned *Moses* across the Straits of Florida. We had perfect weather until we hit the Gulf Stream, where the seas built to choppy six-footers and punched *Moses* in all directions. The churning lasted only two hours, however, and by nightfall we were moored at Base Miami Beach, completing the paperwork and turning the 3 vessels, 6 prisoners, and 3,550 pounds of marijuana over to U.S. Customs.

The commanding officer of Group Miami met us on the pier, excited as a new dad. He told us that *Petrel* had made the Coast Guard's first triple drug seizure. Not one of us had imagined it possible. Three busts at once, and four seizures in our last month of patrol. We'd not only broken our curse but had raised the bar for our SES compatriots.

It was early evening and most of our team had worked nonstop since the previous night, but no one was ready for the rack. Instead, we hit the Gator Den, the base's small, dingy club. Lieutenant Lober ordered a round of drinks, toasting to our success and proclaiming that 1984 was starting off as one hell of a good year for the Red Crew. And as the captain would remind us for the rest of his time in command—and for many years afterward—it all happened at midnight, on Friday the 13th.

————

Red Crew capped off the patrol four days later by making our fifth seizure, this one improbably easy. *Petrel* was skirting the northeast corner of the Cay Sal Bank when the lookout, Seaman Motley, spotted a dim light next to Dog Rocks. The radar showed a small blip and we assumed it was a vessel at anchor. Because the blip was well within the Bahamian three-mile territorial sea, we would have to wait until it headed into international waters to conduct a boarding. We patrolled nearby through the night, keeping close watch.

The sun rose to a beautiful morning, gorgeous pastels painting the eastern sky, with a fluttering breeze from the southeast and the seas calm as a lake. A two-foot, long-period swell surged gently onto Dog Rocks. From our bridge wing four miles away we could see a white lobster boat, typical in appearance, with a forward cabin and open aft deck, sitting next to a rocky cay. Through the "big eyes" we could make out at least three persons on board. They weighed anchor at exactly 0711 and got under way at a brisk pace, headed northwest. *Petrel* followed on a parallel course, remaining just outside the three-mile territorial limit.

The lobster boat was angling toward the Florida Keys. *Petrel* skimmed along the edge of Bahamian waters, no way to hide, clearly visible to the fishing boat's crew. If they were smugglers, we expected them to stay in Bahamian territory or start throwing their load overboard once they saw the Coast Guard nearby. The OOD, Obenland, timed the intercept to nab the lobster boat as she passed through a one-mile gap in the territorial seas.

At 0813 the captain set boarding stations as *Petrel* rapidly closed on the boat. The lookout could read the name *Mary Jo* on her transom, with "KEY WEST, FLA" stenciled in smaller letters underneath. A mile away the lookout said he could see five persons on board, one a woman wearing a bright red blouse. All five were watching us as *Petrel* approached. If *Mary Jo*'s master had been clever, he would have continued another mile to the west or reversed course to avoid being boarded on the high seas. Instead, when Obenland hailed the boat on channel 16, the master instantly complied with the order to heave to. *Mary Jo* stopped just three-and-a-half miles off the rocks, drifting in international waters.

Cliff Boldan led the five-person team that climbed on board *Mary Jo* at 0842. At 0843, the sweep team saw, in plain sight, a large pile of black garbage bags in the vessel's forward berthing area, lumped haphazardly on the deck, with what appeared to be marijuana spilling from one of the bags. Boldan conducted a field test of the material—again seeing our favorite purple hue in the test kit—and seized the vessel at 0845. It had taken three minutes from stepping on board to seizure. No searching for hidden compartments, no crawling around mangrove-like engine rooms, no battered knees, no sweat. These smugglers had made it easy.

After arresting the crew, Boldan patted them down for weapons and transported the prisoners to *Petrel*, and then began a search of the boat. The dope was pathetic, loosely packed into a dozen garbage bags. The marijuana smelled rotten and some was contaminated with salt water. Boldan figured that the bales had been stashed on a Bahamian outcropping, where they had been damaged by weather and waves.

After an arrest it was standard practice to search each prisoner methodically, patting down every surface of his or her clothing, crushing and feeling their pockets, removing their belts and shoes, even looking in their hair and mouths. We didn't want a prisoner to escape by using a small handcuff key hidden under his tongue or in the seam of her collar. Sanders searched the four men, and Carrie Corson patted down the female prisoner. They confiscated the prisoners' wallets and combed through their pockets, seeking any information that could help in the prosecution.

Mary Jo's master was a forty-seven-year-old Cuban-American from Stock Island, just north of Key West. He was muscular and deeply tanned, with a thick brown mustache and a thin silver beard. He looked weathered, like someone who had spent his life on the water. The woman in the red top was twenty-five and lived with him as his common-law wife. One of the other men was a resident alien, also from Cuba, and the remaining two were U.S. citizens. Sanders read them their Miranda rights and started to ask questions, but they all refused to talk. "Don't say anything," the master muttered to his wife.

That was fine with us. It would mean less paperwork. *Petrel* took *Mary Jo* in tow, but the boat's bow cleat sheared away, so our custody crew motored the seized vessel to Key West. We moored at sunset and transferred the prisoners, contraband, and boat to a Customs officer from the South Florida Task Force. Red Crew called it a day and headed to our homes, our streak of good luck continuing.

———

A month later our compatriots in the Blue Crew, sailing on board *Shearwater*, had the opposite experience. Group Key West passed along urgent intelligence reporting that a drug-laden vessel had transited the Windward Passage en route to South Florida. The forty-foot boat, named the *Owl and the Pussycat*, reportedly was carrying a large load of marijuana, and her crew, supposedly members of the Hell's Angels motorcycle gang, was considered armed and dangerous. Red Crew was under way in *Sea Hawk*, near Cay Sal, and *Shearwater* was seventy-five miles to our southeast, patrolling the Old Bahama Channel. Both SES crews kept a sharp lookout through the afternoon.

Blue Crew found them after sundown alerting Group Key West that *Owl and the Pussycat* was riding low in the water and refusing to stop. On our bridge, steaming at full speed toward *Shearwater*, Lieutenant Lober, Senior Chief, and I listened on the high-frequency radio to Blue Crew's play-by-play. Our imaginations went into overdrive, gaming out the dangers that Blue Crew was facing as it closed on a boatload of potentially hostile gang members.

Transmissions were sparse. A minute after the first report that *Owl and the Pussycat* was riding low, Blue Crew said it was sending over a boarding party. Then came silence. A minute later: "Group, this is *Shearwater*, we've launched our small boat. There are six people visible on deck of the subject vessel." Four minutes went by with nothing but high-frequency static. Lober's face was a billboard of frustration and concern. Senior Chief and I stood nearby, fidgeting. Then came another transmission: "Group, *Shearwater*. The subject vessel appears to be sinking, our boarding party is on board, the crew is uncooperative and will not allow us below decks. The main cargo hold appears to be locked. Boarding team is attempting to access."

More silence. Then, tragedy. Blue Crew's radio operator spoke rapidly, his voice pinched tight: "Group Key West, *Shearwater*, the suspect vessel has capsized, we have people in the water, I repeat, we have people in the water." Then came another long pause—painfully long. Then: "Group, stand by. The suspect vessel has gone under."

It seemed that hours passed as we huddled around the radio, waiting for a break in the static to hear *Shearwater*'s next report. I guessed that Jim Sartucci, my friend and mentor, had led the boarding team, and likely was on board when *Owl and the Pussycat* turned turtle. The seas were choppy, and it was well after dark, hampering any potential search. The captain looked out the pilothouse window, his brow knotted. Senior Chief was mute, toying with the chart, a deep frown on his face, not making eye contact. I stared forward, trying to will my friend and his Blue Crew shipmates to safety.

Then: "Group, this is *Shearwater*. We've rescued the crew of the suspect vessel and placed them under arrest. Our boarding team is in the water, but accounted for. I repeat, the boarding party is accounted for. We're recovering them now. More to follow."

Relief—Blue Crew's team was safe. *Owl and the Pussycat* was gone, taking her contraband with her, sinking in more than one thousand feet of cobalt-blue water. *Shearwater* stayed in the area until midnight, hoping that a bale would pop to the surface, but all Blue Crew saw was a few bubbles and blobs of oil. Without knowing exactly what cargo *Owl and the Pussycat* had carried, the U.S. attorney prosecuted the master and crew for hazarding their vessel and failing to comply with a federal law-enforcement official's order to stop.

Lieutenant Sartucci told us later about the experience. It was the stuff of fiction. *Shearwater* had found the boat limping northwest at eight knots, already visibly low in the water. *Owl and the Pussycat* looked bizarrely out of place—a ramshackle design, the type of vessel built for a river, not the deep ocean. Most likely she was a converted harbor tender, with a wide-open forward deck and a cramped pilothouse all the way aft. When Blue Crew called the boat on channel 16, the master claimed that he couldn't stop, since their main hold was flooding and the bilge pump ran off the rotation of the propeller shaft. It was an absurd excuse, but the master was adamant: "Don't send anyone over," he had said. "Don't make me stop, or we'll sink." Sartucci later surmised that when the smugglers saw the cutter they had opened a bilge valve to scuttle their boat intentionally.

Captain Bradford realized they only had a few minutes before the vessel would slip underwater, and he told Sartucci, the boarding officer, to head over as fast as he could. Only one other boarding-team member, MK2 Oscar Perez, was dressed out, so he and Sartucci jumped in *Shearwater*'s small boat. The coxswain whisked them to the sinking vessel. As Sartucci began climbing on board, one of *Owl and the Pussycat*'s crew members rushed toward him, screaming that it wasn't safe. Sartucci and Perez ignored the man and scrambled on deck, finding the six crew members to be a motley mix of young and old, men and women, all wearing life jackets and ready to abandon ship. The decrepit boat was settling by the stern and listing to port, her bow rising up, coasting to a halt as her engine sputtered and died.

In the middle of the forward deck was a square cargo hatch, secured by a thick set of padlocked chains. Perez grabbed the chains, yanking on them, but the hatch was impossible to open. Perez hadn't had time to grab a tool kit from *Shearwater*, so he ran aft to the pilothouse to look for a fire axe, only to find the entry door also padlocked. Meanwhile, Sartucci corralled the six people and ordered them to abandon ship over the port side. The master and other crew members started howling at Sartucci and Perez to stop the search, bleating at the top of their lungs, with the scene devolving into chaos. By this time the boat was listing more than 10 degrees to port, the fantail nearly under water, and the crew members began jumping into the RHIB, some of them missing it and hitting the water. Sartucci made sure that everyone had left the sinking boat safely and then ran to the cargo hold, where he and Perez tried again to break the padlock so that they could lay eyes on the contraband they knew was hidden below. They heaved and pulled, but to no avail. The padlock wouldn't budge.

Now *Owl and the Pussycat* was listing 20 degrees. The Coast Guard duo was only inches away from a large cache of drugs and needed time and tools to break loose the padlock. No matter—survival came first. Sartucci looked at his shipmate, still working furiously on the chains, and gave the order. "Oscar, we gotta go—now," he said.

And go they did. Sartucci and Perez ran toward the port rail, now almost under water. They didn't stop to think or look behind. They just kept running, jumping hard, launching themselves into the air and toward the dark waters below. They knew that the suction from the sinking boat could drag them to the bottom, and they needed to get as far away as possible.

Swimming was difficult, with the twenty pounds of body armor, .45, and law enforcement gear hindering their movements. The RHIB, already crammed with the coxswain and the six rescued crew members, shuddered to a halt alongside Sartucci and Perez. They grabbed onto the polypropylene lifeline that ran the length of the boat, keeping their heads above water as the coxswain pivoted the RHIB and dragged them away from the sinking vessel. *Shearwater* was hovering close aboard, adding to the insanity of the scene, with the roar of the lift fans and spray from the air cushion filling the night. Sartucci looked up at the cutter and thought, "I sure hope they can see us down here."

Then *Owl and the Pussycat* gave her death-gasp, her stern now completely underwater, her bow rising higher and higher until it was vertical, pointed straight at the stars above. There the boat sat, probably for just an instant, but for what the Coast Guardsmen in the water must have felt was eternity. Then she began to sink, stern first, headed straight down to the desolate ocean floor a quarter-mile below. She was gone in less than a minute.

––––––––

Blue Crew's close call showed the nexus of drug interdiction and search-and-rescue. Sometimes it was hard to tell where one mission ended and the other began. That was the case a month later as *Petrel* headed offshore, steaming at full speed toward a disabled sailboat whose crew was squawking "Mayday" on the HF radio. The weather picture was gray and somber, with overcast skies, a stiff breeze, and frequent rain squalls. *Petrel* punched through eight-foot seas.

The disabled boat had been sailing from Cozumel to the States when she was hit by a strong weather front. Gale-force winds had shredded her sails, and her small inboard engine refused to start, rendering her adrift. Ironically named *Lucky*, the sailboat was manned by an amateur crew— one man and two women, none of them a deep-water sailor. Their battery had just enough juice to permit a distress call. The three crew members were cold, wet, scared, and hungry. They wanted to be off their boat— *yesterday*, as the saying went.

I had stopped by the Group Key West Operations Center before *Petrel* got under way, and the watchstander passed along some interesting news. "Sir, we know the boat's in trouble, but there's intel that says it may be carrying some coke—not a huge load, maybe three to five kilos. It's pretty sketchy intel, and I'd give it a fifty-fifty chance at best, but once you get these guys to port, Customs is gonna tear them apart. You might want to give them a good search if you get on board." He knew how rare cocaine seizures were, and how eager we all were to make one. Great, I thought. This should be a fun mission—SAR and law enforcement, all rolled into one.

It took *Petrel* eight hours to reach *Lucky*, which was adrift 110 miles southwest of Fort Jefferson. The waves were rough, but the northeasterly winds were easing and the forecast was for diminishing seas. The sailboat sat in the trough, snapping side to side, its damaged sail flapping uselessly and its halyard twanging methodically off the aluminum mast, a makeshift metronome.

Obenland, Hartsock, and I headed to the sailboat in the RHIB, and as we closed, we got our first view of the crew members. They looked miserable. The women were bundled in rain slickers, shivering, their hair matted, eyes red and desperate, fatigue lining their faces. The master, tall and thin, appeared to be in better shape but barely so. As we pulled alongside, he spoke, his voice cracking and thick with emotion. "Thank God you're here," he said.

Lieutenant Lober had devised a simple game plan: if the master agreed, we'd transfer the three people to the cutter, and Hartsock and I would stay on board to rig her for tow. Then, we'd have all the time in the world to conduct an inspection, and when that was complete, we'd head back to *Petrel* in our small boat.

Hartsock and I climbed on board. I told the master we thought it best that he and his two passengers board the cutter, and he instantly agreed. Then, with a flash of inspiration, I asked: "Sir, while you're on the cutter, do you mind if we search your vessel? We're going to be towing you into U.S. waters and Customs will be searching the boat then, so maybe we can get some of it done out here." He didn't hesitate. "Sure, look wherever you want, check our goddam underwear drawers if it makes you happy," he said. "Just get us the hell off this boat." I winked at Hartsock. Piece of cake, I thought.

The three beleaguered sailors scooped up some personal effects, and Obenland shuttled them back to *Petrel* while Hartsock and I prepped for the tow. The rolling motion of the sailboat was lulling, almost pleasant. *Petrel* crossed close ahead, Sanders tossed over a messenger line, and Hartsock and I hauled in a three-inch towing hawser, securing it to a cleat on the bow. Then *Lucky* was under tow, crashing through the seas as we headed northeast, making five knots through the water, *Petrel* some four hundred feet ahead.

It only took an instant to realize that, under tow, *Lucky*'s motion was nauseating. Her bow pitched rapidly, the strong vertical accelerations bringing back dreaded memories of battling seasickness during training stints on patrol boats when I was a cadet. Hartsock started to turn pale, and my brow beaded with sweat, stomach in a churn. Crap. We had a job to do—to search the boat for drugs—and we got to work, trying to keep our minds off the violent motion. Focusing on the search helped, holding the queasiness temporarily at bay.

The main cabin was littered with soggy clothes, a few empty food cans, charts, shoes, and just about anything that wasn't tied down. It smelled of sweat and sickness. An inch of salt water swirled across the deck, sloshing forward and aft as *Lucky*'s bow rose and plummeted.

Hartsock and I probed the bilges, searched every cabinet and drawer, measured each space, and sounded the fuel and water tanks. Nothing. I noticed some thick trim around the outside of the cockpit, possibly hiding a hollow section of hull. We took out the eight long screws holding the trim in place and removed it. Behind it was just a thick fiberglass hull. Nuts. On top of the cabin was a yellow life raft. Hartsock deflated it, crushing and feeling to see if anything was hidden inside the thick rubber skin. It was just a normal life raft, empty, so we pumped it back full of air. For two hours we looked into every corner, covering every inch of the sailboat, and came to the conclusion that there was no cocaine on board. If the intelligence had been right, the crew must have pitched the drugs before we arrived. More likely, though, there had never been dope on board in the first place.

Back on *Petrel*, Sanders had given the three rescued sailors sets of coveralls and let them take showers to shed the crusty salt and grime that covered their bodies. Once they were cleaned up, Goodrum laid out sandwiches and bug juice. All three dove in, famished. Sanders and Weatherby sat down with Dave, the master, asking him about the voyage and trying to discern any inconsistencies in his story, probing for signs that he'd been smuggling. After that they talked with the women, individually, and got the same story.

Sanders called on the radio. "XO, we've talked to these folks and don't have any suspicions. They're all from Denver and don't know squat about sailing. They were on vacation down in Cozumel and were going to head back to Tampa on the sailboat with a friend, you know, on a big adventure. The friend got sick but talked this guy, Dave, into sailing the boat for him. The girls went along for the ride and didn't realize how inexperienced Dave was. I think he'd lied a bit about his skills, maybe to impress the girls, but that's another story. Anyway, when the weather got bad they were in way over their heads, and then the sails ripped out. They spent a full day bouncing around and probably would have gone crazy if we hadn't gotten to them. Unless you've found something over there, I'd just call this a straight SAR case."

I concurred. We'd completed the search, and I asked Sanders to send the RHIB back to pick us up. Hartsock and I sat amidships, on top of the cabin, letting the breeze cool our faces, helping to ward off seasickness. We both craved to get back to the rock-solid deck of the SES. On *Petrel* we could see our shipmates readying the RHIB for launch. Then, they fiddled with the crane winch, but they never put the boat to the rail. Cliff Boldan appeared, tinkered with the winch controller, then put a hand on his head, looking exasperated.

Lieutenant Lober called on the radio. "XO, bad news. It looks like the winch is inop, and we're going to need to leave you there for a while 'til we can fix it. MK1's not sure we have the right part on board, so you may need to stay on board all the way to the beach. You guys'll be okay—right?"

Of course. We were SES sailors. Nothing could get us down—except a really crappy ride. The OOD had increased speed, and *Petrel* was dragging us toward shore at seven knots. The sailboat's bow plunged wildly over the top of the waves, a fiberglass anti-gravity chamber, free-falling into the troughs, our stomachs in our throats, spray soaking us to the skin. I fought my best, but lost. After three hours of resistance I was barfing over the leeward rail, feeding the fish below, too sick to care if Hartsock had also succumbed. It was my first bout of seasickness since early in my tour on *Active*. I curled up in the cockpit, cursing the weather, the broken winch, and life in general. Hartsock sprawled on top of the cabin, spread-eagle, muttering to himself. It would be a long trip to Key West.

On board *Petrel* it was a different story. Dave, exhausted, went to sleep in a spare rack, not waking for fifteen hours. The two women, meanwhile, had cleaned up nicely. Both were in their early twenties and fun-loving. They sat on the mess deck, playing cards with the crew, telling stories about their time in Mexico, charming the guys and asking about the best bars in Key West. They were already planning their next party.

The seas abated, yielding a more relaxed ride, but Boldan wasn't able to fix the small boat winch. *Petrel* pulled into the Key West ship channel the next morning, shortening the towline to fifty feet, and once we were in the turning basin a 41-footer from Station Key West came alongside. Hartsock cast off the towline, and the utility boat snuggled up, dragging us on her hip to the Coast Guard pier. Once moored, I surveyed Hartsock. He was a mess, red-eyed, unshaven, and covered with streaks of salt. He said I looked like a really bad dream. A Customs agent with a dog team came on board, and we showed them around. The dogs searched, and the agent came to the same conclusion that we'd reached. There was no coke on board.

As Hartsock and I stepped onto the pier, hungry, exhausted, and looking like death warmed over, the two women from *Lucky* walked toward us, perky in their borrowed Coast Guard coveralls. The taller one waved and shouted, now running to greet her rescuers. "Hey guys, thanks *so much* for saving us!" she said. "We were gonna die out there. You Coast Guard guys are great!" She moved in to give me a hug, stopped, took a hard look and then reconsidered, taking a step backwards. "Uh, we're gonna get our stuff off the boat now, is that okay?" she asked. The Customs agent nodded yes. Hartsock rolled his eyes, cursing under his breath, and he and I shuffled back to *Petrel*, our minds only on food and warm showers.

That night, on Duval Street, we ran into *Lucky*'s crew among the swarms of tourists. We shared some drinks and laughs. It was hard to tell who'd been more frazzled by the bad weather. Dave caught a flight for Denver the next day, but the girls fell in love with Key West and stayed. The taller one, a nurse named Diane, eventually got a job at the local hospital and later earned a commission in the Air Force. She proved it was a small world. Diane met a Coast Guard Falcon pilot from Miami and married him the next year. She had run the gamut—from being rescued by the Coast Guard to marrying into it.

———

The one universal constant among Coast Guard cutter crews is a cadre of fanatical fishermen. Red Crew's enthusiasts spanned rank and age, from Jerry Lober at the top to Stan Elliot at the younger end, with Senior Chief, Cliff Boldan, and a handful of others in the middle. Fishing was their catharsis—a way to unwind from the monotony of a quiet patrol, an adrenaline rush as they hauled in a dolphinfish or a grouper.

Surface-dwelling species such as dolphinfish—also called dorado or mahi-mahi—congregated near drift-lines, tangles of seaweed that floated with the current. Captain Lober issued a standing order to alert him whenever a decent-sized drift-line was spotted. When things were slow, it wasn't unusual to find our cutter motoring slowly back and forth across a string of seaweed, a half-dozen fishing lines trailing astern. The beauty was that we could fish and keep an eye out for dopers at the same time.

Petrel was patrolling twenty miles north of Cuba, in a lull, when the OOD spotted a massive line of seaweed and piped "fish call." It was mid-afternoon. I'd been up since 0300 and hit the rack for a few hours of shuteye before my next watch.

Sleep never came. There was a racket on deck, just outside my stateroom window, voices shouting, feet shuffling, fading away then growing louder, gone and back again, over and over. Annoyed, I climbed the ladder to the bridge. Boldan was on the bow, struggling with a thick deep-sea fishing pole, the fiberglass bent 90 degrees, its thin clear line stretching out almost horizontal, with three shipmates alongside encouraging him to keep up the fight. He'd snagged something big, really big, and had been trying to haul it in for forty minutes, circling twice around the deckhouse as the fish darted and pulled. The battle lasted another half-hour. Sweaty and red-faced, Boldan used a gaff hook to snag the fish and hump it over the rail. It was a huge dolphinfish, its blunt head and powerful tail slapping the side of the ship, finally flung onto the deck where it lay exhausted, twitching and flapping. Its next stop would be the frying pan.

The dolphinfish weighed in at sixty-two pounds. Although it was an unofficial measure, we later learned that this was the second largest mahi-mahi caught by a Key West–based fisherman that year. The captain stood next to Boldan, admiring the catch, beaming, congratulating him, laughs all around, a great bonding moment, nature's gift to a hardworking crew.

Over dinner Senior Chief made a prediction. "MK1's dolphin's a sign of good luck, you can bet on it," he said. "Something good's headed our way. Just wait and see." He looked at his shipmates, intensity in his eyes. "Maybe tonight, maybe tomorrow, we're going to have some real damned fun."

Two days later we intercepted a thirty-nine-foot lobster boat named *Miss Marilyn* as she headed from Elbow Cay toward the Keys. It was sunset, and Dan Sanders was the OOD. He maneuvered *Petrel* alongside the vessel and got close enough to question her master using a loudhailer. Where was *Miss Marilyn* headed? Key West. Purpose of voyage? Fishing. How many people on board? Just three. Any weapons or cargo? None. The captain set boarding stations, and I suited up. Walt Goodrum served as my assistant, along with Bill Hartsock and Carrie Corson. This was a good team: Goodrum had great judgment and was small and nimble, able to crawl into tight spaces, and Hartsock and Corson were battle-tested professionals. I'd trust all three with my life.

We climbed into the RHIB and headed for the lobster boat. She was sitting dead in the water, fifty yards off the cutter's bow, rolling gently in the mild swell. There were three fish traps on *Miss Marilyn*'s aft deck, but the winch on the boat's port side—used to haul in the traps—looked rusted and unserviceable. The boat herself was grimy, with orange streaks dripping from her metal fittings and soot smeared around her exhaust ports. Black rub marks decorated her port side. We scurried over the rail and faced the three-person crew on the aft deck. I made a quick scan—there was no line on the winch spool or other signs of activity. Whatever these guys were up to, it wasn't fishing.

I introduced myself to the master, Allen Strong, a taut, dark-haired man wearing long-sleeved fatigues. Following standard procedure, I repeated the questions Sanders had asked, to validate the consistency of the master's story.

Last port-of-call? Key West. Next port-of-call? The same. Nature of voyage? "We went fishing down by the Bahamas." Any weapons on board? No. How many people on board? Three. How many of you speak English? Strong looked uneasy, pointing to his two crew members. "Just me; these guys only speak Spanish." He paused, seemingly torn, then pointed forward toward the cabin. "None of *them* speak good English, either." What? Them? Who the hell are them? My heart jumped.

Goodrum was positioned forward on the open deck, near the portside winch, and I stepped toward him. He was glancing into the dark cabin, his hand resting on his holstered .45. He spoke tersely, in a forced whisper: "XO, I think there's someone in there!" A chill sprinted up my spine as I reached for my gun, sensing movement in the murky darkness ahead of us. "Draw weapons," I told him.

The cabin on *Miss Marilyn* extended the width of the vessel, with the throttles and steering wheel forward on the port side, and bench seats running down the starboard. Ahead of the cabin, tapered into the boat's bow, was a berthing area, two steps lower than the main deck. A narrow opening led from the cabin into the berthing area. The opening was pitch black.

I spoke as forcefully as my tightening throat would allow. "In the berthing area, this is the United States Coast Guard, step out now with your hands in plain view." I repeated the command. Nothing happened. Goodrum and I inched forward, .45s drawn, safeties off. We were greeted only by silence.

The ambient light was almost gone, making it hard to see in the unlit cabin. There was a flash in the berthing area, like the eyes of an animal reflecting the headlights of a car, and I pointed my .45 directly toward the opening. Goodrum did the same. Our world was now focused on whatever lurked in the dark space. Behind us, Hartsock took charge, ordering Strong and his crew to sit on the deck, hands in plain view, to ensure they didn't make any hostile moves.

Goodrum and I crossed slowly into the cabin, my heart racing, thoughts jumbled, wondering if we were about to be ambushed. Instinctively, Goodrum stepped to port and I moved to starboard, creating a wider gap between us and presenting less of a silhouette to anyone intending to attack. We crouched low and I grabbed for my flashlight, finally pulling it free, and pointed the beam forward. A shadow moved in the berthing space. "Don't move! Put your hands above your head!" I yelled, speaking as assertively as I could, trying my hardest to sound authoritative. "This is the United States Coast Guard. Show yourself—*now!*"

The movement stopped. Goodrum and I crept further forward. We were ten feet from the opening into the berthing area. My flashlight beam sliced the darkness. We could see the forward bulkhead—a crumpled pile of laundry, a soda can, the side of the port bunk. I tilted the beam upward. It illuminated an arm, a torso, a man lying on the bunk, shielding his eyes from the light. Goodrum and I took one more step, weapons pointed at the man. I swept the flashlight to the right, revealing a second person, lying face up on the starboard bunk, and then another man, curled up on the deck. The third man was facing the bow, his back to us, and we couldn't see his hands. He started to stir, arms flat along his sides and hands together near his stomach, as if he were manipulating something. My throat cinched. Was he pulling a knife? A gun?

"You on deck—get up—put your hands above your head!" I shouted. "Slowly! Slowly! Let me see your hands!" My finger was on the trigger of the .45. I was ready to chamber a round and squeeze. The man on the deck stopped moving. I yelled again. "No sudden moves—show your hands—slowly—now!"

For seconds that felt like years, nothing happened. Then, in a violent flash of motion, the man twisted his body 180 degrees, quickly thrusting both arms directly toward us, as if to aim a gun.

Goodrum and I had less than a second to decide whether to shoot. Neither of us did. The man completed his twist. His hands were empty.

I took a breath, relaxed my trigger-finger, and swept the flashlight beam side to side, checking to see if anyone else was hidden in the space. My palms were slick with sweat. Goodrum clicked on his own flashlight to provide more light. Aside from the three men, there was nothing there. I barked: "Come out with your hands up; keep your hands in plain sight!" The men rose, filing toward us and dipping their heads to exit the space. All three were dark-skinned, thin, and shoddily dressed, wearing stained, worn shirts and the black pinstripe pants popular throughout the Caribbean. I assumed they were Haitians.

The men stepped from the berthing area, hands held high, passing between Goodrum and me. Guns still drawn, we had them sit next to Strong and his crew. Once they were under the control of Hartsock and Corson, I stepped up to the doorway leading into the berthing space.

Crossing inside, with Goodrum providing cover, I looked under the bunks; there were no other people. Goodrum and I then walked aft and peered into the hatches leading to the engine room, fishhold, and lazarette, also finding them empty.

Now we knew what we were dealing with. No drugs, no weapons— just three undeclared passengers, most likely being smuggled into the Keys. The men who'd been hiding looked scared, one of them trembling, biting his bottom lip, his eyes teary. Emergency over, we holstered our weapons.

Hartsock called *Petrel* on the secure handheld and filled them in. The cutter had already nudged closer and we could see Obenland manning the M-60 on the bridge, ready to blast away if trouble broke out. I asked the six men for identification, and only Strong and one of his crew could produce driver's licenses. The rest said they had no papers with them. We frisked them to make sure they weren't armed. Goodrum and I pulled Strong aside, talking to him in low tones. "Who are these guys?" I asked. "Where'd they come from?" Strong was slow to reply, his eyes shifting left and right. "They're just fishermen. They've been with us since we left Key West. Our boat broke down last night. We just got it fixed and are heading back home." Goodrum looked disgusted, his thoughts clear: what a liar.

We separated the men, talking to each individually, asking them their date of birth, nationality, and home address. Allen Strong was from Key West and his two crew members were resident aliens, originally from Cuba but now living in Miami. The three others, paperless, spoke with a thick Caribbean accent, touched with British. They weren't Haitians; they were from Jamaica. Two of the men were my age, in their early twenties, and the third was forty. The older Jamaican and one of the youngsters said they were resident aliens, but couldn't produce green cards. The other Jamaican, Travis Lafeve, was shivering, and said he was an American citizen.

"Sir, where do you live—what's your address?" Goodrum asked. He was polite and brotherly in his questioning. It was the perfect approach.

"I live in White Plains." Lafeve's voice was warbling, unsure.

"Where?"

"I live in White Plains."

"Sir, thank you. What's your street address?"

"My address is White Plains, U.S.A."

I interjected. "And what state do you live in?"

"White Plains."

This was going nowhere. I conferred by radio with Lieutenant Lober, telling him that we had probable cause that *Miss Marilyn* was smuggling aliens and that we should arrest the master and crew. He concurred but asked that we not place anyone under arrest until he had briefed Group Key West. Goodrum and I took a closer look around the vessel, seeking evidence. There was a chart spread out near the steering console. On it, written in pencil, were tracklines, one from Key West to Cay Sal Island, and a second from Cay Sal south, ending about five miles north of the Cuban coast. The chart would be helpful in court.

At 1930 Lieutenant Lober gave us the green light. I arrested all six men and the coxswain whisked them to the cutter. Goodrum and I seized the chart, along with a small blue tote bag from the berthing area. Inside the tote was a scrap of paper with addresses and phone numbers in White Plains, New York. Returning to *Petrel*, I asked whose bag it was—Lafeve claimed it as his.

We read the prisoners their rights and took them into the captain's cabin, one by one, for interrogation. All six spoke willingly, at least for a while. We talked to the Jamaicans first. The older man said he was a Jamaican national but refused to answer any more questions. We got better cooperation from the second Jamaican, who admitted they were being smuggled into the country. He said that the three had ridden north on a Jamaican fishing boat called *Captain B* and had transferred to *Miss Marilyn* the night before. The third man, Lafeve, was distraught, sobbing, and couldn't offer any help.

It was a sad scene. In less than an hour I'd gone from almost shooting one of these guys to feeling sorry for them. Both Cuban Americans said that the Jamaicans hadn't been part of *Miss Marilyn*'s crew when she departed Key West. Neither man would offer any details on how the Jamaicans had come on board. One said he'd slept most of the trip and woke up to discover the men sitting on deck; the other just said that the Jamaicans were the master's problem, not his.

Our final session was with Strong. Apparently looking for sympathy, he talked about how he'd enlisted in the Marine Corps but now worked as a fisherman out of Key West. He stuck with his claim that all six men had been on board for the entire trip and denied any knowledge of a boat named *Captain B*. After that, he declined to talk further, and we shackled him in the prisoners' chairs for the six-hour voyage to port.

I was so pumped up on adrenaline that it took me the rest of the night to decompress, the boarding replaying in my mind on a continuous loop, realizing how close I'd come to shooting a man. In more than a hundred boardings, it was the only time I'd pulled my .45. Goodrum told me later it was his first time as well.

We never learned why the prone Jamaican had ignored orders and twisted so violently toward us, but it had almost been his last moment on earth. If he'd been holding anything that resembled a gun when he spun at us, he'd be dead. Goodrum said the same thing. There'd been only microseconds to make a decision, but until we saw an actual threat, neither of us was going to shoot. That is how we'd been trained, and the training had paid off.

It was the tensest boarding that Red Crew had carried out. I was blown away with how well Goodrum, Hartsock, and Corson had performed, thankful for their skills, grateful for their judgment, and blessed to have them as shipmates.

That night, as I was lying in my rack and fading toward sleep, it struck me that it was the one-year anniversary since I'd reported aboard as XO Red. Drug seizures, illegal aliens, Mexican gunboats, rough weather—what a year it had been. And, hopefully, there was much more to come. But first, Red Crew had to get a new captain.

6

Double Vision

May 1984

t. Cdr. Bob Council had a problem. As division commander, his job was to provide the personnel and resources to keep the four SES crews in top form. But by the spring of 1984, the Blue and Green crews had been in commission for almost two years, and their captains, XOs, and senior enlisted sailors were all due for transfer. This meant a serious brain-drain for both teams. As a partial remedy, Lieutenant Commander Council decided to move the experienced captains from the Red Crew and Gold Crew over to Green Crew and Blue Crew. That way, the Red and Gold crews would both get fresh captains, and no crew would be disadvantaged. It was a smart fix, but I dreaded losing Lieutenant Lober. He was a great captain, and we worked together effortlessly in a comfortable, productive senior-junior partnership.

Red Crew's new commanding officer had the perfect name, and the perfect résumé, for the job. Lt. Wayne Justice was joining us from the Seventh District operations center in Miami. Before that he'd commanded the 95-foot cutter *Cape Shoalwater* (WPB 95324), out of West Palm Beach, where he'd set a Coast Guard record by making twenty drug seizures in a two-year stint. Lieutenant Justice was a Seventh District legend, a true drug warrior, and he'd be our new boss.

Initial impressions of the new captain were uniformly good. He looked the part, with his broad shoulders, trim waist, sharp features, and movie-star tan, and he was friendly and eager to get to work. Lieutenant Justice told the crew that he intended to push the limits to make as many drug busts as possible. The crew was glad to get another hard-charging captain. I was grateful that he sought my advice and even more pleased when he asked about my family, background, and career goals. He was an open book, introducing me to his wife, sharing his command philosophy, and describing his ultimate goal, to rise through the ranks all the way to admiral. Talk about long-range planning—I was lucky to be thinking a week ahead.

But unlike my relationship with Lieutenant Lober, which had been solid from day one, I felt off-frequency, somehow out of sync, with the incoming captain. Lieutenant Justice was a quick thinker and a fast talker, ideas bubbling off his lips, and I had a hard time keeping up with him. Red Crew spent two days under way with him, walking through emergency evolutions and training exercises, explaining the strengths and quirks of the SESs, but the new captain and I seemed to talk past each other and didn't fully mesh.

I knew that a captain and XO needed to be on the same page, in lock-step, with a solitary vision for how they'd lead their crew. There couldn't be friction or competing priorities. My job as XO was to short-circuit any problems before they got to the captain. But in order to do that I really needed to figure him out.

On May 9, 1984, the SES Division held an unusual event—a dual change of command—on board *Petrel*, which was moored in Key West. The formal invitation told the story: "The Commander, U.S. Coast Guard Surface Effect Ship Division, requests the pleasure of your company at the Change of Command Ceremony, at which Lieutenant Mark A. Fisher, USCG, Commanding Officer, Green Crew, will be relieved by Lieutenant James J. Lober, Jr., Commanding Officer, Red Crew, who will be relieved by Lieutenant Wayne E. Justice, USCG." It read as though there were one too many lieutenants to go around.

The Division and the four SES crews also received an unexpected honor. The Commander of Coast Guard Atlantic Area, Vice Adm. Wayne Caldwell, awarded us the Coast Guard Unit Commendation, the highest unit award normally given in peacetime. The citation centered on the SESs' contributions in the war on drugs, highlighting notable seizures, and saying that the accomplishments reflected "tireless dedication and teamwork in support of Coast Guard operations" as well as "unique aggressiveness and professionalism on behalf of the crews involved." Red Crew was proud to see that our triple seizure was specifically mentioned in the citation. In their first eighteen months the four SES crews had interdicted more than 174,000 pounds of marijuana from twenty-nine smuggling vessels. Operationally, "El Tiburon" was off to a fast and fruitful start.

———

Red Crew was three days into its first patrol with our new captain, sailing in *Shearwater*, transiting from Fort Lauderdale toward the southeast. Just after noon Group Miami called with hot intelligence and directed us to a spot south of Bimini, where it said a vessel loitering there might be packed with Haitian migrants. Bimini was only fifty miles from Florida, and it would be crucial to intercept the boat before it got into the Gulf Stream, where rougher seas could put the migrants in peril. *Shearwater* headed east at full speed, skimming over a nasty five-foot chop and buffeted by twenty-knot winds. Bands of rain showers were coursing through the area, reducing visibility and turning the normally brilliant blue waters into a dreary gray seascape, more akin to the English Channel than to sunny South Florida.

Group Miami passed along a more precise position of the vessel and said that District Seven wanted a close-up look to see if the boat was dangerously overloaded. Senior Chief charted the coordinates. The boat was on the Great Bahama Bank, southeast of the Cat Cays, straddling Bahamian territory in less than eight feet of water. *Shearwater* couldn't operate in those shallows. There was no way to get the cutter close enough to check out the Haitian boat.

An hour later *Shearwater* approached the Cat Cays from the west, getting to within three miles of the nearest Bahamian island. The OOD detected a radar blip near the Haitian boat's last reported position, on

the far side of a pair of desolate rocky cays, but we couldn't see that far
in the rain.

"All right XO, how are we going to do this? We've got to take a look
at that boat," Captain Justice said impatiently, rocking back and forth on
the balls of his feet, talking in staccato bursts.

"Well, sir, we can't get onto the bank—it's way too shallow—and even
if we did, the target's on the edge of Bahamian waters, so we might not
have jurisdiction," I replied. "I'd say we hang out here for a while and see
if the boat moves. Radar says it's dead in the water."

"No, District wants us to check it out, so we need to check it out," the
captain asserted. "How about using the small boat?"

I shot a glance at the roiling seas and iron breeze. Whoever went
for a small boat ride was going to get wet—really wet. "I don't think so.
It's too risky," I said. "The boat'll take a pounding and we'd have to pass
through Bahamian territory for the last couple of miles, and if the RBDF
sees us they'll raise a stink." The Royal Bahamian Defense Force had
a small fleet of patrol boats and a love-hate relationship with the U.S.
Coast Guard, and it was always on the lookout for cutters encroaching
on Bahamian sovereign territory. We could pass between the two small
cays under the concept of "innocent passage," but that wouldn't stop the
Bahamians from complaining to the U.S. Embassy in Nassau. "Legally,
we're okay, but we'll get the Bahamians riled up if they see us," I advised.
"It's best to wait."

Captain Justice lowered his voice and stepped in close. "XO, screw
the lawyers and screw the RBDF," he said. "There's a boat over there that
might be filled with a hundred or two hundred people, and if they get out
into the Stream and capsize, they'll all be dead. No one wants that, not
even the damned lawyers. So, XO, I want you to head over there in the
RHIB and check them out. See what you can find. Get as close as you
can. District wants this done, and damn it, we're going to do it."

I blanched under his glare. Orders were orders, and he wasn't asking
for anything improper. Sanders volunteered as coxswain, and we headed
below to suit up, donning yellow foul-weather gear. I wondered how we'd
explain ourselves if a Bahamian patrol boat crew pounced on our RHIB
joy-riding through their country's waters. I really didn't understand where

the captain was coming from. The Haitian boat wasn't moving—why not just wait?

After we'd been in the small boat for thirty seconds, the RBDF faded to a distant concern. Survival became the priority. *Shearwater*'s four-meter RHIB just wasn't up to the task of making speed through the five-foot chop. As Sanders steered the boat east, directly into the waves, it pounded and smashed, casting thick sheets of spray that hovered in the air and then got caught by the wind, flying back into our faces and soaking us to the skin. We punched forward, slamming hard with numbing repetition, like a car driving through deep, jagged potholes at highway speed. I crouched in the bow to protect myself from the spray and felt every impact, hitting my shins, elbows, and forearms on the boat's console as I ping-ponged back and forth. The slamming was so intense that I feared the rubber pontoon might separate from the RHIB's fiberglass hull and made a mental note to have Sanders inspect the seam once we got back to the ship.

What should have been a ten-minute trip in calm weather took four times as long—forty cold, wet, rotten minutes. To add to our misery, a thick, charcoal-colored cloud passed overhead, as dark as my mood, dumping torrential rain on us and lowering visibility to a hundred feet. Sanders pointed out that at least it was fresh water and would wash the crud off our faces.

The rain slowed as we crossed onto the bank, and Sanders eyeballed his way through the rocky islets, now at clutch speed, chest-deep shoals all around. Once we got past the line of cays, the water deepened, and we picked up speed to twenty knots, scanning the eastern horizon for the Haitian boat. There, through the rain, about two miles ahead, was a gray silhouette. Sanders pointed the RHIB directly toward it. From a mile away we could see it was a freighter, wooden hulled, maybe sixty-five feet long, typical for the island trade. Sanders looked over his shoulder at the uninhabited rocks behind us. His eyes twinkled. "Looks to me like the boat's exactly three-point-one miles off the beach," he said, nodding toward the freighter. "Ready to give it a buzz?" I had no idea how far we were from the rocks, but I was too wet and rattled to care. "Sure, Boats," I said. "Let's go."

We approached at full tilt, and Sanders slowed to clutch speed and circled the vessel twice. The ship was at anchor, and three slender men sat under an awning on the forward deck, smoking cigarettes and playing cards. There was a small charcoal grill on deck, with chunks of meat roasting on spits. One of the men waved to us, a what-the-hell-are-you-doing-here look on his face. We must have been a pathetic sight, in our bright-yellow rain gear, hair matted and bodies drenched, a pair of big wet lemons. As we circled the freighter, Sanders and I peered into the pilothouse and saw that it was vacant. So was the aft deck. One of the doors on the superstructure was jacked open, giving us a view of an empty room. I shouted to the men, and one yelled back that they were running empty, waiting for better weather to head to Miami to pick up a load of shoes. They would return to Haiti with the cargo. I asked how many people were on board, and the man replied, "Just the three of us."

Sanders said everything looked legitimate: there was no sign of migrants, and the crew didn't show any concern that the U.S. Coast Guard was circling their vessel. I'd come to the same conclusion. Our hand-held radio had stopped working, undoubtedly from getting soaked, so I wrote down the boat's name, homeport, and documentation number in a notebook, and we headed back to the cutter.

The six-mile trip back to *Shearwater* was infinitely smoother; the RHIB surfed down the front of the waves, occasionally burying its bow but making good time. Miraculously, the handheld started working again, and I passed along the Haitian vessel's particulars so the quartermaster could run an EPIC check. I still was confused as to why our captain had pursued this wild-goose chase. We were pushing our luck by skirting through Bahamian waters and had punished our small boat to the point where it could have sustained damage—all to check out an innocent freighter. I started to fume. Once we got back, I'd let him know what I thought of his decision.

Sanders pulled the RHIB alongside the cutter. I stomped up to the bridge, my face flushed, trying to control my emotions. The captain was on the radio, talking to Group, and by the time he finished Sanders had joined me on the port bridge wing, both of us still dripping, looking like schoolboys in our yellow slickers. The captain put down the transmitter and strode quickly toward us. I was about to ask for a minute of his time to talk in private, but he beat me to the punch.

"Hey, everyone, listen up," he told the group. The watch was being relieved and half the crew was on the bridge, and they all turned toward the captain. "I just want you to know how proud I am of XO and BM1 for checking out that freighter." He looked at us and smiled, totally sincere, and then put a hand on my shoulder. "We could tell what a hard ride it was to get over there and know it must have hurt. Sorry about that. But you got the job done, and now we know there's nothing to worry about with that boat." He turned to the crew, explaining. "That's really important because otherwise we would've been sitting here forever waiting for the freighter to come out from the islands. Now we can get back to work and find ourselves a doper." He paused, smiling even more broadly. "District's happy, Group's happy, and I'm happy. Great job, guys, great job." He slapped both of us on the back, and for a second I thought we were going to get man-hugged. "Thanks for your hard work."

BM1 stared at me, his face a blank slate. He knew I'd been ready to argue with the boss, and he probably would've enjoyed the show. I was flummoxed, at a loss for words, realizing in a flash that the captain had been right all along. He'd made the right call. Sure, we'd taken a beating and risked antagonizing the Bahamians, but we had solved a mystery that otherwise could have kept our cutter and crew tied up for hours, maybe days. "Uh, sure thing, sir," I stammered. "It was a rough ride, but Boats got us there okay. I'm just glad to be back." Lieutenant Justice's chipper attitude and kind words had completely disarmed me.

Back in my stateroom, peeling off sodden clothes, I suddenly understood our new captain. Lieutenant Justice was a binary thinker, with a single goal of mission success. Only results mattered, and everything else was a distant second. Justice was a bottom-line kind of guy, pushing boundaries to accomplish the mission, and completely unwilling to take no for an answer. Now he made sense.

Thus enlightened, I was able to see the world through his prism. All doubts about our relationship melted away. Sure, he was different from Jerry Lober, but in his own way he was another top-flight officer. Where Lober had been involved in the entire span of shipboard life, the new captain didn't like to be dragged down by the sideshows—the paperwork, the discipline, the maintenance—and expected me to handle the "fluff" so that he could concentrate on operational victories. I just needed to adjust my focus, and my habits, to accommodate his. That's what good XOs did.

Just as it had been with Lober, I ended up enriched from Lieutenant Justice's hard-charging tactics and willingness to take risks. I'd have several future successes that were built on his never-say-die attitude. We ended up friends and as often happened in the tight Coast Guard universe, served together again near the end of our careers. It was a genuine honor when I retired from active duty twenty-four years later that Rear Adm. Wayne Justice, still leaning forward and still passionate about the Coast Guard—and, as planned, having earned his flag—served as the master of ceremonies.

————

Assigning new SES captains meant there also would be new SES executive officers. I had spent the past year shadowing Jim Sartucci at work and enjoying the Key West high life with him, often alongside the Gold Crew XO, Mark Hoesten, a fellow Connecticut Yankee. Now Sartucci was headed north for a stint at Coast Guard headquarters, where he'd be working on the replacement patrol boat project. Al Bernard, the plank-owner XO of Green Crew, also was headed to shore. Sartucci and Bernard were both SES rock stars, smart, talented, and fearless. Sartucci's bravery while rescuing the doper crew on *Owl and the Pussycat* was legend, and Bernard's vibrant personality had its own zip code. "El Tiburon" wouldn't be the same without them.

Fortunately, through the good graces of Coast Guard headquarters, their replacements were cut from similar cloth. Mike Cosenza and Bruce Gaudette were members of the Coast Guard Academy Class of 1982, one year behind Mark Hoesten and me. Cosenza was short and powerful, with a razor-sharp wit and an intense professional ethos, and later was handpicked to teach nautical science at the U.S. Naval Academy. He took over as Green Crew XO, working for Jerry Lober. Gaudette, the new XO of Blue Crew, was a natural-born sailor—clever, crafty, and coy, with a droll sense of humor. He was an intense competitor, and the only time I could beat him at tennis was the rare occasion when he was wiped out from too many long nights at sea. For the first time, all of the SES executive officers—Hoesten, Cosenza, Gaudette, and I—were single, and over the next year we spent most of our off-duty time together, a gang of four, pub-crawling on Duval Street or hanging out at one of our houses. I was losing a best friend in Jim Sartucci but gained two in return.

Sartucci's and Bernard's departures meant one more thing. I was now the senior SES executive officer, having graduated from the Academy a few rungs above my classmate Hoesten. That meant added responsibility. I would act as a mentor to the new XOs and lead the informal network that solved problems between the crews. If the division commander had a problem for all of the XOs to handle, it would come through me. And in the churn of busy operations there was no way to tell what other fun might pop up for the senior SES XO.

————

It took our new captain exactly thirty-three days to get his first drug bust. Even better, he got two for the price of one. Red Crew was back on board *Shearwater*, patrolling the Great Bahama Bank, ninety miles southeast of Bimini. It was a picture-perfect morning, with light winds and clear skies, the aqua water sparkling in the sunlight. At 0830 a Coast Guard Falcon reported that it and a Customs Citation aircraft were tracking two go-fast boats, twenty-five miles farther east. Both vessels were carrying bales recovered from an air drop and were headed northwest, toward the island string south of Bimini and, beyond that, Florida. *Shearwater* turned to an intercept course, blasting due north at thirty knots.

I'd stood the midwatch, and Chuck Meisner woke me up, pounding on the stateroom door. "XO, get up, we've got a hot one, couple of go-fasts with bales. Captain says to get ready to board." I threw on a set of coveralls and scrambled up to the bridge, arriving just in time to hear the Falcon crew report that crew members on one of the speedboats were throwing bales in the water and that the other vessel had split off, now heading southeast, with the Customs jet in pursuit. I scuttled down the ladder to grab a bite to eat and dress out. Senior Chief hollered after me, saying that we'd be intercepting the first boat in half an hour.

I was back on the bridge in fifteen minutes, dressed, fed, and ready for action. On the horizon, off the starboard bow, was a dark, cigar-shaped blob, shimmering like a desert mirage. It was the first go-fast, the one that had dumped her bales, still headed northwest, rocketing across the shallow water. An occasional white cloud erupted in its wake. Captain Justice had his face in the radar, tracking the go-fast, and said it was making forty-two knots. "If we both hold steady, looks like eleven minutes to intercept, close aboard." He chuckled. "Hopefully, they don't know they're faster than us."

The go-fast flew straight as a cruise missile, getting closer, three miles, two miles, 1,500 yards off *Shearwater*'s bow. Senior Chief was plotting furiously, the edge of shoal water only minutes away. All the speedboat had to do was head farther north into the shallows, forcing us to break off the chase, or else zig left under our stern, and we'd never be able to catch her.

Instead, she kept coming, straight and true, now 1,200 yards away, with constant bearing and decreasing range. *Shearwater*'s blue light was flashing, our police siren wailing. The OOD blasted the ship's horn, over and over. The Falcon screamed past, rattling the pilothouse windows, cutting directly across the go-fast's bow, flying so low that its jets churned up a wall of spray. It was an awesome show but had no effect. The go-fast punched through the salt plume at full speed, never slowing down.

A thousand yards, seven-hundred-fifty, five hundred—we were close enough to see three men on board, one of them pointing at us. Our vessels were on a collision course, in a nautical game of chicken. The captain stood on the starboard bridge wing, arms crossed on his chest. His orders to the OOD were simple: "Hold your course and speed."

Shearwater wasn't budging. The go-fast wasn't either. In thirty seconds both vessels would pass through the same spot at the same time, coming together at a 45-degree angle. The dynamics were frightening. If we collided, the go-fast would bounce off hard and maybe puncture our hull. People could die.

I estimated twenty seconds to impact. Surely the go-fast would turn away. Fifteen seconds—why weren't they turning? Twelve seconds, ten— were they suicidal? The go-fast was only 250 yards away, still holding her course. Our OOD had one hand on the throttles and the other on the helm, ready to yank them back and turn hard to avoid a wreck. The quartermaster was poised to punch the collision alarm, watching the captain, waiting for a signal.

Two hundred yards. The go-fast hit a swell and went airborne, thumping like a bass drum when it smacked back onto the water. Now the boat was 150 yards off our bow; a second later, 120 yards; another second, 100. At 50 yards, the man driving the go-fast snatched back his twin throttles and the boat slowed, instantly, as if a parachute had opened behind her, pitching forward and snowplowing the water, a thin translucent wave breaking over her bow. Captain Justice signaled to the OOD and *Shearwater* fell off lift, decelerating and sliding alongside the go-fast a few seconds later. It was 1009.

At 1010, Bill Hartsock and I jumped from *Shearwater*'s step deck onto the go-fast. I shouted: "U.S. Coast Guard, don't move, keep your hands in plain sight, stand away from the helm!" The three men stared, not understanding. Damn, they only spoke Spanish. I put my left hand on my holstered .45 and pointed at them with my right, and then thrust it into the air. All three raised their arms in defeat. Standing near the transom, we could smell the lingering odor of marijuana and saw an army of green buds littered across the deck. I told the three men that they were being detained and ordered them onto *Shearwater*, gesturing toward the cutter. Stan Elliot, standing on the step deck, translated the command. Sanders, shotgun in hand, herded them on board.

The go-fast was a sleek vessel, thirty feet long, Florida registration number FL-3699-DE, with twin two-hundred-horsepower engines and a red racing stripe complimenting a deep-blue hull. It was a typical go-fast layout, with an enclosed sleeping compartment taking up the forward third of the hull and the rest open to the weather, with a steering console aft. Hartsock peered into the berthing area and said: "Good to go, XO, no one else on board." I field-tested one of the buds and it produced the vaunted purple color. I seized the vessel and, on board *Shearwater*, Sanders arrested the three men. It was 1013.

The Customs aircrew radioed that it was chasing the second go-fast, still loaded with contraband, six miles to the south. Lieutenant Justice cupped his hands and bellowed from the bridge wing: "We're gonna go after the other boat—you go get the bales from this guy!" Hartsock was an experienced coxswain and stepped up to the helm, revving the engine and clutching the go-fast into gear. I gave an exaggerated shrug and mouthed back, "Which way?" Justice pointed southeast and said the Falcon had marked the spot with a smoke flare before heading home to refuel. Hartsock jammed the throttles forward, and we jetted toward the hazy funnel of smoke on the horizon.

The go-fast was incredibly powerful and blasted across the light chop. It felt as though her hull was barely touching the water, giving an intense sensation of speed, like a rocket in flight. Standing next to Hartsock, the wind slapping our faces, we both began to chuckle and then laugh, soon hysterical. Hartsock peeled off a string of rebel yells. Not bad duty for a kid from upstate New York.

It took seven minutes to get to the bales, and we found eight of them bobbing lazily in the water, strung out like stepping stones in the crystal-blue ocean. Hartsock jockeyed the go-fast alongside each bale, and I leaned over the side, wrestling it into the boat. Each weighed about fifty pounds; fortunately, the tops of the bales were dry, making the burlap easy to grab. I cut into the first bale and tested the material: purple again. Hartsock spun the boat in a circle, searching for more contraband, but we came up empty, and then he called *Shearwater* for instructions.

Lieutenant Justice's voice flared from our handheld radio, heavy with static. "Boarding party, this is *Shearwater*, we're pursuing the second go-fast. It's steering various courses, now headed northeast. The target is four miles ahead and moving away. Request you assist in the chase. We have you on radar. Head 280 degrees magnetic for your initial course. Over."

Bloody brilliant. The captain wanted us to run down the second doper using the seized go-fast. I thought, what the hell, the FL-3699-DE was now in the custody of the United States government—why not use it for law enforcement? Hartsock swung the bow to 280, using the round bubble compass on the console as a guide, and slammed the throttles forward. I started laughing again, realizing this was my first command at sea.

Hartsock steered a beeline, our boat making forty-plus knots, chipping across a brilliant blue sea. In the distance, just forward of our port beam, was a gauzy haze of exhaust from *Shearwater*, and, closer to the bow, flashes of sun reflected from the Customs jet as it circled high overhead. All else was empty horizon. The Citation reported that the second go-fast's crew was tossing bales over the side. That was a mistake— the smugglers had waited too long to dump their load, sacrificing speed. They were also making a second mistake—steering erratic courses, first to the northeast, then to the northwest, then westerly, and a few minutes later back to the north, allowing us to close.

Then we saw the second go-fast—a blurry smudge, followed by a contrail of spray, three or four miles out, almost directly ahead, slowly drifting to the right as she crossed ahead of us. Hartsock nudged our boat to starboard, falling into a stern chase behind the smugglers. Far to port, *Shearwater*'s smoke plume was barely visible, lagging farther behind. I called on the handheld but got no response. Hartsock and I were on our own. It was up to us to catch the smugglers before they reached the shelter of the Bahamian territory looming ahead.

The chase was exhilarating. Hartsock kept our boat at full throttle, skimming across the wave tops, a frothy white wake spreading out behind us. He worked the trim tabs expertly, settling the go-fast onto a perfectly aligned plane, maximizing speed. The wind was ripping at our coveralls, drops of spray stinging our faces like buckshot, sharp jolts buckling our knees as the boat clipped across the light seas. Hartsock let off another loud yell, howling like a teenager, and I screamed in his ear: "Life doesn't get any better than this!"

We could see the second go-fast more clearly and were closing on her, now only a mile away. The boat was creamy white, powered by twin outboards. Suddenly, the smugglers turned hard to port—too hard—and their boat sent a shower of spray into the air and slowed momentarily. Hartsock edged our boat to the left, keeping up our speed and closing the gap to 1,500 yards. The white boat steadied on a westerly course and then turned back to starboard, creating another white plume and settling on a northerly heading. We closed even further. The smugglers seemed confused, as if looking for something, not sure where to go. "Hell," Hartsock hollered, fighting the wind, "they might not even know we nailed their buddies and that we're chasing them." We were now only one thousand yards away.

Hartsock pointed to the left: in the distance was a string of rocky cays, desolate and weatherworn, the nearest Bahamian territory. If the smugglers had any sense, they would have headed directly for the rocks and stopped, since we had no search or seizure authority there. But they didn't, instead continuing their high-speed run to the north, on a tangent to the outcroppings.

The white boat's stern was low in the water, not properly trimmed, slowing it by a few knots. We crept forward, steadily gaining, the gap now closed to five hundred yards. We could see two men. The passenger was staring at us and started slapping the driver on the shoulder, yelling in his ear. He'd just realized they were being chased by the Coast Guard.

Without warning, the second go-fast turned hard to port and headed directly toward the rocks. Hartsock made a wider turn to keep up our speed, but almost lost control when our boat slammed into their wake, going completely airborne, then thwacking hard onto the water. I held onto the console, the impact driving me to my knees as Hartsock somehow maintained control and continued the chase.

The white boat angled toward a string of desolate cays, rocky and windswept, sprinkled north-to-south over a mile of knee-deep shallows. We followed in hot pursuit, closing the gap. The smugglers headed straight toward the rocks and, when their boat was impossibly close to shore, curved sharply to port, throwing up a curtain of water. We were two hundred yards behind. The white boat maneuvered wildly, arcing left and right, trying to shake us, now heading south. Hartsock matched their every turn. They turned 90 degrees to starboard and settled on a straight line to the west, passing between two of the craggy outposts, thirty yards separating the jagged rocks, the water beneath us shallow enough to wade ashore. Once we were through the gap, the white boat pivoted right, to the north, and skirted close along the line of islets, which were just off our starboard side, one hundred yards out. The smugglers came to starboard again, heading east between another set of cays, powering forward at full speed, rocketing past a twenty-foot cliff of crumbling brown rock, almost close enough to touch, spooked seabirds taking flight, starfish and patches of seaweed flashing by just feet beneath our hull. The men on the other boat were glancing furtively over their shoulders, watching as we closed the gap. I told Hartsock to stay directly behind them and keep some distance. That way if they ran aground we'd have fair warning. He feathered the throttle to match their speed, fifty yards in their wake.

For the next ten minutes we continued the chase, the smugglers turning and twisting among the rugged cays, our boat unshakable, trailing behind. I scanned the horizon, trying to find *Shearwater*, but the cutter had disappeared. The white boat made another hard maneuver, turning to port and then back to starboard at full speed, a huge S, then settled on a westerly heading, passing close by the tallest rocky island, a lonely sentinel thirty feet high that bore a vague resemblance to a Stonehenge monolith. We followed, hoping that the dopers would make their third big mistake of the morning and head onto the high seas.

They did. The smugglers continued west at a full sprint, and within four minutes they'd left the shelter of the Bahamas and were now on a direct course for Key Largo. Hartsock maxed out the throttles and cursed at the engines to give him more power. Out of nowhere, the Customs Citation flew over us, coming up from behind, startling Hartsock and jolting me, the plane's belly only fifty feet above our heads, its jet engines churning out a deafening metallic roar. The white go-fast continued to run.

Now our boats were in deep water, jostling through three-foot chop and a long-period swell. I pointed at the smugglers, only thirty yards away, signaling them to stop, almost blinded by the spray as we punched through the waves, the ocean surface ripping past at breakneck speed. The smugglers signaled back, one giving us the finger and the other grabbing his crotch and laughing. The pounding became intense, jarring, with the bows of both go-fasts casting huge swatches of white spray as they serrated the wave tops. Hartsock pushed even harder on the throttles: in the rougher waters we'd lost some speed but were still creeping closer, now only twenty-five, twenty, fifteen yards astern.

We were so close to the white go-fast that the torrents of spray blasting out from under her hull rained onto us. I squinted, scanning the horizon, face drenched, glasses spotted and nearly opaque. Emerging from the mist was a bulky black object, a vessel, directly ahead, no more than a mile and a half away. I took off my glasses and squinted harder. It was *Shearwater*. I pointed toward the cutter, and then Hartsock saw her and yelled, "The goddam cavalry's here!"

More tactical brilliance—while we'd been circling and pirouetting near the rocky cays, *Shearwater* had looped around the lower end of the string of islands and into the deep water, guessing that the smugglers would make a run for Florida. They'd cut off the white boat at the pass.

The smugglers saw the cutter and made a wide turn to port and then another to starboard, trying to shake their pursuers, throwing a heavy wake and sacrificing more speed. *Shearwater* matched every maneuver, pivoting directly at the smugglers. We followed in the white boat's wake, never losing a knot. *Shearwater* was looming closer, larger by the second, her broad bow a wall of shiny black aluminum and glistening rubber, the white deckhouse crisp and bright in the midday sun, a tiara of water droplets shimmering around the bow seals.

The relative speed between the SES and the two go-fasts was almost seventy knots. It was another collision situation, this time head-on. Here, the laws of physics were brutal: if the smugglers and *Shearwater* hit, we wouldn't have to arrest anyone—we'd be scooping up whatever pieces floated. *Shearwater* was half a mile out, bearing down on the white boat, bow-on-bow, with Hartsock and me only fifteen yards behind the smugglers.

I did the quick math. The cutter was closing at forty yards each second, maybe eight hundred yards away, still coming full bore. That meant twenty seconds to impact. The white go-fast held her course. *Shearwater* was four hundred yards away. Hartsock pulled back on the throttles, broadening the gap to the white boat. Two hundred yards. I tensed, expecting to witness a collision. Hartsock slowed our boat even further and yanked the steering wheel to starboard. Our go-fast heeled hard as she bit into the waves. We didn't want to be in the crossfire when the one-hundred-ton cutter crunched over the top of the white boat.

One hundred twenty yards—three seconds. The man driving the second go-fast snatched back her throttles, and the boat crashed to a stop, smashing into a four-foot swell, burying her bow and flooding her cockpit with a glassy surge of water. *Shearwater* came off lift and turned to starboard, decelerating rapidly. Sensing his cue, Hartsock gunned our boat's engines and pivoted to port, and within a few deep breaths we sidled alongside the white go-fast.

I glanced at my watch. It was 1130. The Citation buzzed us again, flying low and slow, the high-pitched whine of its engines shattering the air, its fuselage almost brushing the water. The Citation dipped its wings in tribute to the successful intercept. I saluted the plane, hatless and dripping but grateful for the tenacity of the Customs air crew.

Hartsock nudged FL-3699-DE against the white boat, and I ordered the two men to stand near the console and keep their hands in plain sight. Both of the men looked ashen, one of them shaking, clearly terrified. No one was laughing now. The boat was a thirty-foot Scarab, a high-end speedboat, powered by twin 235-horsepower outboards. The men were wearing expensive clothes and had layers of gold chains around their necks. *Shearwater* maneuvered alongside and Cliff Boldan and Chuck Meisner hopped on board the white boat, quickly searching the berthing compartment and collecting residue samples from the deck. More field tests: more purple. Boldan arrested the two smugglers and had them climb on board the cutter. It was 1133.

Shearwater drifted as we tied off the two seized vessels to her transom, enabling Hartsock and me to help with the search and interrogation of the five prisoners. During the search we found clumps of marijuana stuck in the treads of the men's running shoes; even a novice prosecutor could use that to prove that they had been handling large amounts of pot. As it headed for shore, the Customs aircrew radioed that they had taken photos of both vessels dumping bales, more compelling evidence for the courtroom.

I climbed the exterior ladder to the bridge, where the captain and Senior Chief were clowning around, offering broad smiles and high fives. Lieutenant Justice grabbed my hand with both of his and pumped it hard, crowing over our good luck, thrilled by the moment. The captain had shown nerves of steel. I asked him when *Shearwater* had intended to turn away from the head-on collision, and he said he had just given the order for right full rudder when the white go-fast stopped. "Damn, XO, I think we just scared the hell out of them, don't you?" he asked rhetorically. I couldn't have agreed more.

Shearwater steamed back onto the bank, the two seized vessels in tow, to recover the bales tossed by the white go-fast. After that it was a six-hour trip across the Florida Straits to Miami, Red Crew's morale sky-high and our captain in the clouds. By sundown we were at the Gator Den, toasting the improbable nature of our success—running down two faster smugglers and using the first go-fast to capture the second. No one knew if that had been done before, so we assumed that we'd broken new ground and established bragging rights. Red Crew was on a roll.

————

Three nights later, *Shearwater* was steaming southwest along the Keys, eighty miles from home and hours from a mid-patrol break. We were still on the prowl. Jerry Lober had burned into our minds the motto "never waste a minute under way"—a sentiment that our new captain fully embraced. In the Florida Straits, the next high-interest boarding, rescue, or migrant intercept could be just over the horizon.

Patrolling south of the reef line at night was nerve-wracking, like a rabbit crossing a highway, as the cutter dodged a steady stream of tankers, freighters, and cruise ships following the arc of the Keys. The northbound vessels stayed five to ten miles offshore, using the power of the Gulf Stream to add a few knots, with the southbound ships hugging the shallows a mile off the reef, north of the prevailing current.

In more desolate areas we usually patrolled dark, without navigation lights, but here the constant presence of merchant and cruise ships made it a terrible idea. It wasn't just a collision that we had to worry about. Six months earlier we'd been steaming along the reef line, dark, when a bright spotlight lit up our pilothouse. We'd been intercepted by a U.S. Customs go-fast, whose crew had seen us running without lights and thought we were a smuggler. Lesson learned.

At midnight, tired of playing dodgeball with the merchants, the captain changed plans. We'd swing south toward Cay Sal, look for smugglers headed north from the Bahamas, and then zip back to Key West.

I was sleeping when the phone rang at 0125. Senior Chief was on the line, almost breathless. "You've got to hear this, XO, we have a cruise ship that thinks it's found a doper." I hustled up to the pilothouse to hear Senior Chief talking on the VHF radio: "Motor vessel *Nordic Prince*, this is the U.S. Coast Guard cutter, please repeat your position. Over." The captain pulled me aside and gave the lowdown. *Nordic Prince* was alongside a disabled fishing vessel, and the people on it were tossing bales over the side. Senior Chief plotted the coordinates and saw that the disabled boat was only twenty miles away, northeast of Dog Rocks. He pushed home the throttles. Full speed ahead.

The weather was getting ugly as we arrived on scene, with a strong line of thunderstorms five miles off and headed our way, lowering visibility and freshening the breeze. Off our bow, the outline of the cruise ship was as distinct as day: she was a massive vessel, lit from stem to stern with thousands of lights, a solitary city on a dark sea. Behind her was the black void of the approaching squall, lightning shimmering high in the clouds.

When we were a mile away, Senior Chief slowed *Shearwater* to twelve knots. The cruise ship's master spoke to us in a strong Scandinavian accent: "Coast Guard, thank you for coming. We found this vessel drifting an hour ago and provided some supplies, and then saw they were throwing packages in the water. We witnessed at least eight packages being thrown." Senior Chief thanked the master and obtained contact info for *Nordic Prince*, and then released the cruise ship to resume her voyage.

I briefed the boarding party on the port bridge wing as *Shearwater* closed on the forty-foot lobster boat. The captain ran through the pre-boarding questions over the radio.

"Fishing vessel *Mabelu*, this is the U.S. Coast Guard vessel that has you in its spotlight, channel 16, come in and shift to channel 22. Over."

Silence. Then, a gruff reply: "Yeah, Coast Guard, this is *Mabelu*, channel 22, what do you need?"

"*Mabelu*, this is the Coast Guard, please describe the nature of your distress."

"Yeah, um, we broke down, but I think we can fix the problem. Our fuel pump died, but the guys from the cruise ship gave us some parts, and we have plenty of battery. We're good—no need for any help."

"*Mabelu*, thank you. What was your last port-of-call?"

"Uh, Islamorada. We were fishing, but our engine died and we've been drifting for a couple hours. I think we can get it fixed, though, so we won't need a tow."

"Roger, sir, what's your next port-of-call, and how many people are on board?"

"Coast Guard, it's just me and one other guy, and we're heading back to Islamorada tomorrow."

"Roger, understand two people on board. Please muster yourself and your crew on the fantail in plain sight. A Coast Guard boarding party will be arriving shortly."

A jagged bolt of lightning streaked across the sky, followed by a thick growl of thunder. Before heading to the boat deck, I glanced at the radar screen. To the northeast was the large blip of the departing cruise ship, headed toward Miami, and just to our west was a heavy band of green. The storm was almost on top of us. As the boarding party climbed down the Jacob's ladder into the RHIB, we felt the first fat drops of rain. Halfway to *Mabelu*, the skies opened up like a carwash, instantly drenching. At least the rain was warm.

Thick clouds blotted out the stars. The only lights visible were the bright beam of *Shearwater*'s spotlight and the specter of *Nordic Prince*, fading rapidly, obscured by sheets of rain, a vanishing ghost. The fishing boat was totally dark, but we could see two men standing amidships, underneath the cabin roof, silhouetted in the spotlight beam.

Mabelu was a typical lobster boat, with the pilothouse forward and the roof extending aft to cover the working area. The roof didn't run all the way to the stern—a design that left the aftermost three feet of deck open to the elements. The boat's name was crudely lettered across her transom, the homeport of Miami stenciled underneath. *Mabelu* was grubby, her white hull marred with black soot and rust streaming down from around the pilothouse windows. I climbed over the boat's transom, followed quickly by Chad Weatherby and a two-man sweep team.

It was quarter after two in the morning, and a stray thought flashed through my mind: who else had the pleasure of boarding a suspect smuggling boat, in the eye of a thunderstorm, fifty miles from shore, in the middle of the night? The Coast Guard provided a decent paycheck, but hell—I'd have done this for free.

I approached the master. He was middle-aged and thin, with chunky cheeks and a Yasser Arafat scrub of beard, and had the same look on his face as a three-year-old caught stealing candy. The photo on the green card that he presented as identification showed a clean-shaven visage under his name.

"Sir, we're here to inspect your vessel for compliance with all applicable U.S. laws. What's the purpose of your voyage?"

"Uh, we're lobster fishing. Our boat broke down, but we're going to head back home once we have it fixed." I scanned the deck, seeing no fishing gear, no traps, no lines. The rain intensified, pummeling the roof like a drum.

"Sir, I need to see the vessel's documentation. Is it handy?"

"Sorry, we don't have papers with us. I think we left them in Islamorada."

"Where's your fishing gear, and how much ice do you have on board?"

He hesitated. "We lost all our traps in a storm, and I think most of our ice has melted." I gave him a look that said: "What a load of crap."

"How much lobster do you have on board?"

More hesitation. "Uh, we ate most of the catch. I think they're all gone."

I normally hated liars, but this guy wasn't even a good one.

"What were you throwing over the side when the cruise ship spotted you?" I asked.

"Um, we didn't do that. I think he was looking at another boat that was here a little while ago. They left right before you got here. It wasn't us throwing anything."

Enough was enough. "Sir, I need you and your crew to step aft and sit on the railing, over there." I pointed to the transom, which was being pelted by the monsoon. "Please keep your hands in plain sight." The master gave me a death stare, incredulous, and walked aft, the rain instantly soaking him. His shipmate joined him in the deluge. Neither of them looked particularly happy. Senior Chief told me later that it was a moment for the XO hall of fame.

Our security team made a quick sweep of the vessel, finding the boat empty of other people or obvious signs of contraband. They reported two oversized fuel tanks in the engine room. I walked toward the pilothouse, along the starboard side, and felt my foot stick to the deck. Huh? It was as though I'd stepped onto a monster-sized wad of gum. I lifted my leg, leaving a footprint in the blue paint. I bent over and touched the deck, pushing down: the paint was tacky, the deck underneath doughy. Bingo. I looked up and saw the master put his hands over his face, not sure if he was protecting himself from the rain or didn't want to watch the proceedings.

The radio on my hip came to life. "Boarding party, this is *Shearwater*, be advised we've spotted bales floating in the water off your starboard side, about seventy-five feet out. It looks like at least three packages. We'll have the small boat retrieve them as soon as you're ready. Over." I told *Shearwater* that we had the situation under control and that the RHIB could start recovering the bales any time.

I continued to examine the deck. The wet paint covered about two feet square, near the starboard rail, fifteen feet forward of the transom. Weatherby found a second soft patch on the opposite side of the deck. I unfolded my knife and pushed it straight down into the edge of the doughy area. It penetrated an inch. I probed with the knife again, then again, moving it outboard by a quarter-inch every time. There—the knife slid into the deck up to its hilt. I began sawing with the blade, guessing that the knife was in a groove between the original deck and a hatch that had been covered with putty. I sawed in a straight line until the blade hit resistance, and then turned the knife 90 degrees, cutting for another two feet. After sawing all the way around the square, I tried to use the blade to pry up the hatch. It didn't budge.

Bright blue paint covered my hands and coveralls. *Crap*, I thought. I'd just bought these. On the port side, Weatherby was using a screwdriver to pry up the putty in small chunks. I looked at him and cussed out loud. Somehow, he had managed to keep his uniform clean. I pulled a crowbar out of the boarding kit and jammed it into the gap in the deck, popping loose the hidden hatch cover. Back on the stern, the master and his crew sat in the rain, long-faced and dripping.

Tossing aside the hatch cover, I shined my flashlight into the hole. I could see straight down into a large, empty fuel tank, three feet wide, four feet top to bottom, and twelve feet long. There was a strong stench of bulk marijuana, and the bottom of the tank was littered with chunks of leafy material and stringy shreds of burlap. Weatherby held onto the back of my coveralls and I slid down into the tank, holding my breath while scooping up clumps of residue. I stuck my head up out of the hatch before taking a breath; the last thing I wanted to do was take in the air from the confined space. I climbed back on deck, and Weatherby popped the hatch on the port fuel tank, which also was empty, and then tested the residue with a drug kit. No surprise. The reagents turned bright purple.

Captain Justice agreed that we had enough evidence for prosecution, and I seized the vessel and arrested the crew. The master gave me a cold, wet stare as we snapped on the cuffs. Most likely *Mabelu* had broken down carrying its load of pot, and when the cruise ship stumbled across them, the smugglers had panicked and tossed the load, and then tried to cover up the crime by patching and painting the deck.

The coxswain shuttled the prisoners to *Shearwater* as Weatherby and I conducted an in-depth search of the vessel, seeking additional evidence. There were no charts and no documents, but we did find a can of blue paint and a gummy paintbrush. The captain called and told us the small boat had recovered four bales, each fifty pounds. The bales had been floating within thirty yards of *Mabelu* and were fresh, not yet saturated with salt water. Good enough. We headed back to the cutter to start the paperwork as Dan Sanders and deck force prepared for a tow. Within an hour we were headed to Key West, with *Mabelu* streaming four hundred yards astern and the two prisoners shackled to the chairs in *Shearwater's* main deck passageway, their sodden clothes replaced by dry paper coveralls and warm blankets. It was almost daybreak.

We'd worked through the night, but no one cared. Red Crew had made three drug busts in the past four days, and eight in the past six months. I remembered the long days after commissioning *Petrel*, when we'd worked our tails off but couldn't buy a seizure. Now we were riding high, at the top of our game. And with the help of the good people on *Nordic Prince* we'd placed two more smugglers into custody, taking them off the street and notching another small victory in the endless war on drugs. For that, it was worth losing a little sleep and trashing a new pair of coveralls.

———

During our mid-patrol break one of the electronics technicians from the division staff gave me a strange gift—a part from one of the ship's radars. He'd been walking down the pier when he bumped into me, a purely random encounter. I asked about the anonymous gray box and jumble of wires cradled in his arms. "It's a magnetron," he explained. "It uses a really strong magnet to steer the electron beam inside the radar. A connector burned out and I had to replace the whole unit." He pulled a periwinkle blue object out of the gray box, a thick, U-shaped magnet, three inches wide. "Hey, you want this? It's kinda cool." The ET said he was going to throw out the magnet unless someone took it.

Hell, yes—I wanted it! The magnet would make a great conversation piece. I walked to my office in the division compound, put it on my desk, and tossed a handful of paperclips at it. The clips snapped onto the magnet in a volley of sharp clacks. Dang, it had pull. On a whim, I threw the magnet into my underway kit, figuring it could keep pens and other metal odds and ends from sliding around my desk on the ship.

That night we shoved off for the second half of the patrol. The weather was perfect, with a microscopic swell and a feathery breeze, and we headed toward the Cuban coast. We carried out one routine boarding, a sailboat, over the next two days. Lieutenant Justice became antsy, thirsty for action, but as was his way, kept a positive vibe, telling me, "Don't worry, XO, we'll find one tonight—I can feel it." We'd been lurking west of Cay Sal, and now the OOD steered *Shearwater* closer to shore, to patrol twenty miles south of the Keys.

At five in the morning the captain woke me from a sound sleep, calling on the ship's telephone. "XO, get up," he said. "We're coming up on an unlit boat, dead in the water. We might have a mothership here." I pulled on my pants and boots and ran to the pilothouse, tucking in my shirt. The captain and OOD were huddled on the bridge wing, night vision scope in hand. The lookout pointed to the radar, which showed a blip a mile ahead of us, solid but compact—the right size for a lobster boat. Outside, the night was clear, and we couldn't see any light in the direction of the contact. In the night scope, a hazy object bobbed in the swell. It looked like a western-rig shrimper, probably sixty feet long. It seemed too big a boat to generate such a modest radar return.

In a conspiratorial whisper the captain asked: why would a shrimper be sitting dead in the water and unlit in the middle of the Florida Straits? This had to be a smuggler. The OOD called the duty engineer and had him wake the boarding team. I'd be the boarding officer, with MK1 Pat George as my assistant and two others as the sweep team. George had just joined Red Crew to replace Cliff Boldan, who'd been promoted to chief petty officer and was awaiting a new set of orders. I'd be helping George refresh his law enforcement qualifications during this and other boardings.

We changed into our boarding uniforms and broke out the weapons, locking and loading as the cutter slowly crept toward the darkened boat. Now only a half-mile away, we still saw no lights, no movement. The captain considered waiting to see if other vessels showed up, but with sunrise only an hour away, he decided it would be better to board the mothership—if that's what it was—before her crew saw us. Once our boarding team was fully dressed and the small boat was ready to launch, *Shearwater* picked up speed and headed directly for the shrimper.

We pounced. At 150 yards the OOD brought the cutter to all stop and lit up the shrimper with the spotlight, hailing the boat on channel 16. There was no answer, and for good reason—the boat appeared to be a derelict, riding low in the water and rolling sluggishly in the mild swell. She was an old wooden fishing boat, with a two-story pilothouse forward and no outriggers, nets, or antennas visible. The low freeboard and lack of metal appendages explained the weak radar return.

The boat was bigger than we had thought, closer to seventy feet. *Shearwater* circled the shrimper to inspect her from every angle. There seemed to be no people on board. There were faded numbers on the superstructure and a name on the stern—it appeared to be a Spanish word, written in a swirling cursive script—but it was so faded that it was impossible to read. We suspected that she was an abandoned fishing boat from Cuba or Central America, broken free of her moorings and swept north in the Gulf Stream. Our hopes for a drug bust faded. The captain decided that we'd board the vessel anyway to look for signs of life. Then, if the boat were a derelict, we'd sink it as a hazard to navigation.

We launched the RHIB just as dawn began to break. It was a stunningly beautiful morning, a vision of paradise, with small whitish-pink cumulus clouds drifting overhead in the growing light, the dark azure sky slowly brightening. The light swell rocked the shrimper gently, but the boat had a sluggish, lurchy roll, as if it were heavily overloaded, reminding me of *Gulf Express'* lumbering propane barge. The boat's main deck was only a foot above the water, and occasionally a larger swell would push through the scuppers and wash across the deck. The period of the boat's roll was abnormally long, a sure sign of instability.

This was dangerous. We were boarding a decrepit, waterlogged boat that could capsize or sink without warning. Even with our life jackets, the suction that would be created if the vessel went under could take us with it. I didn't want to relive Jim Sartucci's nightmare on *Owl and the Pussycat*, so I decided we'd make a quick sweep of the vessel, confirm that there were no people, and then hustle back to the safety of the cutter.

The boarding team climbed on board, gingerly. The sweep team checked the aft compartments, peering into them from the main deck, while MK1 George and I headed forward, climbing six steps to a compact bridge wing. We looked inside the pilothouse, discovering an eerie world. The bridge was completely gutted, with no equipment, chart desk, seats, or electronics of any kind. Even the ship's wheel was gone. We stepped inside, my weapons belt snagging on a broken doorframe. On the aft bulkhead of the pilothouse was a doorway that led below to the berthing areas and galley, but we couldn't inspect those spaces because the ladder down to them had been ripped out.

I shined my flashlight aft into the passageway between the berthing compartments. It was totally dark and completely empty, devoid of equipment, clothing, personal effects, or other signs of human activity. The boat had been stripped clean of everything and anything of value. Even the light fixtures were gone. The scene was haunting, like being on board a ghost ship. Despite the cloying air, I suppressed a shiver.

MK1 George and I walked back to the main deck, with only the main fishhold left to inspect. The six-by-six-foot hatch cover was missing, allowing us to peer directly down into the hold. It was the largest compartment on the boat, probably twelve feet wide, twenty feet long, and ten feet deep, and typically would be filled with ice to keep the vessel's catch fresh. The sun had almost broken the horizon, and there was enough light to see that instead of the usual ice the hold was filled with sludgy, black water, eight or nine feet deep. The sweep team said the aft compartments were also pressed full. That explained the lethargic roll of the boat: she was flooded, stem to stern.

The four of us stood around the open hatch, peering into the nasty muck below. The water in the hold seemed to be covered with a thick layer of goopy oil, and there were small clumpy particles floating in it, about the size of peas. A few of the small clumps looked like plant residue. Wait a second, I thought: were those buds of marijuana? Maybe this boat had been used for smuggling before being stripped clean. Maybe this was a law enforcement case after all.

The surface of the oily water was two feet below the lip of the hold, and I bent down to take a closer look. I still couldn't identify the clumps. I bent farther, leaning forward as far as possible, thinking of a way to scoop up some of the particles to run a field test for THC. Then *splash!*

What was that? Something had fallen into the hold. I looked up at MK1 George. His face was ashen, frozen with surprise. So were those of the sweep team. George was staring at me and pointed feebly toward my waist. It couldn't be. I felt my weapons belt, making sure that the equipment was secure. Flashlight, handcuffs, pepper spray, ammo clips— all good. What was George pointing at? Wait—I moved my hand to the holster on my left hip. Where the hell was my .45? George pointed down into the murk, and I realized that my gun had fallen from its holster into the oily mix. The holster snap must have popped loose when I snagged the door frame entering the pilothouse.

I fell to one knee as the weight of the situation sank in. My .45 was at the bottom of the fishhold, under eight feet of turgid oily water brew, on board an unstable derelict vessel, fifty miles from the nearest port. What a mess. I sighed out loud. I'd lost my service pistol, one of the military's cardinal sins, and there was no way to get it back. This was not going to go over well. I radioed *Shearwater* and briefed the captain. He remained calm, albeit with a frosty edge to his voice. He had to be furious, but he was professional enough not to let off steam in front of the crew.

The captain asked for a description of the hold—was there a ladder to climb down into it? No, it had been removed. Could someone swim down to retrieve the gun? Not without dying of sludge poisoning or getting snagged on an obstruction. Could we tow the boat to Key West and pump out the water? No way—the wasted boat couldn't withstand the strain of a tow. As we brainstormed, George began looping together a set of flexible handcuffs, rigging a makeshift grapple to try and snag the pistol. I knew it wouldn't work, since the gun would be impossible to lasso, but it was our only option. I resigned myself to spending the next few hours fishing for the pistol and then giving up in shame, only to face a mountain of paperwork and a wedge of embarrassment for my crew.

Then, something sparked in the back of my mind: The magnetron. What were the odds? I'd never owned a powerful magnet, but the day before this very sortie I'd been given one on a whim. And what had prompted me to take it under way? I never took extra gear to sea; it'd be just another thing to pack up and lug on board. Now, it seemed that the planets were aligning. I radioed back to *Shearwater* and had the quartermaster retrieve the magnet from my desk, along with twenty feet of shotline. The coxswain whisked them to the shrimper. Damn, there was even a hole drilled through the center of the magnet. How convenient! I passed the shotline through the hole, tied a bowline, and dipped the magnet into the hold. The boarding team stood around the hatch, not breathing as I lowered the line through the muck, five feet down, six feet, seven. This might take a while, but now there was a real chance to recover the gun.

Snap! The magnet jumped as it clamped onto something. I pulled up the line, slowly at first, and then more quickly. I thought there was no way it was the gun, especially on the first try, and that it had to be a piece of debris. George crossed his fingers. I kept pulling. The magnet broke the oily surface, the .45 firmly attached, dripping blobs of sludge. The grin on George's face was so wide that I thought he'd swallow his ears. One of the sweep team guys gave a shout. I said a few very bad words and then radioed *Shearwater*. Across the water, I could hear Captain Justice say some very bad words of his own. The .45 was safe, and we weren't going to have to waste half a day trying to recover it. We could get back to Coast Guard business, and I was off the hook for all that paperwork. It sure was a beautiful morning.

We headed back to the cutter and focused on sinking the derelict vessel. From *Shearwater*'s bridge wing, our gunners pumped hundreds of M-60 rounds into it, with no discernable effect. We broke out the .50-caliber, firing from the port bow, and ran through two full ammo belts before calling a cease-fire. The shrimper was so waterlogged that the holes didn't make a difference. She rolled sluggishly, taunting us. We tried setting her ablaze with a few buckets of gasoline and a flare, but the wood was too wet to maintain a flame. The derelict simply wasn't going to die. She would sink when she was good and ready.

After the thrill of shooting machine guns and setting fires had devolved into drudgery, the OOD reported the derelict's position to Group Key West, and *Shearwater* headed back on patrol. I sat in my stateroom and lovingly cleaned my .45. The sludge gave it a unique sheen, and it probably was the best-oiled small arm in the fleet.

That magnet became my good-luck charm, and it stayed with me for the rest of my career. But it didn't bring good luck to everyone. More than one person, while playing with the magnet, would pry it loose and then get his or her finger pinched as it snapped back onto a metal surface. One friend waved it too close to his wallet and wiped clean the magnetic strips on his credit cards. And a few years later, a shipmate would make the unfortunate mistake of picking it up and holding it near his groin: even through the thickness of his uniform, the metal clamps inserted into his nether region during his recent vasectomy were drawn to the magnet—quickly, and with force—and he had a hell of a time prying them loose.

I had never been a believer in fate, but the magnetron incident changed that. Without the chance encounter that had led to the magnet being handed to me, my .45 would have stayed on board the derelict vessel, adrift at sea. Losing the weapon would've put a black mark on my service record and, in the make-no-mistakes culture of the Coast Guard, would have hurt, if not crippled, my chances for promotion and future command. Fortunately, luck found me first and cemented my belief that sometimes good things happen but for no worldly reason.

7

Seeing It All

June 1984

Two days later, Red Crew was finishing up the patrol, steaming south-east of Anguilla Cay. Since the encounter with the derelict we'd gone without a boarding, and Lieutenant Justice was spring-loaded for action. When *Shearwater* came across a forty-foot lobster boat headed southeast, the captain decided to board her, even though she was steaming in the wrong direction. You never knew what you'd find in this stretch of water.

Macabi was a typical Keys-based lobster boat, white-hulled and well maintained. I led the boarding team, introducing myself to the master, Narciso Perez-Caro of Miami. Perez-Caro was in his sixties, weathered and rugged, with curly silver hair and a stubbly gray beard, looking like a rougher version of Hemingway. I took an instant dislike to him. He bossed around his two-man crew with an angry arrogance and answered my questions with a sneer. Our sweep team reported nothing out of the ordinary except for oversized fuel tanks, just as we'd seen a week earlier in what Red Crew now proudly called our "cruise-ship seizure."

It didn't make sense for *Macabi* to be carrying a load of dope, since she was headed away from the States. If anything, Perez-Caro seemed to be challenging us to find something wrong with his boat. He gave a reasonable story, saying they were headed around the eastern end of Cuba, bound for Jamaica, where they'd be fishing for the next month. During the compliance inspection we saw plenty of supplies to support his claim. Still, something didn't seem right. My instincts said "trouble." After the compliance inspection I slid down the hatch into the engine room to take a closer look at the boat's twin fuel tanks.

Damn, they were big. Filled with diesel, this boat could pull a Magellan. The tanks were nearly flush with the deck above them, with a layer of insulating foam along the top, making it impossible to see their upper surfaces. The foam seemed unnecessary and out of place. Fireman Elliot and I crawled through the bilge, methodically inspecting the vertical faces of the tanks, trying to find an entryway where drugs could be hidden.

Elliot traced the fuel lines from the engine and saw that they were attached to the forward end of the tanks. Nothing out of place there, I thought. But there was a seam welded into the side of each tank, three feet aft of where the fuel hoses were connected, and it was ground down and polished as if it were meant to be unobtrusive. We'd never seen that before. Were the tanks segregated, carrying fuel in their forward sections and empty aft, where a few thousand pounds of pot could be hidden? Customs recently had seized another boat rigged like that. Elliot did some rough calculations and figured *Macabi* would have plenty of diesel fuel to get to Jamaica, even if she were drawing just from the forward third of the tanks.

I rapped my flashlight along the inboard face of the port tank. If the tank were uniformly hollow, without any internal modifications, the sound would be consistent along the entire length. To my ear, the tapping produced a deeper, duller tone forward of the welded seam. That was another clue.

We climbed back on deck. Elliot unscrewed the caps of the fuel fills and lowered a flexible steel measuring tape into each pipe. Both tanks were almost topped off with diesel—at least in their forward part. There was no way to check if the fuel ran all the way aft. I examined the main deck above the fuel tanks, looking closely at the fiberglass for any imperfections or signs of a hidden hatch, as we'd seen on other seizures. The deck was worn, with dirt ground into the fading blue paint. If there was a patched-over hatch, it was camouflaged by the grime.

Elliot and I reviewed the facts. Hefty tanks. Unnecessary insulation hiding the upper tank surfaces. Unusual welds. Inconsistent tone. The suspicions piled up: I hypothesized that there were hidden openings on the main deck leading down into the aft sections of each tank. We needed to look further.

I called the captain to talk through the evidence. He agreed that the tanks were suspicious, and we considered the options. We could drill a series of holes in the deck, hoping to find a hatch, but without knowing where to start that could make a pretty big mess. More surgically, we could drill a single hole into the aft end of one of the tanks and inspect it with a borescope. I recommended the second option, and the captain gave us his blessing.

The coxswain delivered an access kit from *Shearwater*, which included a battery-powered drill equipped with a carbide steel bit. Elliot and I climbed down into the engine room and crawled around the back end of the port tank. I picked a spot at eye level, about eight inches below the top of the tank. By drilling high on the aft face, we'd run less of a risk of hitting fuel if the tank actually were in use. Elliot handed me safety goggles and I put them on, sliding my glasses into the front pocket of my coveralls.

The engine room was stifling hot, and sweat was pouring down my face when I pulled the trigger and leaned into the drill. The carbide bit dug into the aluminum, spewing out a waterfall of shavings. A thin spiral of metal emerged from the hole, encircling the whirring bit. The bit broke through the quarter-inch metal plating, and I pulled it back, already thinking of inserting the borescope.

Almost instantly, a thin, pressurized stream of diesel fuel shot out of the hole, hitting me on the cheek and splashing in all directions, down the front of my coveralls, into the air, and onto Elliot. The safety glasses saved my eyes, but I learned the bitter taste of diesel. Startled, I jammed my thumb over the hole, staunching the flow. I wiped the diesel off my face with my free hand, the fuel stinging where it hit some razor burn, and spit repeatedly into the bilge to clear my mouth. Elliot dug into the access kit and found a wooden plug, which he tapped into the hole, sawing it off flush with the tank surface. What an embarrassment. Not only had my theory proven wrong, but I'd damaged the boat and trashed another pair of coveralls. At least this pair could be salvaged.

Elliot and I hoisted ourselves back onto the main deck, stinking to high heaven of diesel. Trying not to blush, I explained to Perez-Caro that we'd drilled a hole into the tank, described the exact location, and assured him that the plug should hold long enough for him to make a permanent repair. He was simmering and demanded the claim forms, saying he'd seek reimbursement from the Coast Guard, his surly attitude ramped up to a new level.

Boarding complete, we headed back to *Shearwater*. As usual, Lieutenant Justice thanked us for our work, venturing a guess that the boat and crew were dirty, but we just hadn't caught 'em at the right time. I skulked below to clean up.

Like the boarding, the patrol ended quietly—no law enforcement, no search and rescue, no migrant cases. We sped home across calm waters to enjoy our status as the only crew with two multi-boat seizures. Red Crew had proven itself under two captains, each with his own style, but each equally successful. If there were a few bumps in the road, or squirts of diesel in the face, it was a fine price to pay to sail with such a team.

————

Twelve days later Red Crew was back on patrol, working our way from Key West to the Old Bahama Channel. The weather was idyllic, with a wispy easterly breeze and seas like a bathtub. We saw a pack of freighters and three cruise ships headed north but nothing of interest, and we continued tracking to the southeast. By the next morning *Shearwater* was south of Andros Island. The captain didn't want to head any farther out, so we diverted to Cayo Lobos, a small island sitting twenty miles north of Cuba. From Cayo Lobos we could monitor the deep-water shipping lanes to our south and the Great Bahama Bank to our north. And for morale, we'd drop the anchor and enjoy some fishing, maybe even snag some grouper for the grill.

Cayo Lobos was quintessentially Bahamian, a roughly hewn hole-in-the-wall. A mile-wide, uninhabited, sandy oval, the island sported a grove of scrubby trees and a tall, decrepit lighthouse at its center. The light, built in 1869, was still active, although the structure was severely weathered and in disrepair. The brilliant blue waters surrounding the island were shallow out to two miles from shore; on the south side, they then dropped precipitously into the cobalt depths of the Old Bahama Channel.

Senior Chief and the captain squirmed over the chart, looking for the best fishing hole, and found a spot just outside of Bahamian territory, on the edge of the channel. There, the boatswain's mates threw *Shearwater*'s anchor over the side, and Pat George shut down the engines. The water was 120 feet deep, the perfect habitat for the really big grouper. Whistling, the captain headed aft to try his luck, followed by Senior Chief, Meisner, and Elliot—the core of Red Crew's fishing mafia. I took a nap.

Neither the fishing nor the nap lasted very long. I'd just fallen asleep when the OOD, Dan Sanders, called on the phone. "XO, we have a westbound boat, about six miles away and closing. Looks like a small fisherman. I told the captain and he said to get under way and intercept. You've got the next boarding, so I wanted you to have a heads-up."

Great, a hot target. I climbed up to the bridge and studied the boat in the "big eyes"—white hull, about forty feet, lobster rig, throwing a wake and making good speed, maybe twenty knots. The boat was steaming on the shallows of the bank, a few miles north of Cayo Lobos, avoiding the merchant traffic in the ship channel to its south.

We weighed anchor and *Shearwater* headed north for the intercept. Three miles away, Senior Chief joked that the boat looked like the one I'd drilled, rubbing salt in the wound. "Hey, XO, maybe this time you can poke a few holes in its bilge," he said. Very funny, I thought. At two miles away, I began to think he was right. At one mile, it was confirmed: on the transom, in bold blue lettering, was *F/V Macabi*, and in smaller letters underneath, "Key West, Florida." It took Lieutenant Justice less than a microsecond to decide that we'd go on board and see why the boat that was supposed to be spending a month in Jamaica was already heading home.

Our preboarding questions found that nothing had changed. Narciso Perez-Caro was still the master, and the same two crew members were on board. Perez-Caro was agitated, on the verge of hostile, and made it clear he didn't want to stop for a second boarding in two weeks. "Hey, you guys were just on this boat, I'm in a hurry to get home," he radioed. He said they'd had some engine problems and decided to cut short the trip to Jamaica. After more haggling, the vessel hove to, and our boarding team climbed on board, cautiously eying the three men and again checking their IDs.

The safety sweep took only a few minutes—nothing found—so I set out to see if there were any alterations to the fuel tanks, which we knew were the only space on the boat where a large load of drugs could be hidden. I slid down through the hatch into the engine room, spider-crawling toward the transom. There, at the aft end of the port tank, was Elliot's wooden plug, still in place, not leaking a drop. Everything else looked undisturbed, exactly as we'd seen it twelve days earlier.

I climbed out of the hatch and looked closer at the main deck, viewing it from different angles. The deck looked crisp, with only the slightest bit of weathering. I didn't remember it looking this fresh. Hadn't it been grubby and worn two weeks ago? Maybe they'd scrubbed it down, washing away the grime and fish guts that could accumulate on a working boat. I paced slowly down the port side, trying to see any sign of a patch job hiding an entryway into the top of the fuel tank below. The entire aft deck was uniform and undisturbed.

Walking forward, I crouched on one knee and titled my head closer to the deck, like a golfer lining up a putt, my chin only two feet above the blue-painted fiberglass. The sun was low in the sky, and at that angle it cast shadows that exaggerated the slight ridges and imperfections on the seemingly flat surface. I scanned slowly, looking for anything unusual. Nothing. There were ribs in the deck where the fiberglass was slightly warped from the structural beams underneath, but that was normal. I stood up and moved to the starboard side, scanning again, even more slowly, as *Macabi* rolled gently in the placid sea. The deck was solid, unblemished. I took three steps toward the bow, dipping low for a final look.

Wait. There, on the port side, was a minuscule rise, an almost imperceptible hump in the deck. The lobster boat rolled to starboard and the hump disappeared, then became visible again, just barely, when *Macabi* listed again to port, the size of the hump oscillating with the boat's side-to-side motion. Was it an illusion? The hump was completely invisible when viewed from above and could be seen only from a lower vantage point, with the sun at a certain angle.

I asked Chuck Meisner, the assisting boarding officer, to take a look. At first he didn't notice anything, but then, on his hands and knees, he picked out the raised area. He began rapping the deck with the butt of his flashlight, moving from the centerline outward, toward the slight hump. The retorts were sharp and crisp, like miniature rifle shots, but when he got to the elevated spot the sounds became slightly muffled. Very slightly. What would cause the sound to change? Maybe the foam insulation on top of the fuel tank created a different echo. Or maybe the deck in that spot had been replaced with putty or new fiberglass to hide an access point into the tank below. We had to find out.

Meisner began tapping around the periphery of the hump, inboard and outboard, fore and aft. The sound was consistently sharp except for a two-foot square, right at the hump. I asked Perez-Caro if the deck had been repaired. He said no, that everything was the same since our last boarding, only they'd added a skim coat of paint to cover up the dirt, since he hoped to sell the boat when they got back home. Meisner and I walked to the transom. I spoke in a low murmur, my back to the fishing boat's crew. "Chuck, what do you think? That spot looks like it's been repaired, and they repainted the deck to cover up the work." He nodded and said: "That's what I think, too. And hey, did you see the master tense up when I started tapping? His nonverbals were through the roof." I hadn't caught that. Meisner was a great judge of people, so if he said the master was getting nervous, it was a guarantee. Time to talk with our captain.

I spoke with Lieutenant Justice over the comms headset, letting him know that we suspected a repair job in the deck right above the fuel tank. With that and Perez-Caro's nervous reaction, we had enough suspicion to perform a limited search. I gave the bottom line. "Sir," I said, "we're going to have to drill a few holes and see if there's a hatch underneath that spot in the deck. The master won't be happy, but we know where to search, so it won't be a wild-goose chase. There's definitely something going on here." Justice said he didn't care about pissing off the master and gave the go-ahead to drill.

I told Perez-Caro that we'd be poking a few small exploratory holes in the deck. Like triggering a switch, he became livid, his creased, tanned face turning beet red, his eyes narrowing. He started cursing, spittle flying, vowing to get me fired for harassment and sued for illegally damaging his boat, his property, his livelihood. I asked him to remain calm and not to impede the boarding, or else he'd find himself in cuffs. His voice got louder, more intense, so I cut him off mid-rant, and in my bossiest voice ordered him and his crew to move to the bow of the vessel, where they'd be out of the way and more easily controlled by our security team.

Perez-Caro stopped talking and stared at me, clenching and unclenching his fists, a vein pulsing in his neck. I thought he was going to throw a punch. My right hand instinctively grabbed for my flashlight, and I tensed to deflect the blow. Perez-Caro just stared, seething. Then, abruptly, he turned on his heel and climbed around the pilothouse to the bow. His shipmates followed, casting angry stares our way. Fistfight averted. Now we could get to work.

Macabi was rolling lazily, a soft breeze coursing over her decks, sunset approaching. It was perfect weather for a pleasure cruise—or for an intrusive search. Meisner handled the drill. He made five marks on the deck, eight inches apart, laterally across the suspected patch job. Revving up the drill, he pressed the bit into the deck at the first mark. He pulled out the drill and then moved to the second spot, repeating the process four more times. "These three," he said, pointing at the second, third, and fourth holes. "The drill went in a lot harder here." We examined the shavings from the five holes, and saw differences in color and consistency. The shavings for the three holes Meisner had identified included a chalky material, as if he'd drilled into fiberglass body-filler. Meisner drilled another hole near the three suspicious ones, and as he withdrew the bit it seized on the decking. As he tugged on the drill, the deck underneath distorted, an area the size of a dinner plate deflecting upward a quarter of an inch, as though a fiberglass patch were being pulled off the deck. Definitely a repair job.

We'd have to cut a hole a few inches across to see what was underneath the patch. I called back to *Shearwater* and asked them to deliver a coping saw. As I was talking, Meisner took a hammer from the boarding kit.

"Hey," he said, "while we're waiting, how about we try a little brute force?" I nodded and he smacked the deck, striking the edge of the suspected patch. *Whack*. Nothing happened. *Whack*. Again, nothing. *Whack*. The deck cracked, the edge of the nearly invisible hump peeling upward an eighth of an inch. The crack was five inches long.

Meisner looked at me, surprised that his caveman method had worked. He struck again. *Whack*. The crack widened. He shifted his aim a foot to the left, hitting even harder. *Whack*. A slab of fiberglass patching material ten inches wide bent upward. Meisner slid a crowbar underneath it and lifted. The patch began peeling up, revealing a glint of metal. I shined my flashlight into the crack and saw the aluminum top of the fuel tank six inches below, along with the head of a bolt. Meisner crammed the crowbar further underneath the fiberglass, lifting harder, ripping the patch part way from the deck. Three bolts and the corner of a metal plate were now visible. Hallelujah—we'd found a hidden entrance into the tank.

The coxswain delivered the coping saw and Meisner cleaned up the opening in the deck, expanding it to a square eighteen inches across. Beneath the hole was the top of the fuel tank and a rectangular metal covering, held in place by ten half-inch bolts, two on each of the short sides and three on the long ones. Meisner used a socket wrench, and after five minutes of ratcheting he had twisted off all the bolts. He wedged a flathead screwdriver between the access plate and the top of the tank. There was a thin rubber gasket between the two, probably to cut down on odors leaking from the tank, a sign of a high-quality, professional installation. Whoever was making these illicit fuel tanks was a craftsman, no doubt. Meisner lifted the screwdriver, and the plate popped free.

It didn't take a flashlight to see that the fuel tank was filled with dope. Only two inches below the rectangular opening was a burlap-wrapped bale, and the intense odor of the marijuana made both of us gag. For however long the pot had been sitting in the tank, the Caribbean sun and the warmth from the engines had put it into a state of near-fermentation, creating an overpowering stench. I looked forward to see if *Macabi*'s crew was still under control. No problem—they were sitting on the stubby bow, feet dangling over the side. I mouthed "Stand by" to the security team to let them know that arrests were imminent.

But first, the drug test. Meisner reached in and pulled out a bale. It was a miniature package, about a foot square and eight inches deep. He sliced it open, revealing a compact mash of dark, leafy matter. Test positive. I looked back in the hole, trying to estimate how many bales were inside the tank, but couldn't make a rudimentary guess; the bales were so tightly packed that it was impossible to see how far the secret compartment extended. I called *Shearwater* with an update. The captain was gleeful at the news.

Meisner and I walked to the bow and told Perez-Caro and his crew that they were under arrest for drug-smuggling. The master was no longer argumentative, arrogant, or bullying. He complied meekly with our orders, a distant, consigned look on his craggy features. We cuffed and frisked the prisoners. The coxswain transported them to *Shearwater*, where they were shackled to the prisoners' chairs. Meisner and I searched *Macabi* stem to stern, photographing the bale, the secret compartment, and the general layout of the boat, all for the prosecuting attorney's benefit.

Tenderly, wearing latex gloves, Meisner began removing the bales from the tank. We quickly realized that it was the most complex secret compartment that Red Crew had yet encountered. The fuel tank, twelve feet long and forty inches wide, had a smaller tank built inside it, accessible only from the top. Surrounding the inner tank, on all sides, was a buffer of diesel. Anyone in the engine room drilling into the tank would hit fuel. Twelve days earlier, had my drill bit been a foot longer, it would have passed through the fuel and found the wall of the inner tank.

Meisner found a chart that showed that *Macabi* had steamed only as far south as the Ragged Island chain, 120 miles from Cayo Lobos. We surmised that after loading the marijuana they'd carefully rebuilt the deck with the fiberglass patch, then painted the entire deck for consistency. They'd done quality work, and we weren't surprised to learn that one of Perez-Caro's shipmates had been a carpenter in his native Cuba before heading to the United States during the Mariel Boatlift four years earlier.

Later that night I stood on *Shearwater*'s bridge wing, enjoying the smooth ride and soothing weather, the seized vessel in tow astern. This had been another unique case, with an extremely well-hidden compartment.

We'd found the dope, but I wondered: had we been lucky, or good, or a combination of the two? If we hadn't boarded *Macabi* on the southern leg, we wouldn't have seen the difference in the appearance of the deck, one of the clues that led to the discovery of the fiberglass patch. Also, the angle of the sun had been just right for us to see the slight hump, so if we'd boarded *Macabi* earlier in the day, or at night, we could have missed it. There wasn't a clear answer to the lucky-or-good question, so I headed down to the mess deck to grab a snack, a single truth settling in my mind: in the drug-infested waters off South Florida, it was better to board a profile vessel twice than not at all.

Red Crew spent the next day towing *Macabi* to Miami and inventorying the goods. The starboard fuel tank also had a built-in compartment, and the two tanks held ninety-five compact bales, yielding 1,300 pounds of high-grade marijuana. The Customs agents from the South Florida Task Force were impressed with the tanks and took photos to help train their fellow agents on the complexity of the hidden compartments.

When the case went to trial a year later, Perez-Caro and one of his shipmates would be found guilty, sentenced to four years in prison, with three more years suspended. The third crewman wouldn't serve time. He never showed up for trial. Later he was found dead, shot in the head. The drug cartels suffered no fools.

Macabi was an indicator of a troubling trend. The tactics used by the smugglers to hide their contraband were growing more creative and increasingly complex. During every boarding we had to think in three dimensions, conceptualizing every place where drugs could be hidden. Each vessel was different. Each boarding was unique. Fuel tanks, water tanks, crew quarters, underhull compartments—even on a small boat, the possible hiding places were almost endless. The smugglers had really stepped up their game. To win the fight, we'd need to do the same.

———

Later in July my tenure as XO Red took an unexpected twist. Wayne Justice and I were summoned to a private meeting with Commander Council, who explained that the division would be short a commanding officer until Halloween. Blue Crew's new captain, Bob Eccles, had been handpicked for temporary duty in Grenada and would be heading south later in the week. Because Bruce Gaudette, the XO of the Blue Crew, had just reported aboard, Wayne Justice would temporarily shift over to command that crew and provide a bridge of experience. Council smiled. He said that as the most senior executive officer, I'd assume temporary command of Red Crew in Justice's absence. That would give me more than three months acting as captain. I was startled, humbled, and excited beyond belief to have such a golden opportunity so early in my career.

The surge of euphoria lasted only seconds as Council kept talking. "Just so you know, we're going to keep Red Crew on *Shearwater* to handle its yard period this summer," he said. "You'll be taking the cutter up to South Carolina for ten weeks, and then you'll spend another week in Miami for a new radar install. By the time you get back, Mr. Eccles should've returned, and we can give you your old captain back. That way you won't have to worry too much about the operational side of things."

A yard period? I was deflated, the bright sun of euphoria replaced by a dark thunderhead. For a cutterman, there was nothing more mind-numbingly awful than to spend months on end sitting in drydock, away from the action. Council looked at me, squinting, and seemed to know what I was thinking. He threw a bone. "Since Eccles is leaving right away, we need to make these swaps by the end of the week. *Shearwater* has one more patrol left before you head to Charleston. It's only a couple of days long, but you'll be in command." The dark cloud parted. It was better than nothing—a short patrol before the tedium of the yard. I thanked the commander and headed back to the ship, my mind swirling.

The patrol came and went in a flash. Bruce Gaudette sailed with us, providing a sounding-board as we discussed the strengths and quirks of the surface effect ships. Bruce had a good head on his shoulders and played the sponge, absorbing everything he could about the temperamental cutters. Fifteen months earlier, I'd been doing the same under the tutelage of Jim Sartucci. It was remarkable how much a person could grow in a year.

One thing was for certain: command was a different beast from serving as XO. For the first time the decisions were all mine. Head east, west, or south? Run dark at night or with normal running lights? Board a vessel or let her sail past? Postpone scheduled training to give the crew a rest? I'd never appreciated the swirl of decisions that were made by a ship's captain.

I chose familiar ground, and *Shearwater* headed to the shallows west of Andros Island. The bank was deserted so we steamed across Santaren Channel toward Cay Sal, boarding two sailboats. Nothing found. The next night, we intercepted a cabin cruiser, and EPIC reported that her crew was armed and dangerous. Our boarding party saw nothing suspicious during its inspection. They found no weapons, and the master and crew members were cooperative, so we sent the boat on its way. On the last day we towed a disabled sailboat from the middle of the Florida Straits toward Islamorada, our deck force now experts on the evolution. After passing off the sailboat to a Coast Guard 41-footer, *Shearwater* steamed back to Key West, the mini-patrol complete.

The operations had been routine, but I'd made an essential discovery: I liked being in command—a lot. It felt natural, as if it were the proper state of things. I'd always harbored a deep-seated fear that command at sea would be overwhelming, with the weight of responsibility too much to handle. Instead, I had the opposite reaction. The five days commanding *Shearwater* were liberating, freeing me to make choices—responsible for a hundred decisions a day, yes, but enjoyably so. Command brought out an inner strength, an intense desire to excel, a crisp focus on the crew's well-being, and a newfound appreciation of the joys of leadership. Ten weeks in the yard? Bring it on. It would be a blast, so long as I had the privilege of serving as the temporary captain of Red Crew.

We sailed for Charleston a different team. Two of the plank-owners had transferred, promoted and headed for new assignments. Walt Goodrum left the area, but Chuck Obenland would serve as executive petty officer in an 82-footer further up the Florida coast, and we'd have the good fortune to run into him every now and then. The departures left a big hole in the crew; Goodrum's culinary magic and Obenland's law enforcement expertise had been a foundation of our success. Saying goodbye was tough. Red Crew was diminished without them.

The transit up the coast was uneventful. After a two-day hike, *Shearwater* entered Charleston Harbor, steaming past Fort Sumter, with the crew gathered along the port rail, drinking in the history. We crossed the inner harbor and headed west, up the Ashley River. *Shearwater* glided slowly along the Battery, the 1800s-era neighborhood that sat on the river's edge. Red Crew gawked at the stately homes with their white columns, brick porticos, and wide porches, surrounded by sumptuous lawns and graceful palmetto trees. I'd never visited Charleston, and at first glance it exceeded expectations. The ten weeks were looking better by the minute.

Shearwater moored at Base Charleston, and after a night of exploring the city we got under way, bound for the Delta Marine shipyard. Delta was a new facility, a spinoff of a larger yard, Detyens Shipyards, Inc. We headed back to the main harbor and then turned north, passing the downtown bustle, the pastel row houses and cobblestone streets oozing southern charm.

On its north side, Charleston Harbor was fed by the winding Cooper River and, to its east, the shallower, sluggish Wando. The Navy had a large base on the Cooper, which dozens of warships called home. We went the other way, up the Wando, with *Shearwater*'s destination ten miles to the northeast. Delta Marine sat on a small tributary to the brackish river, and the approach to the yard was so shallow we had to time our transit to coincide with high tide. After an hour of snaking through the twists and turns of the low country, we made the final run into the yard's turning basin, only two feet of chocolate water separating *Shearwater*'s propellers from the puff mud underneath.

Charleston's beauty had taken my breath away, and so did the yard—but for the opposite reason. It looked like an industrial wasteland. Sitting on a dozen acres carved out of thick pine forest, it appeared to be little more than a staging ground for rusty machines, large scraps of metal, and lumpy heaps of rock and gravel. At one end sat a boxy, white metal storage shed, the only respectable building on the grounds. Haphazardly littered around the yard were piles of construction scraps, oddly shaped compressors, and an uneven row of faded 40-foot cargo containers, most of their doors open to the elements. Next to the 150-foot drydock was a tall lattice of rusted metal, topped by a rectangular hopper that held tons of sandblasting grit. A thin layer of the black abrasive covered every surface in sight. Our lucky crew would call this place home for the next ten weeks.

Once *Shearwater* was in drydock, the yard workers could replace her driveshaft bearings and propellers, clean her hull, service her rudders, and make a close inspection of the wet deck. The Coast Guard also mandated changes to improve the original design of the ship. There were dozens of minor tweaks and two major upgrades.

First, *Shearwater* would be outfitted with a larger, five-meter RHIB, as well as a stouter launch crane, replacing the underpowered four-meter boat and its flimsy davit. We'd learned a hundred times over the need for a more capable RHIB and were excited about the change.

The second upgrade was far more intrusive. As the ship was originally built, the exhausts for the main diesels and lift engines exited the hull amidships, just above the waterline, which led to an unhealthy swirl of exhaust on the main deck and carbon build-up in the engines. The Coast Guard solution was to install smokestacks. The new exhaust pipes would run vertically from the engine room, discharging fifteen feet above the main deck. To house the heavy iron piping, the superstructure would be extended twelve feet aft on both the port and starboard sides of the lift fan plenum, adding five tons of bulk to the ship. The project would require the disassembly of the entire aft bulkhead of the superstructure and a tremendous amount of cutting, grinding, and welding to fabricate and install the expanded deckhouse.

Floating the ship into the drydock was a straightforward affair. The drydock was a mammoth U-shaped structure, and as the yard team flooded the dock's ballast tanks, the drydock slowly sank to the bottom of the river. *Shearwater* was winched inside. Once the ship was in place, the yard workers pumped out the ballast and the drydock rose until *Shearwater*'s twin hulls came to rest on wooden blocks arranged on the floor of the U. After divers ensured that the hulls were properly aligned, the drydock supervisor continued pumping ballast until the floor of the U was a foot above the river's surface. There *Shearwater* sat, dripping ooze, her bronze propellers shining in the sun, the wet deck fully exposed for the first time since the ship had worn the Coast Guard stripes.

Yard work was hot and noisy. It was the heat of summer and conditions on board the ship were awful, with debilitating humidity and temperatures near 100 degrees. We shut down the galley and the crew moved into a hotel in Mount Pleasant, fifteen miles away on a map, but forty minutes by car on the winding back roads. To beat the heat, the crew started work early, before 0600, but we usually didn't head back to the sanctuary of our hotel until sundown.

The yard workers and Red Crew members worked tirelessly, and the effort became unexpectedly satisfying, as we watched the ship torn apart and then rebuilt. Sanders being Sanders, he decided to give the superstructure a new coat of white paint—a task not covered under the shipyard contract. He and his deck force worked in the blazing sun to sand down every surface of the two-level deckhouse, after which he gave up a weekend, working fourteen hours a day, to spray on two thick coats of high-gloss white. *Shearwater* became the best-looking SES in the diminutive fleet, and Sanders' work was so good that I later hired him to repaint my car.

We ate box lunches for breakfast and lunch—very bad—and dined out in Mount Pleasant or Charleston proper—delectably good. Despite the grueling hours that our crew members were putting in on the ship, most of them relished their time in Charleston. I felt the same way. With its innate hospitality, great beaches, low-key atmosphere, and reasonable cost of living, Charleston seemed like the ideal duty station.

Senior Chief was acting as XO and nannied the crew, making sure everyone got plenty of sleep, stayed off the booze, and kept out of trouble. Earlier in his career he'd served as executive petty officer in a 95-footer in California, and he knew the ropes. When I complimented him on his XO skills, he said that multitasking was his specialty. He could juggle both sets of duties—no problem at all.

He also showed off his inventive side. Our new, larger RHIB had arrived and was sitting on a trailer in the yard, and Senior Chief wanted to test it. Rather than run the new boat up and down the Wando River, he towed the RHIB to Lake Moultrie, an expansive freshwater state park. He arranged a huge spread of food and drink and proclaimed a morale day. Red Crew spent hours in the RHIB, zipping around the lake at full speed, learning about the enhanced capabilities of the bigger boat, all while tossing footballs, playing horseshoes, and gorging on low-country barbecue on shore.

In late September I was called to testify in court for the Friday-the-13th seizure. Five defendants, from *Moses* and *Dino*, would be on trial. The man from the third seized boat, the white go-fast, would be tried separately. Senior Chief assumed temporary command of *Shearwater*, and I flew to Miami for the proceedings.

Testifying was harder than busting them in the first place. I met with the assistant U.S. attorney, James Reagan, and reviewed the case. The attorneys weren't allowed to coach the witnesses, but Reagan described the evidence that he'd present to the jury. He gave a few general hints on how to comport oneself in the courtroom—no speculation, facts only, look the questioner in the eye—and the next thing I knew the bailiff was calling me to the stand.

I hated every minute of it. The defense attorney did everything he could to muddy the water, to cast doubt on our actions, our motivations, and our integrity. Had Red Crew actually seen *Moses'* crew put the marijuana in the fuel tanks? If not, then how did we know the defendants were guilty? Hadn't I overstepped my authority by prying up the deck inside the cabinet without a warrant? Had the cutter been trespassing in Bahamian waters? Did we have it out for these poor immigrants, who'd recently fled Communist Cuba and war-torn Nicaragua and had no idea that some nefarious individual had hidden marijuana on their boat? On and on he went, distorting the facts, planting seeds of doubt, and sparking multiple objections from the prosecutor. By the end of the proceeding I felt unclean, as if the defense attorney had tossed a bucket of bilge slops on me. Once the testimony was complete, it was a relief to fly home to the ramshackle, gritty shipyard on the Wando and rejoin the real world.

It soon was time to wrap up the yard work and send *Shearwater* back to sea. We'd fallen off schedule, delayed when Hurricane Diana passed close by the Carolina coast, and were leaving almost a week later than originally planned. The last few days were barely controlled chaos. Red Crew started work at first light and stayed late into the night, piecing together the engines, the fuel lines, and the insulation around the new exhaust ports. The yard workers refloated the ship, flooding the drydock and putting *Shearwater* back where she belonged—in the water. The engineers checked for leaks, found some big ones, and the yard team raised the drydock. After the workers made adjustments around the drive shafts, the cutter was lowered back into the water, leaking no more. *Shearwater* was a ship again.

More frenetic work: the crew tested the auxiliary equipment and got the air conditioning and potable water back on line. The inside of the ship was filthy, with sandblasting grit in every corner. After cleaning *Shearwater*'s interior, crew members removed the protective deck coverings, finding yet another layer of grit. Red Crew moved out of the hotel and back on board and helped load food and supplies, all of which had to be coordinated around the shipyard work schedule. Our new cook, SS2 Tom Stoltz, prepared his first meal—steaks, broccoli, and baked potatoes—all light-years ahead of the box lunches that we loved to hate.

Pat George oversaw the main diesel and lift engine "lite-offs," funneling their exhaust through the new smokestacks for the first time. There were pinhole leaks in the exhaust pipe junctions, filling the interior main deck with noxious gas; the yard team removed the newly installed insulation, isolated the pinholes, and welded them shut. More engine-testing. Another leak, this one on the saltwater intake line, was quickly repaired with a new gasket. Deck Force exercised the new boat-launching system, which worked like a charm, the beefy new crane easily hoisting the larger RHIB over the side. The crane was big enough to lift a school bus. Finally, the engineers lit off the generators and switched from shore power to ship's power. After ten weeks and five days of being ripped apart and reassembled, *Shearwater* was ready to go home. We'd be leaving the next day on the high tide, at 1500.

Red Crew woke early to ready the ship for sea. SS2 Stoltz served huge omelets, delicious treats, but most of the crew just poked at them listlessly. Everyone was gathered on the mess deck, dog-tired, ragged and on edge, anxious to leave, but burned out from the weeks in the sweltering heat. I scanned the mess deck, worried. Our team members looked used up, not on their game. They'd hit the wall. Senior Chief stood in the doorway, sporting a frown, clearly concerned. This wasn't a good start to what was going to be a long, hot day.

Dan Sanders lit the crew's fuse. He walked over to a garbage can sitting in the corner, looked into it, reached down, and pulled out a half-eaten omelet. "Hey, why'd someone throw this away? It's still good," he crowed. With that, he folded up the omelet and shoved it in his mouth, jamming his cheeks full, like a squirrel, rubbing his belly with his free hand. At first everyone just stared, but then the crew erupted, laughing hysterically, jumping up, high-fiving Sanders, a few with tears in their eyes, one of the seamen pretending to retch into her napkin. The laughs jump-started the team and Red Crew's energy began to flow. It was world-class theater. I'd watched the entire episode but hadn't seen Sanders hide the omelet in the trash can. Certainly he'd staged the whole thing.

Shearwater sailed at 1500, squeaking through the cut into the Wando River, headed for Base Charleston and a final night of liberty before steaming south in the morning. Senior Chief and I met up with Mark Hoesten and the captain of Gold Crew, who'd just arrived on board *Petrel* for her turn in the yard, and we enjoyed a sumptuous meal at a trendy restaurant on East Bay Street. It was late October, the weather a perfect 75 degrees, and the streets were buzzing with tourists. As we left port the next morning I felt hollow inside, unexpectedly melancholy, already missing the vibrant feel of the historic city, vowing to come back.

Bound for Miami, *Shearwater* ran great, at least for a while. The OOD powered up to speed once we were past the sea buoy, heading south into three-foot swells. The big question was, would the five tons of new deck structure slow the cutter down and keep her from coming up on plane? The answer was no—at least not by much. With a full fuel load *Shearwater* was cruising at twenty-eight knots, the South Carolina coast fading away in our wake. The crew walked through a set of fire, man-overboard, and collision drills, getting back into fighting form and ready to face real-world emergencies.

The next morning the port main engine lost power, and forty minutes later the starboard engine died. *Shearwater* coasted to a stop, bobbing in the seas, waiting for the engineering gang to offer a prognosis. We'd been following the coast to stay clear of the Gulf Stream and now sat ten miles off Jacksonville, disabled and adrift. Senior Chief contacted Group Mayport but declined its offer of help, since we weren't in any danger. Nonetheless, Group dispatched two 41-foot utility boats that soon were parading down our starboard side, their coxswains taking a close look at one of the SESs that they'd heard about but probably had never seen in person.

MK1 George called me from the engine room. He'd found the culprit. There was a rag stuffed in the starboard fuel line, apparently left there when the pipe had been disassembled during the yard period. The rag had moved slowly through the pipe and now was wedged in a bend in the line, cutting off the flow of fuel to the main diesel. George found the same problem on the port side and within two hours we were back under way, turning at best speed for Miami. No harm, no foul, but I wondered if any other surprises lay in wait.

Shearwater spent the next five days at Base Miami Beach, where a team of electronics technicians installed a brand new AN-SPS-64 radar, along with more advanced secure radios. The day before we departed, Senior Chief, Sanders, and I paid a visit to the Group Miami operations staff to learn if any new smuggling trends had popped up during our time away. The watchstanders at Group handled hundreds of search and rescue, drug, and migrant interdiction cases each year and had a wealth of knowledge. For the drug trade, they said that both the Coast Guard and Customs were seeing more and more complex secret compartments, mostly in fuel tanks, as we'd found in our recent seizures. They also noted that smugglers were moving cocaine more regularly by sea, although seizures were few and far between and almost always consisted of small stashes found on board merchant vessels.

Finally, they warned that migrant traffic was starting to pick up, with large sailboats and coastal freighters transporting groups of Haitians into the Bahamas, or in some cases, directly toward the United States. One cutter patrolling the Windward Passage had intercepted a fifty-foot sailboat carrying 211 Haitians on board, a staggeringly high number of people to cram onto such a small vessel. I didn't know whether an SES crew could handle such a crowd, and I had no interest in finding out firsthand.

Shearwater got back under way at dawn, my last day in command. Lieutenant Justice had served his time with Blue Crew and would meet us on the pier when we returned to Key West. I knew it was going to be awkward sliding back into the XO role, having come to appreciate the freedom afforded a patrol-boat captain in making day-to-day decisions. Still, it was unavoidable, orders being orders, and I felt confident that the time in Charleston had helped prepare me for a full-time command, should I someday be so lucky.

Back in home port, I sorted through the mail and found a letter from the District Seven legal office, reporting the results of the *Moses* and *Dino* trial. The dirty questions from the defense attorney hadn't swayed the jury, and all five defendants had been found guilty. The judge sentenced *Moses'* master to three years in prison; the other three people on board, including the Nicaraguan women, received probation. *Dino's* operator had fled and was now a fugitive, his sentence pending.

It was hard to imagine that a three-year sentence would be much of a deterrent to someone who'd captained a mothership packed with almost two tons of dope. The jail time just didn't seem very serious, and the probation for his accomplices was a joke. I wondered how we'd ever win the drug war without a bigger legal hammer, hoping that the justice system would catch up to the reality of the smuggling onslaught.

————

Eighteen months had sped by, and now it was time for a new assignment—even though I didn't want to leave Key West. It was the sign of a good ship and a good crew when its leadership wanted to stay beyond their welcome. But Coast Guard policy required officers to move around for experience, and two years was the limit for serving as a surface effect ship XO. There was no choice but to find a new job.

But where? With four straight years afloat, I'd have to head ashore. There were dozens of desk jobs in Washington, San Francisco, and New York, but I wasn't interested. The only thing that mattered was getting the right experience that would lead to future command afloat. That meant one choice: a district operations center, or OPCEN.

The OPCENs were the nerve centers of the Coast Guard's regional commands and a grooming ground for patrol boat captains. Manned by junior officers and senior enlisted specialists, the OPCEN watchstanders, or controllers, oversaw all Coast Guard activities in their areas of responsibility, directing aircraft, cutters, and small boats to carry out search and rescue and law enforcement missions. For shore duty it was as exciting as it came, permitting full contact with the fleet.

My first choice was Boston, with Miami a close second, and the West Coast OPCENs a distant third. OPCEN Boston oversaw the New England coast, from Maine to New York, its controllers handling a strong mix of SAR, fisheries law enforcement, and even the occasional drug case. Serving in Boston would also get me closer to home. It'd be good to see my family and friends in Connecticut more than once a year. It added up to a winning ticket.

I'd visited OPCEN Boston once before, during my junior year at the Academy, and had walked away in awe. The OPCEN was housed in a shabby federal office building attached to the Boston Garden, and inside it was a crowded kaleidoscope of charts, plotting tables, rosters, photos, manuals, televisions, telephone lists, and computer screens. Outside the one small window was an elevated expressway, with cars crawling by, and there was a bullet hole in the glass, its origin a mystery.

The ambiance wasn't important, however. What mattered was the function. The on-watch controller had shown me around and explained the intricacies of search planning. The amount of information he needed to make life-and-death decisions was overwhelming. Cutter, boat, and aircraft capabilities; tides and currents; drift factors; water temperature; life-expectancy; visibility; wind and sea effects; and a hundred more variables all were part of the calculus. Within a few moments I was lost, unable to follow his narrative, and had decided then that it was too much to learn, too complicated, and too much responsibility for me to handle. Now, five years later, with two cutters' worth of real-life experience, I was bucking to have a chance to serve there.

The assignment officer who handled the OPCENs called while Red Crew was away and left a message with Wayne Justice, who talked to me in private once we returned from the yard. He got right to the point. I wouldn't be getting my first choice but instead would receive orders to OPCEN Miami. The captain was jazzed. He said the senior controller in Miami wanted to get an SES sailor on his team, and the folks in Boston were more interested in officers completing a patrol boat command in northern waters. I trusted Wayne Justice completely, and having seen how much he'd enjoyed his time in Miami, I knew it would be a great opportunity. I was perfectly happy with the decision and was glad to know so early where I'd be spending the next three years. There was plenty of time for house-hunting and, with Miami only four hours away, there'd be no problem arranging a smooth transfer. It was settled. Six more months of SES life and then a tour of duty in the Coast Guard's busiest OPCEN. The next few years were looking just fine.

———————

Our next patrol began on November 8, with Red Crew back in fighting trim. Along with getting our captain back, we had a new BM3, Dave McCurry, tall and lanky with a down-home wit and a perpetually sunny disposition. Unfortunately, McCurry was about two inches too tall for the low overheads inside the SES and was continually smacking his head. McCurry turned out to be a solid shipmate, always eager to help out, and showed great skill as a boatswain's mate. We also added two new seamen, Nancy Buttermore and Gloria Denton, the former a hardworking, bright, and sassy college grad who'd spent a year with Green Crew, and the latter quiet and introspective. Buttermore added spice to the crew, offset by Denton's sedate persona.

Red Crew had transferred back to *Sea Hawk*, and we got under way in late afternoon for a ten-day patrol. Trouble started before we got to the reef line. Both main diesels died and the cutter began drifting outside of the main ship channel, the current pulling us toward a five-foot shallow—not good. Then we lost electrical power. That was *really* not good. The captain gave the order to drop anchor and for the next two hours *Sea Hawk* sat, a mile off Key West, within spitting distance of the dangerous shoal at Western Triangle. Pat George clomped up to the bridge, drenched with sweat, and reported he could get a generator and one engine back into service, but the other main diesel would need extensive repairs. *Sea Hawk* crept back into port, arriving after dark, all of us wondering why such capable ships had to be so damned unreliable.

Commander Council met us on the pier and said we'd be shifting immediately back to *Shearwater* so we could head to Group Miami, which was desperately short of patrol boats. We relieved Green Crew as they accepted control of *Sea Hawk*, setting a new speed record for a double change of command—three hours, start to finish. At 2200, we headed back to sea, in our comfort zone on board *Shearwater*, which showed her appreciation by not breaking down and coming up easily on plane in the Gulf Stream. We headed for Bimini.

The post-yard *Shearwater* proved to be a much better cutter than what we'd sailed over the previous year. When she was fully laden, there was only mild speed degradation from the weighty smoke stacks, and the cutter hit thirty knots when light on fuel. The new RHIB and boat lowering apparatus were a vast improvement over the sad rigs they replaced, while the upgraded radar proved far better for detecting small craft. Slowly and surely, the SESs were being transformed into proper Coast Guard cutters, hampered only by the recurring engine failures.

On November 12 *Shearwater* was on barrier patrol west of Bimini. I'd just been relieved of the 2000–2400 watch when the captain called from the bridge. *Shearwater* was responding to a distress call from the pleasure craft *Jolly Folly*, disabled and adrift twelve miles away. We sprinted to the scene and found a well-maintained thirty-five-foot cabin cruiser rocking in a four-foot sea. There were three persons on board. They'd been headed from Miami to Bimini when their engine died. Sanders joked that it wasn't just SESs that had engine problems.

We boarded the boat. Pat George, now fully qualified, led the team, with me as his assistant. We found the vessel immaculate throughout, her master and crew cooperative, with no signs of a drug load or secret compartments. In the forward berthing area, though, next to an ashtray, our sweep team spotted a small clump of green leafy material and some rolling papers. The clump tested positive for THC. It was a minute trace of marijuana, certainly from personal use, but under the law it gave us reason to detain *Jolly Folly* and tow her to Miami for a Customs search.

I called the captain on our new secure handheld radio to discuss our plans. "We could drag this guy back to Miami but there's no evidence of bulk contraband, and we were able to search the entire boat without a problem," I reported. "This boat's not smuggling. I think we should tow it to Bimini and get back on patrol." The captain mulled it over and agreed. George gave the master a stern warning about personal use marijuana and the boarding team debarked.

Jolly Folly was sitting five miles off the beach, and Lieutenant Justice decided that it would be best to tow her to Bimini using our new, more powerful small boat. Chad Weatherby and I boarded the RHIB and hooked up the tow. It was a clear night, with no moon. What sounded like a simple evolution—dragging *Jolly Folly* a few miles into a protected harbor—in reality bordered on harrowing. Weatherby had to steer east, directly toward the beach, until we were one hundred yards offshore, and then make a sharp turn to the north, jogging around a sandbar that guarded the harbor entrance. Miss the turn and we'd run aground in the breakers.

As we lumbered toward shore the RHIB cast sheets of spray, limiting visibility, with *Jolly Folly* bobbing on a short leash seventy-five feet behind. It was slow going. The OOD on *Shearwater* tracked us on radar, vectoring us in: "Maintain your heading, six hundred yards more, then come hard to port, you'll see the Alice Town range lights off your bow."

It was too dark to tell how far offshore we were. We could hear the waves crashing on the rocks, steadily getting louder, an ominous cadence, the dark shore looming up from the surf, a thick stand of trees dead ahead. I suppressed a wave of panic. Suddenly it seemed that we were way too close, almost on the beach. The OOD told us to hold steady, one hundred more yards, fifty, *now*—mark the turn. Weatherby swung the RHIB to port, heading north, but the range marker lights were burned out, and we couldn't see the harbor entrance. I looked toward shore and saw a dance of phosphorescence in the booming surf, so close off our starboard beam that I felt we could wade ashore. The OOD called again, his voice tense: "RHIB, come further to port, *now*, at least 20 degrees—you're too close to the beach." Weatherby compensated, sidewinding back on track. After a minute the radio crackled again: "Okay, that looks better, give it another five hundred yards and then steady on zero-two-zero magnetic."

Ahead was the narrow cut that led into the main harbor. Weatherby threaded the tow through the opening, maintaining a steady strain, and we saw the wooden pier where we'd be delivering *Jolly Folly*, half a mile away. By 0320 Weatherby had nudged the cabin cruiser alongside the pier and after a hearty round of thank-yous we were on our way, full speed ahead, bound for *Shearwater* and for what I hoped would be a few hours of sleep.

Once the RHIB was back on deck, the captain changed the game plan, saying he had a hunch. Rather than loiter off Bimini, *Shearwater* would head south. I hit the rack at 0430, and ten minutes later the phone rang. It was Lieutenant Justice again. "Westbound contact, looks small, making twenty knots, we'll be on scene in fifteen minutes. You good for another boarding?" Absolutely. I'd been too wired to fall asleep, and I hadn't even changed out of my coveralls. I popped open a soda for the sugar rush, guzzled it, and headed to the bridge.

In our spotlight was another cabin cruiser, almost identical to the one we'd just towed to shore. The boat looked clean and well-equipped. We were in deep water, fifteen miles south of Bimini, the Cat Cays six miles to our east, and the cabin cruiser was headed directly for Miami. Captain Justice called her on the radio. "Motor vessel *June Bug*, this is the U.S. Coast Guard cutter shining its spotlight on you. Stop your vessel and respond on channel 22 VHF. Over." It took three tries before *June Bug* replied, her master explaining that he hadn't heard the calls. He said there were three persons on the boat, two men and a woman, all from Miami Beach, and that *June Bug* had been cruising the islands and was headed home, hoping to arrive for breakfast.

By 0530 our boarding party was climbing over the port side of the cabin cruiser, the three persons on board lined up just aft of the superstructure. I checked their IDs. The men were resident aliens of Cuban descent and the woman was from Guatemala. She was forty-one years old, attractive, and wearing tight slacks, a more mature version of the Nicaraguan girls we'd found on *Moses*. Maybe it was a good sign that she was on board. Maybe this was another doper. There were no outward signs of smuggling, but the boat was traveling from the Great Bahama Bank and was by default a prime target. The sweep team headed forward to check the man-sized compartments.

"XO, we've got bales in the forward berthing area." It was BM3 McCurry, his voice low and scratchy on the comms headset. I replied, "Okay, Boats, make sure the area is secure, then take a sample from a bale and bring it back aft." I was standing near the transom and directed the master and his two shipmates to get on their knees with their hands in plain sight. They complied, and BM3 put a sprig of the contraband into the field-test kit. The reagents turned purple. I notified the captain and then George seized the vessel, placing the three people under arrest. It was 0549.

By 0630 we'd transferred the prisoners to *Shearwater*, and Weatherby joined me on board *June Bug* for the sixty-mile trip to Miami. The boat was well outfitted, borderline luxurious, and stocked with food and beer. We witnessed a glorious sunrise, throttled the cabin cruiser to full speed and made twenty-two knots at the edge of the Gulf Stream. Then a steering cable snapped, and *Shearwater* had to take *June Bug* in tow, arriving at Base Miami Beach around 1500.

After transferring the prisoners, evidence, and seized vessel to the South Florida Task Force, I declined an invitation to join my shipmates at the Gator Den, heading instead for my rack and some much-needed sleep. We'd just made our tenth drug bust in less than a year, surely a time for celebration, but after working all night, my first priority was to recharge my batteries.

I lay in the rack, considering our luck. Had we dragged *Jolly Folly* back to Miami, we'd never have seen the second cabin cruiser, and there would've been no seizure. If *Shearwater* had stayed off Bimini and not jaunted south, we wouldn't have encountered the drug-laden boat. Had the captain decided to let *June Bug* pass by due to the early hour and the long day that had preceded it—again, no seizure. There were lessons here.

It also hit me that our drug busts were following a pattern—just an odd coincidence to the random observer but something more to a superstitious sailor. The first seizure, *Miss Leslie,* had been almost effortless, the bales in plain sight, followed by the infinitely more complex triple seizure. After that the busts cycled between easy and hard. If the pattern held, considering how simple it had been to nail *June Bug,* our next drug bust would be a doozy.

We had another week of patrol, and I needed to be fresh. I closed my eyes as one last, wildly off-the-mark thought rang through my head: boy, Red Crew had seen it all.

8

The Gift of Life
November 1984

Shearwater got under way from Miami after dark and headed directly for the Great Bahama Bank, on the hunt for dopers. The next day, near 24° 00' N. Lat. and 78° 30' W. Long., we hit a much different jackpot.

The blip first appeared when the vessel was fifteen miles away. It was making eight knots, heading northwest. We steamed toward the contact at full speed, trying to preserve the element of surprise if she turned out to be a smuggler, knowing that once her crew saw us they could run into the shallows near Andros or pitch their cargo overboard. At eight miles our lookout had the vessel in sight, and at 0600 we all knew she wasn't a typical fishing or lobster boat. She looked like a Haitian freighter.

It was midafternoon when *Shearwater* pulled alongside the motor-vessel *Sainte Bernadette*, which was chugging toward Florida through choppy seas. The weather was cool and blustery, a cold air mass sitting over the Bahamas. The fifty-five-foot wooden freighter was painted white, with bright blue trim along her rail and her official number,

Q-1302, hand-painted on her narrow bow. A typical Haitian rig, *Sainte Bernadette* had an open deck forward and her pilothouse amidships, with the superstructure extending aft to the transom. There was a large, square hatch on the forward deck. The boat was riding low, down by the bow.

The OOD tried hailing the freighter on the radio but got no answer. We mustered a boarding party, led by BM1 Dan Sanders, and conferred on the port bridge wing. Captain Justice gave specific orders. "Boats, head over and take station off their stern," he said. "Once you've got their attention, ask the standard questions and relay the answers to me before going on board. A lot of these small freighters cut across the Bank, but looking at the way it's riding, there's probably a big load of cargo in the forward hold. It might take a while to sort through it." Sanders was enthused, sensing he'd find a stash of dope, and walked aft to the boat deck.

The RHIB whisked BM1 Sanders and his team alongside *Sainte Bernadette*. We could see Sanders shouting up to a man on the fantail, and he called the cutter a minute later. "The master says there are seven crew members, they don't have any cargo, and they're heading to Miami to pick up a load of bicycles," he said. "They left Cap-Haïtien three days ago." Normally the story would've sounded legit, but with the vessel sitting low in the water, they were either hiding something or had a lot of water in their bilge. Either way, Red Crew could be facing trouble.

The captain told Sanders to go on board, and we watched the six-person team scramble over the starboard gunwale, mustering *Sainte Bernadette*'s crew. I relieved the OOD, maneuvering *Shearwater* close to keep an eye on the boarding.

The captain stood on the port bridge wing, cradling a handheld radio, while I jockeyed the throttles. *Shearwater* was 150 feet away from the freighter, and it was like watching a play in pantomime. Sanders and a teammate headed into the pilothouse with the master to inspect the vessel's documents, their dark blue coveralls and bright orange life vests standing out against *Sainte Bernadette*'s garish blue trim.

Sanders was thorough, and watching him was a lesson in how to conduct a boarding. He always positioned himself perfectly, never turning his back to a potential danger or leaving his sidearm exposed, and he projected an air of calm authority. He moved forward onto the bow and said something to the master, who shrugged his shoulders. Sanders stood near the large deck hatch, and then he and Chuck Meisner bent over to lift it up. It didn't move. The hatch was secured with a padlock and the master walked forward, key in hand, and opened it. Meisner popped up the hatch and Sanders leaned over the opening, shining his flashlight down. He recoiled.

Meisner looked into the hold and gestured to the rest of the boarding party to stay back. Sanders fumbled for his radio, yanking it off his weapons belt. "*Shearwater*, boarding party, the forward hold is full of people. I say again, the hold is full of people." He paused, staring into the opening. "There's at least a couple dozen of them." Another pause, as he swept the flashlight beam side to side. "Um, correction, there's a lot more than that—probably fifty or sixty. They're packed in real tight." He paused once more. "We're gonna need a lot of help on this one." It was the understatement of the year.

———

Chasing drug smugglers was a relatively new mission for the Coast Guard, but interdicting Haitian vessels was even newer. The Coast Guard had long engaged in keeping undocumented migrants out of the United States; in the spring of 1980 it had responded to the Mariel Boatlift, when 125,000 Cubans fled their homeland by sea. But only in the past three years had the Coast Guard conducted operations specifically aimed at preventing the Haitian populace from setting sail toward America—a dangerous and often deadly voyage.

The poorest nation in the Western Hemisphere, Haiti was one of the oldest republics in the world, having earned its independence in a slave revolt over its French masters in 1804. Since then, Haiti has suffered from almost continual political and civil turmoil. The U.S. military occupied the country in 1915 and withdrew in 1934. After a number of failed presidencies, Dr. Francois "Papa Doc" Duvalier was elected as the Haitian ruler. Duvalier controlled the citizenry through brutality and depravation. When he died in 1971, his son, Jean-Claude, assumed the presidency. "Baby Doc," as Jean-Claude was known, was a feckless and inept ruler, and each year thousands of Haitians took to the sea, seeking a new life. By 1980 about 20,000 migrants left the island nation each year, most of them crammed into primitive wooden sailboats. Tragically, far fewer than that made it safely to the Bahamas, Cuba, or the U.S. mainland. The rest—several thousand people, year after year—were assumed lost at sea.

To combat this humanitarian crisis, the newly installed Reagan administration directed the Coast Guard to patrol off Haiti to intercept migrant vessels and return their passengers to the Haitian capital, Port-au-Prince. The wisdom of this order became clear on October 26, 1981, when a thirty-foot sailboat capsized off Hillsboro Beach, Florida, drowning thirty-three Haitians. The Coast Guard's Haitian Migrant Interdiction Operation became a top priority in the Seventh District, and at least one medium- or high-endurance cutter patrolled the Windward Passage around the clock. Ashore, the U.S. embassy and Haitian government spread the word across the mountainous country: if you leave by sea, you'll be intercepted and returned home.

The policy was controversial. The Coast Guard was sending people back to an impoverished land, ruled by an oppressive dictator. As a safety valve, every migrant who was brought on board a cutter was interviewed by an Immigration and Naturalization Service (INS) agent to determine whether he or she had a credible fear of persecution. Very few did. The vast majority were repatriated, transferred to the custody of the Red Cross, given a small stipend, and provided a lift to their home village. The Duvalier government gave assurances that it wouldn't harm those who chose to flee, and the U.S embassy monitored the Haitian authorities to make sure that they were living up to that promise.

Within months of President Reagan's order, the migrant flow reduced to a trickle. The cutters in the Windward Passage provided a visible deterrent, patrolling within sight of the jagged Haitian coastline and conducting joint operations with the fledgling Haitian Navy. In the first year the policy was in effect the Coast Guard intercepted only 171 Haitians. But now Haitian migrant activity was on the upswing, and *Sainte Bernadette* had slipped past the cutter patrolling the Windward Passage. Only *Shearwater* and Red Crew stood between the freighter and landfall in the United States.

———

Joan Scott, the quartermaster, set the migrant interdiction bill, rousting the entire crew. While Red Crew had trained for handling an influx of migrants, we'd never actually done so; the three Jamaicans from *Miss Marilyn* had been the largest group we'd encountered. All three SESs were equipped with a stockpile of life jackets, beans and rice, and blankets to sustain up to one hundred migrants for three days, the most the District Seven staff thought the 110-foot cutters could handle. Members of Red Crew began breaking out the supplies and manning their stations.

The strategy was to get the migrants onto the cutter, feed them, keep them secure, and return them to Port-au-Prince. It was an all-hands evolution. We'd need to screen everyone coming on board for weapons and contraband, identify and treat health issues, isolate troublemakers, and care for their needs—food, water, sanitation—as long as they were in our custody. There were sixteen of us and dozens more of them, requiring firm but humane control to prevent trouble from breaking out.

Within minutes the situation spiraled downward. BM1 Sanders and his team began helping people out of the cargo hold, grabbing their arms and torsos as they scaled the wooden ladder that led to the freighter's forward deck. The first person out was a tall, thin man, middle-aged. He shielded his eyes from the sun and his knees buckled as he took his first step. He sat down, cross-legged, his hands over his face. From *Shearwater*'s bridge, it looked as though he was sobbing. Up next was a woman, also middle-aged, wearing a long yellow dress, which even from distance looked soiled. She staggered across the bow, collapsing in a heap near the port rail. A boarding-team member rushed to her side and helped her sit up, but she didn't have the strength and lay back down.

Sanders was back on the radio. "*Shearwater*, these people are in tough shape, weak and dehydrated. We need a large jug of water and one of the EMTs over here ASAP."

Men and women continued to climb out of the hold, some able to stand, but most sitting or lying down. Sanders counted heads. "*Shearwater*, these people are speaking Creole, they're definitely from Haiti. I count ninety, and there may be even more than that down in the hold. It's hard to see all the way back." The first dozen Haitians were scattered about the deck. The boarding team put life jackets on the strongest ones and escorted them to the gunwale, helping them board the RHIB. The coxswain loaded six Haitians and sped them back to *Shearwater*, where they were lifted onto the step deck. After the first group was safely on board the cutter, the RHIB headed back to *Sainte Bernadette* with an EMT, a large cooler filled with water, and a collapsible stretcher.

Senior Chief took over as OOD, and I headed aft to oversee the embarkation. We'd set up an assembly line. As the Haitians came on board, each person was gently frisked, examined for medical problems, handed a gray wool blanket and a cup of water, and led forward to sit near the plenum chamber. There, we could keep an eye on them from the bridge wing, with the superstructure providing a lee from the crisp breeze coursing across the deck.

The stream of Haitians climbing out of the cargo hold continued, almost none of them looking better than the first few. The strongest were unsteady on their feet, several fell to their knees, most laid down, and one passed out cold. Sanders reported that the stench was overwhelming and the deck inside the hold was covered in vomit and human waste. There were no lights in the hold, no food, and no water. As the hold emptied, the boarding team saw people lying unconscious on deck and sent the EMT below to evaluate. Sanders' voice was steady and insistent: "*Shearwater*, we've got five people who are unresponsive and need urgent medical attention." Lieutenant Justice grabbed the radio mike and called Group Miami, requesting an immediate helicopter medevac for the unconscious people. The boarding party, assisted by the crew on *Sainte Bernadette*, lifted the limp bodies out of the hold, carefully laying them on the deck.

Red Crew was facing a worst-case scenario. We had a full-blown medical emergency on our hands, a final count of 120 Haitians, 97 men and 23 women, all dehydrated and unfed, most suffering from exhaustion or exposure, others in dire need of medical care, some on the brink of death. Thankfully, there were no children.

The boarding team labored to get the Haitians on board the cutter, where our EMTs could treat the most severely ill. The unconscious migrants were carried on the stretcher, laid across the pontoons of the RHIB. It took twenty trips, but by late afternoon the transfer was complete. Sanders climbed into the freighter's cargo hold and searched its dark, fetid corners, making sure no one was left behind. The hold was empty.

Our captain faced a harsh decision. The master and crew of *Sainte Bernadette* were engaged in human trafficking and had recklessly endangered the lives of more than a hundred of their countrymen, some of whom might not survive the ordeal. But Red Crew was maxed out, stretched to its limits caring for the ten dozen people on *Shearwater*'s aft deck. We didn't have the manpower to detain the crew and take custody of the freighter, and we couldn't escort the ship to Miami at its maximum speed of eight knots. There were lives to save, and lives came first.

Lieutenant Justice looked at me, his face twitching with emotion. "XO, those bastards belong in jail, but we need to get to shore ASAP," he said. "It kills me, but I'm going to have to let them go." He called Group Miami and told them that *Shearwater* would depart scene at best speed and release the freighter to resume its voyage. Group replied that *Sainte Bernadette* would be reboarded once she arrived in port and that the INS would interrogate the crew. Our boarding team returned to the cutter and *Shearwater* turned toward the northwest, sprinting through the Bahamian shallows at thirty knots.

On deck our EMTs, Hartsock and Weatherby, assisted by McCurry, worked feverishly, conducting triage and providing rudimentary care for the sickest people. The healthiest migrants were lined up in rows, curled up under the thin wool blankets to protect against the chill. Below deck, Tom Stoltz was preparing a vat of black beans and rice, and deck force was passing out extra cups of water to prevent dehydration. *Shearwater*'s water supply was limited, and we'd have to be careful not to run dry.

At 1730 there was shouting on the aft deck. One of the five unconscious Haitians, a frail sixty-year-old woman, had awakened briefly and then passed out. Then she stopped breathing. The EMTs scrambled to her, checking her vitals. The woman's heart had stopped. Hartsock and Weatherby applied CPR—five compressions, one breath, five compressions, another breath, but the woman had no heartbeat. Five more compressions, another breath, still with no response. The woman's thin body was lifeless, her arms splayed across the deck, her eyes wide open and staring toward the heavens. She looked gone. Hartsock glanced up, his face flushed, braced with determination: he wasn't going to let her die. Five compressions, one breath. No response. Five compressions, another breath. Nothing. More compressions. Then, in a spasm, the woman coughed harshly and inhaled, ragged and wheezy, gulping air and spilling tears. She was back from the dead. Weatherby and Hartsock sat back on their haunches, sweat pouring down their faces, monitoring her vitals, too busy for congratulations.

Every one of the Haitians was in sorry shape, weak, dehydrated, and malnourished. Five remained gravely ill. They needed a hospital— immediately. Weatherby pulled me aside and said that some, if not all, of the sickest would perish during the night. *Shearwater* was 150 miles from Miami, and we'd have to cross an angry Gulf Stream to get there. The National Weather Service was reporting twelve-foot seas—a nightmare for a cutter loaded with migrants. Airflift would be the only answer.

Just before dusk, an Air Force C-130 buzzed *Shearwater,* flying low and slow, followed a minute later by a sleek gray helicopter. The OOD slowed *Shearwater* to six knots and pointed into the wind; the helo moved over the forward deck, its powerful downdraft lashing the ship, the sound deafening. The helo crew tossed a long, thick rope out of the cabin and two men slid down, landing upright on deck, casually, almost nonchalantly, as if they did this every day. It was a pair of Air Force pararescuemen—PJs, some of the best-trained rescue specialists in the world—deployed from Homestead Air Force Base. The PJs walked briskly to the bridge and introduced themselves, pleasant but all business, no time for idle chitchat.

The captain and the PJs huddled. The helicopter, Rescue 52, would hoist the five sickest Haitians on board, one at a time, then make best speed for shore. The PJs said they wanted to complete the hoists before dark, in the next thirty minutes. They talked with Sanders and assembled a team to handle the stokes litter, quickly reviewing safety procedures.

The helo crew lowered the litter, and Hartsock and Weatherby strapped the first unconscious Haitian into it. The rotor wash whipped the forward deck. Looking up at Rescue 52, some thirty feet above the pilothouse, we could see the crisp movements of the helo as the pilot manipulated the cyclic, collective, and foot pedals to keep the aircraft precisely centered over the bow. He was a marvel: the aircraft never wavered more than a few feet from dead center, an impressive display of airmanship considering the forward motion of the ship and the winds that were buffeting the airframe.

Within a minute the litter was hauled up, spinning slowly on the hoist-line, and a crewman pulled it inside the cabin of the helicopter. After unstrapping the limp Haitian, a medical technician began to rig an IV. The helo crew lowered the empty stokes and repeated the process four more times. Once the quintet was on board, the helo crew again dropped the cable, and the two PJs clipped on for the final hoist. One waved as they were yanked off the deck, smiling, the other rigid at attention, rendering a crisp salute. The PJs scrambled into the cabin just as the helicopter pitched forward, dipping toward the water as it increased its forward speed, next stop Miami. Total time for the hoists: twenty-nine minutes. Our first crisis was averted, with the gravely ill migrants now headed for world-class medical care.

Throughout the evening *Shearwater*'s crew worked nonstop, feeding, treating, and safeguarding the 115 remaining Haitians. The EMTs hopped from person to person, checking pulses, scanning pupils, and taking temperatures, followed by shipmates offering food and water. Some of the Haitians sat up but most sprawled across the deck, a handful moaning or crying, a few thrashing in discomfort, others praying or talking quietly to themselves—a scene from a disaster movie, played out in real life.

As the sun set, the air temperature dropped into the 50s. The captain and I talked on the bridge wing, shivering in the growing chill. He asked: "Can we keep these guys warm all night? The last thing we need is a hundred cases of hypothermia. Do we have enough blankets?" I had just surveyed the conditions on deck and had an idea. "We have enough blankets, but even if we cram them together, the wind will be brutal. How about this? Let's move everyone into engineering stores for the night." The engineering storeroom, near the transom, was forty feet wide, ten feet fore-and-aft, and had plenty of open deck space to sit or sleep. "There's plenty of room back there," I said. "It'll keep everyone warm, and security will be a snap. We've got the toilet set up right outside the hatch, and there's a fresh water hose, too. It'll keep them from freezing."

Bringing migrants inside the skin of a cutter was against Coast Guard policy and raised serious security, sanitation, and health issues. But housing the rescued throng in a warm, well-lighted space would keep everyone alive. Practicality overruled policy, and the captain agreed with the plan. "Sounds good, XO," he said. "Make it happen." We moved most of the group into engineering stores and left a dozen lingering on deck for medical treatment.

We picked a man named Jean, who spoke broken English and had lived in Boston for three years, to serve as an ombudsman for the migrants, allowing two-way communications between Red Crew and its temporary guests. Jean said the migrants had each paid $300 for the trip and were told the voyage would last forty-eight hours. After they had climbed on board *Sainte Bernadette*, her master ordered them into the hold, saying they needed to stay hidden until they were out of Haitian waters. He'd padlocked them inside, providing neither food nor water, and they'd stayed imprisoned until liberated by BM1 Sanders. Jean had lost track of time but thought they'd been in the hold about three days, which agreed with our calculations of how long it would have taken the freighter to travel from Haiti. Jean was amazed to learn that none of his compatriots had died.

I asked Jean if being housed in engineering stores was working, and he said, yes, that it was "a hell of a lot better than sitting out in that wind." He asked whether migrants who wanted to stretch their legs were allowed to walk on deck, and I told him that would be fine, and that we'd bring everyone back out on deck in the morning, once the sun was up.

The EMTs had completed their medical evaluations and had shifted to port-and-starboard duty, one on watch while the other rested. I tried to get other shipmates to take a break, but everyone wanted to keep pitching in. Fortunately, around 2300, with most of the Haitians dozing, we only needed two security watchstanders to keep an eye on them, along with a cook and an EMT. Everyone else went to bed. Senior Chief and I agreed to stand port-and-starboard OOD watches until we'd disembarked the Haitians and resumed patrol.

Group Miami directed *Shearwater* to head southeast for a rendezvous with a larger cutter, which would take custody of the Haitians and return them to Port-au-Prince. The rendezvous point was near Great Inagua

Island, at the northwest corner of the Windward Passage, two days away at a slow bell. Then, around 0200, District Seven radioed with welcome news. The five people airlifted to shore were in stable condition at Jackson Memorial Hospital, and all were expected to live. I called the captain on the ship's telephone to relay the news, waking him from a furtive sleep. It was a quick conversation. His only response was: "Thanks XO—that's why I joined this outfit."

At 0400 *Shearwater*'s port main diesel engine died, slowing the cutter to a paltry ten knots and limiting our maneuverability. Pat George explained that a turbocharger had seized up, and it would take five or six hours to repair. District changed the plan: the 210-foot cutter *Diligence* (WMEC 616) would now steam further north for the rendezvous. I navigated *Shearwater* toward an anchorage near Cayo Lobos, and we dropped the hook just outside Bahamian waters, close to where we'd seized *Macabi*. George worked through the morning and had the engine back up and running by 0930, but we spent the day at anchor, barely able to keep up with the feeding, medical care, and hotel needs of the 115 men and women who were recovering on our decks.

The weather stayed unseasonably cold, and when our security teams moved the Haitians out of engineering stores in the morning, some of them asked to stay. Most preferred being out of the wind, but others felt more comfortable in the sunshine, and we were able to accommodate both groups, all while guarding their movements. The Haitians outnumbered us seven to one, so we watched for signs of unrest. There was no trouble.

Tom Stoltz hefted pot after pot of beans and rice to the aft deck, feeding his crew in between. The rest of Red Crew provided security, three persons on duty during the day, discretely equipped with pepper spray and flashlights and in constant contact with the OOD by communications headset. Our tanks ran low, and we had to ration the cups of water. Stoltz broke out stockpiles of canned fruit for the migrants, knowing how essential the liquids and vitamins were to their recovery. The captain roamed, helping out on the bridge, in the galley, and on the aft deck—a coach encouraging his team, praising everyone's efforts.

We watched the health of the Haitians improve. Rehydrated and with warm food in their bellies, they bounced back to life, becoming animated and talkative, almost miraculously. I figured that while most of them would have survived another day or two in the locked cargo hold, some certainly would have died. Through Jean, we told them that they'd be transferred to a larger ship in the evening and would have to follow our instructions so that everyone stayed safe.

Diligence arrived at Cayo Lobos around 2100. By then we'd had the Haitians on board for nearly thirty hours, and Red Crew was dragging. The winds were howling from the east, gusting to thirty knots, building the seas to sharp five-foot breakers and adding a layer of complexity to the transfer. The OOD weighed anchor and maneuvered *Shearwater* alongside the larger cutter, approaching slowly, one hundred feet away, seventy-five, fifty. Our fenders were rigged along *Shearwater*'s starboard side, and when we were twenty feet off *Diligence*'s port quarter her crew tossed us a thick sea painter, which one of our seamen secured to a bitt on our starboard bow. *Shearwater* fell back on the sea painter and settled alongside *Diligence* amidships, surging up and down in the surf, with our thin aluminum hull only inches away from her thicker steel plating. *Diligence* was rolling freely, and the fenders couldn't keep up. Our hulls mashed together, scraping paint and bending our lifelines, the ear-bending howl of metal-to-metal contact ripping through the air.

The transfer was dizzying. *Shearwater* was surging up and down and *Diligence* was rolling 7 or 8 degrees, sometimes 10, creating a jerky, unpredictable motion between the two ships. *Diligence*'s massive white superstructure loomed over the SES like a three-story building swaying over our decks. *Diligence*'s embarkation point was a few feet higher than our aft deck, so her boatswains laid a wooden gangplank between the cutters, angled upward from *Shearwater*. They secured the gangplank at the top, and its lower end skittered back and forth across our white nonskid deck as the ships shifted and rolled.

As each Haitian stepped onto the gangplank, one of our crew members would grab the back of the person's life jacket and hold tight as he or she walked across the gap between the cutters. A *Diligence* crew member would then grab the strap on the front of the life jacket and half-guide, half-pull the person on board. One by one we led the Haitians across the two-foot-wide chasm, with the crew on *Diligence* talking to the Haitians to get their attention and trick them into not looking down, where they'd have witnessed a terrifying scene of our fenders being smashed flat in the grinding motion between the hulls. We'd saved these people from potential tragedy, and the last thing we wanted was for one of them to slip and fall during the transfer.

It took more than an hour, but as the last Haitian stepped onto *Diligence* I began to relax for the first time in two days. Looking at the relief on the faces of our crew—Sanders, Hartsock, Elliot, George—I knew they felt the same. The evolution hadn't been perfect: we'd bounced off *Diligence*'s hull several times, and there would be one heck of a mess to clean up in engineering stores, but somehow no one had been hurt, and every one of the Haitians was now safely on their way home.

We took on fuel and water from *Diligence*, which enabled us to finish the patrol without another port call. *Shearwater* returned to Key West on November 19, Red Crew exhausted but proud for having added a tenth drug bust to our list of seizures, five each under the command of Jerry Lober and Wayne Justice. Somehow, though, those accomplishments paled in significance to our encounter with *Sainte Bernadette*. Without any doubt, we'd helped 120 of our fellow humans live another day.

The *Sainte Bernadette* rescue rekindled memories from two years earlier, when *Active* had spent a month patrolling the Windward Passage. We'd made a four-day port-call to Port-au-Prince over Christmas. It was a haunting trip into a desperate universe. Twenty miles offshore, as *Active* steamed toward the port city, the sparking blue Caribbean waters turned cloudy, discolored by effluent and runoff from the capital city. Small fishing skiffs and rowboats headed toward us, following in the cutter's wake, the people on board shouting, offering trinkets or fish for sale. Ahead, Port-au-Prince sprawled under a fog-like haze, its low buildings and huts covering every nook and cranny of the hills, many tiny houses clinging perilously to the sides of mountains. You could see and smell the poverty.

Active moored at the stripped-down seaport terminal adjacent to Fort Islet Park. Awaiting our arrival were dozens of city policemen, a few toting machine guns and the rest carrying stout clubs. In the arrival party were officials from the U.S. embassy and the International Red Cross. They came on board and briefed the officers on the latest migrant intelligence and then gave the crew an eye-opening lecture on how to act when on liberty, focusing on the many dangers particular to Port-au-Prince. Stay in groups of at least four people. Don't drink the water. Don't eat anything locally produced. Under no circumstances give a cop a hard time, unless you were looking for a beating, or worse. Uncharacteristically, *Active*'s Boston-tough crew looked anxious, casting nervous glances, some of the men jittery. This was no place to bend the rules.

Along with two other officers, I was invited to Christmas Eve dinner at the home of the embassy's military attaché, a Marine colonel. He picked us up in a rusty Jeep and headed toward a mountain on the south side of the city. Beyond the confines of the pier, the city bustled with energy, thousands of people swarming the streets, clouds of beggars, clusters of merchants, dilapidated cars and taxis zipping through the throng. We stared at the cityscape—the streets lined with cinderblock houses and decrepit shanties made of wood and metal sheets, most with rusted tin roofs, the buildings jammed together, block after block, an endless parade of deprivation.

As the Jeep scaled the side of the hill we saw more palm trees and unkempt clumps of thick vegetation. The road skirted the edge of a steep canyon, and in the valley below were cramped rows of rickety shacks, covering every inch of the hillside, stacked on top of each other like cordwood. Up the Jeep climbed, the road twisting wildly, the four-wheel-drive getting a workout. Occasionally, amid the poverty, we could see a decent-looking house, usually behind a high iron fence and set far back from the road.

The road got narrower and steeper. To our left were a dozen make-shift huts in a row. Then to our right was a large house overlooking the city, painted cranberry red, two stories high, with fancy turrets flanking wide balconies on the upper floors. The colonel pulled up to the gate and a thin old man hobbled out to greet us, opening the gate to allow the Jeep through. We had arrived.

We spent the evening swimming in a deep oval pool, enjoying the company of the colonel's family as his wife and two teenage daughters regaled us with stories about living in the hemisphere's poorest nation. We ate as the sun set, sampling a smorgasbord of exotic dishes, from pickled fish to roasted cauliflower to salmon casserole. The view of the city below was spectacular. Spread out as far as we could see were dense clusters of small homes and shanties, dotted with islands of vegetation, the squalor incredible, yet from a distance somehow orderly. The colonel said that there was little violent crime, with the police force and the thug-like Tontons Macoutes, the dictator's secret police, ruling the streets.

It was just after dark when we said our goodbyes and headed down the mountain. The colonel's driver shepherded us back to the seaport. He was the same old man who'd let us in the gate and, after some friendly banter, he asked if we wanted to visit a slum and see how the poorest of the poor lived. Intrigued, we said yes. He took a circuitous route to the north side of the city, the Jeep coursing through nearly deserted streets, making good time, bounding up and down the rolling hills and bouncing through the potholes.

We thought we'd seen it all on the trip up the mountain, but the driver showed us an even grimmer world, with swarms of dilapidated huts, most only a dozen feet wide, some barely upright, many the color of drab metal sheeting or whitewashed cement but others, inexplicably, painted bright Caribbean hues. Just when it seemed that the scene couldn't be any more depressing, the Jeep crested a ridge, and spread out before us were waves of smaller hillocks, each a replica of the other, thousands upon thousands of ramshackle homes crammed together, sitting on pockmarked dirt streets with no running water or electricity, sewage floating through shallow ditches, mounds of garbage piled high.

The scene seared into my brain. The scope of the poverty was staggering, breathtaking, almost incomprehensible. A million people lived in Port-au-Prince, probably more, almost all of them desperately poor, scrapping for food and water and the necessities of life, with little hope of improving their lot. No wonder people wanted to flee this place.

Now I understood why a city-dweller or farmer or struggling merchant and his family would give up all their belongings—house, livestock, and land—and turn over their life savings to a smuggler offering the promise of a quick trip to America, risking death on board an overcrowded, unsafe boat. One Christmas in Haiti had explained everything.

———

As 1984 came to a close, the flow of Haitian migrants continued to spike. Our rescue of the 120 souls from the floating prison on *Sainte Bernadette* had been the tip of the iceberg. Every week or two a cutter made a major rescue—most of them in the Windward Passage but a few trickling through to the Bahamas.

Red Crew's last patrol of the year started right after Thanksgiving, on board *Sea Hawk*, her engine and generators now repaired. We patrolled east and south, boarding a tug and barge near Cayo Lobos, then made our second trip through Blossom Channel—this time in daylight—and headed for a four-hour port call at AUTEC. After topping off on fuel and water and hitting the Navy Exchange for a few bottles of tax-free liquor, *Sea Hawk* headed north, to patrol near the Berry Islands, to catch a lee from an oncoming cold front. The weather forecast wasn't pretty, with winds expected to top twenty-five knots.

We'd cleared the sea buoy off AUTEC when Group Miami handed us a new mission. A Falcon jet had overflown a wooden sailboat to our east and reported that up to fifty persons might be on board. The boat looked like a typical Haitian sail freighter, packed with migrants. Our orders were to get to it and rescue the people before the cold front blew through.

The captain ordered full speed ahead. The eastern side of the Tongue was home to an endless array of sand bores and coral heads. The Falcon crew had spotted the sailboat in one of the larger fields of coral, far from land, a desolate graveyard for those who failed to negotiate the dangers lurking below.

Sea Hawk arrived in late afternoon, the sun behind us, low in the west. The coral reef stretched out to the east as far as the eye could see, a postcard of tranquility, the light blue shallows empty but for a distant, brown bump sitting halfway to the horizon, miles from navigable waters. The captain studied it through the "big eyes," adjusting and readjusting the focus, and turned to me, clearly concerned. "It looks like a Haitian boat, all right— too far to tell if its overloaded, and the sail's not doing much," he said. "The water looks really shallow, tricky. Here, take a look." I stepped up, pressing my eye to the lens.

From a distance it was hard to see detail; the boat was a hazy blob. It might have been thirty-something feet long, with a dirty brown hull and a single mast, surrounded by a jeweled sea that sparkled in mottled hues of blue. There was a fuzzy dark mass along the top of the hull, probably people sitting on deck—dozens, for sure. The sail hung limp and useless. Senior Chief, standing over the radar, called out: "Got a good lock on it, four-point-seven miles. It's not moving at all."

Sea Hawk crept toward the shallows, closing the distance. Then, all stop. The cutter drifted four hundred yards off the reef. The captain, Senior Chief, BM1 Sanders, and I huddled around the chart table to work up a plan. "We can get the RHIB in there," Sanders said. "Looks like there's enough water—we'll just have to watch out for coral heads. We can escort the boat through the reef line, or if there's only a few dozen people on board, we can bring them back to the ship seven or eight at a time."

The captain agreed, adding a note of urgency. "We need to get moving and get this done before dark," he said. "XO, you take charge in the RHIB, and be sure to take a good look when you get there. Make sure their boat's seaworthy. If it sinks inside the reef, we've got real trouble."

Sanders, McCurry, and I would head into the field of coral. We dressed out in standard boarding gear, minus body armor, weapons, and helmet. Sanders threw sixty life jackets into the RHIB, thought about it, and then tossed in another twenty. We'd use the jackets for transferring the Haitians to the cutter. They also were a hedge—to be used if the sailboat were to sink or capsize.

We cast off from *Sea Hawk* at dusk, with a bold crimson sunset behind us, belying the old trope, "Red sky at night, sailor's delight." The forecast called for the cold front to pass through early in the morning, with the seas expected to grow from glassy calm to six feet, maybe higher. Sanders gunned the engine until we saw the water lighten, and then slowed to clutch speed, making three knots. The shallows were so still that it looked like plastic wrap had been stretched over the water, the glossy surface reflecting the purple, red, and magenta clouds in the western sky. We could make out hazy dome-shaped objects underwater, first a few random ones and then dozens more, scattered in every direction. Sanders joked that we'd have to be careful not to nick one of the coral heads with our propeller. It was a long paddle back to the cutter.

McCurry leaned over the RHIB's bow, resting his chest on the V of the rubber pontoon and scanning the water ahead of us. The sailboat was two miles away. McCurry guessed that there was six feet of water between our hull and the coral, so Sanders kicked up the speed a notch and aimed directly for the sailboat. He held his course and speed for ten minutes. Now a mile away, we looked toward the sailboat but couldn't make out any details in the failing light—only a murky silhouette.

"All stop!" It was McCurry. He pointed toward a jagged wall of coral directly ahead. This mass looked closer to the surface than the other coral we'd seen, forcing Sanders to jockey around it. As the last traces of sunlight faded away, McCurry shined a handheld spotlight into the water ahead, and Sanders nudged the RHIB slowly forward. As we got nearer to the sailboat, the path became more treacherous, with the gaps between the clumps of coral increasingly tight. McCurry called out the dangers, and Sanders twisted and turned the RHIB continuously, seeking safe passage. Some of the coral heads were almost brushing the surface. The circuitous route was costing us time. We'd be making the rescue in the dark.

The RHIB passed over an open area, the bottom ten feet below. We were able to approach to within two hundred yards of the sailboat when the coral loomed up again, blocking the way. McCurry kept the light pointed into the water ahead, and I shined my flashlight to the side, gauging the distance to the hazards passing by.

We could hear a crowd murmuring from across the calm water—the sound of an audience just before the lights go down. Sanders slid the RHIB between two coral ridges, and after a dozen doglegs we were only seventy-five feet from the sailboat. The murmuring had grown more intense. Sanders pulled back the throttle, letting the RHIB drift. "BM3, light up the boat for a second, I need to see how they're sitting," he said. McCurry nodded. He shined the spotlight beam onto the sailboat.

My first thought was that we were going to need a helluva lot more life jackets. In the spotlight was a solid mass of humanity. The sailboat was crammed with more people than I'd ever imagined could fit on a single hull. From stem to stern, faces stared at us, their eyes reflecting coolly in the spotlight beam, the people packed so tight that it was hard to tell which head went with which body. I caught my breath and then did a quick count, pointing my flashlight at the stern and slowly tracking it toward the bow. There were 25, 40, 75 faces. One hundred, 120 . . . *Damn!*—there were 140 Haitians, maybe more, on the cramped wooden boat, most sitting, some standing. I knew how unstable a boat like this could be.

Only six months earlier, the cutter *Hamilton* (WMEC 715) had encountered a grossly overloaded sailboat seventy-five miles north of Haiti. *Hamilton* had dispatched her motor surfboat, and as the Coast Guard team stepped on board the sailboat, a group of Haitians rushed to one side. The sailboat settled by the stern, and then capsized in the five-foot seas. Treading water, the boarding party saved scores of Haitians from drowning. Tragically, despite their heroic efforts, more than a dozen people were lost.

Here we faced a similar dire situation. Sanders, McCurry, and I were completely on our own. If the sailboat rolled or swamped, more than a hundred people could go into the sea. *Sea Hawk* was a prisoner of the deep water and couldn't do anything to help, and the most our RHIB could carry was ten or twelve persons at a time. If the boat sank, dozens would die.

It was amazing that the sailboat was even afloat. She sat so low in the water that a one-foot wave would have lapped over the gunwale. The boat was old and homemade, with a ragged wooden hull and a single mast made of a rough-hewn timber. The sail was completely limp—nothing more than a flag of surrender.

I spoke loudly and slowly, trying to sound calm and in command: "Does anyone speak English?" I asked. There was a low commotion, then one voice from amidships: "Yes, I can, what do you want us to do? Our boat is stuck." I asked the man his name and he replied, "Gabriel." He said they were from Haiti and had been at sea for a week. I told him that we were the United States Coast Guard and would help them, but needed everyone to remain where they were. No standing, no shifting, no movement at all. Gabriel said okay, and began shouting orders in Creole. The murmuring increased as everyone sat down. So far, so good.

The sailboat was stuck in a pen of coral heads, an underwater dead-end street, the only exit behind them. Gabriel told us they'd been there since midday. The Haitians had been sailing east to west, moving slowly, and had run smack into the coral, their boat bouncing off an underwater ridge. The impact had widened a seam in the hull, which was slowly flooding the boat, and the Haitians hadn't been able to maneuver out of the maze. Then the wind had died, stranding them.

That was how we found them—becalmed, surrounded on three sides by thick coral heads, and barely above water, 2 men bailing with wooden bowls, 140 persons sitting on the edge of disaster. Their salvation, *Sea Hawk*, was four miles and a forest of razor-sharp coral heads away.

McCurry, Sanders, and I reeled through the options. If we freed the boat from the coral cul-de-sac, there was no way she could sail toward deep water in the calm air. We could pluck the Haitians from the sailboat, cramming eight or ten, maybe twelve, into the RHIB, but it'd take at least a dozen round trips to the cutter, and at an hour per trip, the storm would hit before we'd saved half the people. That left only one solution—a tow.

Sanders eyed the sailboat, taking in her contours, studying her freeboard. "It's going be a slow pull," he said. "They can't rock the boat at all or it'll swamp. We'll have to toss the line and have them loop it around the forward bitt. It looks like it'll hold." The crucifix-shaped bitt was made of thick wooden pillars, three feet abaft the sailboat's bow, surrounded by a swarm of bodies.

Sanders nudged the RHIB alongside the sailboat as Gabriel ordered everyone to stay seated. McCurry passed out the life jackets, distributing them to women and children first. He tied a bowline in the end of our three-inch hawser and handed it to one of the Haitians, who draped the knot over the crossbar near the top of the bitt. Slowly, Sanders edged the RHIB ahead, putting the towline under light strain, careful not to lurch. McCurry paid out twenty feet of line to keep the sailboat close. The Haitians remained seated, a respectful audience, quietly watching as Sanders swung the boat 180 degrees, now headed due east, directly away from *Sea Hawk*.

McCurry controlled the towline while I leaned over the RHIB's bow, shining the spotlight into the depths, on the lookout for hazards. We crept ahead, making two or three knots over ground. Behind us the sailboat was barely afloat, inches away from shipping water. One big bump and all hell would break loose.

There was no wind, and the sea remained supernaturally calm, a shallow, long-period swell the only motion on the water's surface. It was like motoring through a huge swimming pool, the edges lost in the darkness. The quarter-moon in the west had been obscured by high-altitude clouds, a sure sign that the cold front was getting closer, rendering a dark, impenetrable night. The scene looked fake, staged, like a cheap movie set. Beyond the arc of the handheld spotlight was inky blackness, absolute dark, as if there were a thick curtain holding back all illumination. In the western distance sat *Sea Hawk*, the only visible light, her deck floodlights ablaze, the cutter framed in black. She looked like a child's bathtub toy. Behind us, the Haitians began talking quietly, one singing in a deep voice, accompanied by rhythmic splashes of water as the two men continued bailing the slowly sinking boat.

Sanders threaded the tow through the coral reef. The sailboat drew twice as much water as the RHIB, and we had to find deep channels, at least ten feet wide, so that the boat could pass through. I swept the spotlight side-to-side to see the obstructions in our path and reported each lump of coral as it became visible. Sanders looped the boats around them. He navigated as if he did this sort of thing every day, gently adjusting the throttles and making minute course corrections—the skilled hands of a surgeon.

We traveled fifty yards away from the cutter before the channel opened, and Sanders could curve south and then back to the west, dodging a gaggle of coral heads, keeping the sailboat and its hundred-plus souls safe in the gaps between the craggy underwater ridges. I kept my voice low and emotionless, so as not to spool up the migrants.

"Big one, forty feet out, zero-one-zero relative, close to the surface."

"I see it, coming to port. McCurry, keep the line tight."

"Got it, Boats."

"Two more dead ahead, fifty feet, looks like it's best to keep them to port. A whole bunch of them five yards to the right of those two."

"Okay, got 'em in sight. Coming right. Gonna be a tight squeeze."

The RHIB and its tow passed through an underwater alleyway, with massive coral heads four feet away from tearing the sailboat's hull. Sanders maintained a slow bell, weaving around villages of coral, steering a serpentine course, with the trip toward *Sea Hawk* painfully slower than the ride out had been. We'd been under way for half an hour when the RHIB entered a canyon made up of a dozen coral heads on one side and a thicker, solid ledge on the other. Sanders steered the RHIB around a left-hand bend and then we saw with horror that the canyon narrowed sharply. It looked like there was barely enough room for the sailboat to squeeze through.

As we entered the canyon, the sailboat's starboard side scraped against the ledge—a gentle kiss, bouncing off the coral. The murmuring picked up. Sanders pulled back the throttle, letting the RHIB drift. On the sailboat, three men stood up, one pointing into the water, his voice rising, babbling in Creole. Gabriel shouted "*Chita, chita!*"—"sit down, sit down!"—until the men sat, one heavily, jostling the crowd around him, the shifting bodies causing the sailboat to rock side to side, her gunwale pivoting closer to the water's surface with every roll. The murmuring become a gaggle of voices, the sailboat again clipping the ledge, harder this time, sending a shudder through her wooden hull. Gabriel screamed for calm.

We were inches from catastrophe. Sanders, his voice brisk and urgent, told McCurry to shorten the towline. He twisted the sailboat away from the coral, inching the RHIB forward, the boat only ten feet behind us, gliding through the canyon. The beam of the searchlight lit up the ragged underwater ledges. The Haitians quickly fell silent as they watched their boat slip through an opening that was thirty feet long and only a few feet wider than their hull, their boat still rolling side to side, the oscillations slowly fading. I held my breath. Sanders and McCurry probably held theirs, too.

The sailboat didn't touch the coral, safely clearing the jagged walls. The far end of the subsurface canyon came into sight, the ledge peeling away, and ten yards beyond it a huge, solitary coral head sat directly in our path. Exiting the canyon, Sanders turned the wheel hard to starboard and then, when abreast of the coral head, twisted it all the way to port, adding a shot of power, enabling the transom of the RHIB and the sailboat to loop gracefully around the underwater mass. We cleared the danger and continued the slow glide through the coral maze. The Haitians stayed quiet.

For almost an hour the RHIB dragged the tow and her passengers toward *Sea Hawk*, looping and twisting around a city of obstructions.

It was delicate and nerve-wracking work, making time stand still, every coral head a tragedy waiting to happen.

The fate of the Haitians was in our hands—140 men, women, and children. I gave thanks for Sanders' boat-handling skill, and McCurry's sharp eyes, and for the Falcon crew that had spotted the sailboat. Without them the Haitians would still be stranded in the reef, only to face the high winds and seas from the cold front bearing down from the west. There was no doubt that if the radically overloaded boat met heavy weather, every last one of the Haitians would die.

Then, our minds numb from the tension, the reef began to thin, the coral heads appearing less often, the water a touch deeper. Sanders had gotten us through the worst of it. The Tongue of the Ocean—safety—was close aboard. McCurry lengthened the tow to thirty feet and sat on deck, leaning back against the pontoon, staring at the sailboat. He exhaled slowly. "Damn, XO, that's the hairiest damn thing I've ever done. Type of thing that'll give you a heart condition. Hard to believe that boat's still floating." He grinned. "And hey, Boats—nice job getting through that maze, you really ought to be a reef tour guide. Maybe there's a future in it for you." Sanders chuckled, blushing.

Captain Justice called from *Sea Hawk*, asking for a status report. Sanders told him we were doing fine and crossing into deeper water, and should be alongside the cutter in a few minutes. I felt enormous relief, leaving the coral in our wake, and the steely look on Sanders' face began to soften. The captain called again and said *Sea Hawk* was ready to receive the migrants, our crew thoroughly tested from the 120 whom we'd saved from *Sainte Bernadette*, just two weeks earlier. We all knew the drill, and thankfully, this group seemed to be in better health.

The RHIB approached the cutter from astern, the Haitians talking louder, some pointing, Gabriel urging calm. Red Crew was waiting on the main deck, our ranks thinned due to illness and out-of-town training. Although we'd been augmented by a chief storekeeper from Group Key West, there were only 15 of us, needing to care for more than 140 migrants. That could make security difficult if there were instigators. I hoped everyone on the sailboat was friendly. We quickly found out that some of them weren't.

The captain decided to take advantage of the calm seas by tying the sailboat to the step deck, parallel to the transom. Sanders towed the vessel until she was fifteen feet from the cutter, directly behind and perpendicular to *Sea Hawk*, and McCurry cast off the towline. Sanders pivoted the RHIB and used its soft bow to push the sailboat sideways until it contacted the four cherry fenders hanging over the cutter's stern. The evolution was smooth and effective.

That's when one of the Haitian men, a tall, scrawny twenty-something dressed in a tattered *Hard Rock Cafe* T-shirt, jumped up and started screaming in Creole at the top of his lungs, thrusting his thin arms above his head as if he'd won the lottery. Instantly, a dozen of his fellow passengers started yelling back, several standing, pulling at him, trying to force him to sit. The man fought back. The tussle looked like it was growing into a major scrum when the scrawny man suddenly sat down, holding his face in his hands and whimpering in a high-pitched tone, like an injured dog. Gabriel said the man had been trying to incite his shipmates to riot.

Quickly, our deck force tied the sailboat's bow and stern to the cutter and began unpeeling the mass of people, taking them off one at a time, gingerly, so as not to upset the delicate balance. The sailboat's gunwale was barely above water. Our crew walked the people up the short ladder from the step deck onto the main deck for a quick search and medical evaluation.

We'd only removed the first dozen people when the scrawny man jumped up again and began shrieking and moaning, this time in a pained, agonizing tone. He sounded like he was on fire, and he looked possessed. Maybe he was. The man thrashed his arms wildly in all directions, striking the people around him. They struck back. It was bedlam, men pushing and shoving, one woman screaming and another smacking the man repeatedly with the palm of her hand. The sailboat began rocking side to side, her gunwale dipping into the water. After a thirty-second frenzy the man stopped his rant, paused, and then leaped off the boat, running across *Sea Hawk*'s step deck, then up onto the main deck, headed toward the bridge, shouting nonsense at the top of his lungs.

Red Crew had seen enough. Pat George tackled him, a perfect take-down, and with the help of two shipmates secured the man's arms and dragged him to the starboard side of the deck. George frisked the man and then handcuffed him to the rail, shackling his legs to a stanchion so he couldn't jump overboard. The Haitian continued to alternate between screaming and silence and after a while fell into a catatonic state. Senior Chief, our purveyor of nicknames, dubbed him Captain Crazy.

I stood on the aft deck, watching as we peeled Haitians off the boat, one after another, our crew moving cautiously to preserve the vessel's equilibrium. The sailboat stretched the exact width of our transom—forty feet. She was longer than we'd first thought.

There also were more people than I'd estimated. Our crew had taken 50 Haitians on board the cutter, and as I scanned the sailboat now from a perch slightly above it, I still counted another hundred-something bodies. For every person we removed, another head popped up. Where in the world were they coming from? I walked down to the step deck and leaned over, now looking directly into the boat for the first time, using my flashlight to peer through the crowd, and was dumbfounded to see that beneath the Haitians sitting on deck was another layer of people, many women and children, wallowing in a mire of garbage, seawater, and spent clothing that was sloshing in the sailboat's bilge. It was almost too surreal to comprehend. I did some quick math, guessing the number of people in the lower layer, concluding that we'd actually found at least 225—maybe 250—migrants on board the boat. I feared that we could be in over our heads.

Captain Justice made a command decision. Instead of housing the Haitians behind the superstructure, we'd put as many as we could fit on the bow, which would allow the bridge watchstander to help keep an eye on them and would free up space aft for medical treatment and security. Our crew already had picked out four men from the crowd who were growling and sputtering in Creole, goading others to rebel. Our deck force roped off a section of the fantail and put the troublemakers in it, cuffed, to separate them from the rest of the population.

Our EMTs were treating others for various maladies, mostly dehydration or acute seasickness. In general this crowd was in better overall health than those we'd found locked in *Sainte Bernadette*'s hold, although now we had children and infants to deal with. As before, Hartsock, Weatherby, and McCurry stayed busy through the night.

And the Haitians kept coming. There were now 110 of them on deck. The sailboat still looked completely full. Ten minutes later, we'd removed another 50. When we hit the 200 mark, I was amazed to see a large crowd still sitting on the sailboat. Five minutes later we'd crossed the 225 threshold. Then, the last Haitian came on board, a frail man, probably 70 years old. He'd been sitting in the middle of the deck, holding onto the mast, refusing to leave. Gabriel coaxed him onto *Sea Hawk*, promising a warm meal and a cup of water. Tenderly, the man stood, his creaky legs shaking, and 2 of our crew members gently guided him across the gap between the sailboat and the cutter. He was number 265.

We didn't know it at the time—and wouldn't have had time to care— but *Sea Hawk* had just found the largest group of Haitians yet encountered at sea by the U.S. Coast Guard. The incident became a national story, gracing the pages of newspapers across the country. *USA Today*'s headline read, "A new wave bound for Florida's shore," and described the "biggest boatload ever seized by the Coast Guard." Had we written the story, knowing firsthand the deadly hazards that the Haitians had faced, we'd have said "rescued" rather than "seized."

Our fifteen sailors now had to care for a population almost twenty times larger, all while safely navigating the cutter one hundred fifty miles to rendezvous with the 210-foot cutter *Reliance* (WMEC 615), which would transport the migrants back to Haiti—in churning seas. The cold front was just hours away, and the lake-like waters of the Tongue were poised to roar into tumult and confusion when the winds began blasting.

First, we had to dispose of the sailboat. With the bailing stopped, the boat had settled lower in the water, the gunwale now even with the surface. The vessel wasn't going to sink on her own, though, and Red Crew needed to give her a nudge. One look at the boat's thick wooden hull told us that bullets wouldn't do the trick. That left burning the hull as the only option.

Weatherby and I stepped on board the boat to make sure no people or valuables remained. It was a sickening task. On deck was a scattering of soiled clothing, chicken bones, and two large cooking pans. The lower hold was filled with garbage and debris, floating lazily in the fetid water. We shined our flashlights into the hold, examining every corner, probing the water with a gaff, trying to shield ourselves from the overpowering odor, a mixture of illness, poverty, urine, and sweat. There was nothing to save.

Weatherby splashed five gallons of gasoline across the upper deck. We stepped back onto the cutter as Sanders and McCurry cast off the boat, pushing her with their boots. When the sailboat was ten feet away, Weatherby tossed a lit flare onto her, amidships, sending the coarse wood into an inferno. The Haitians on *Sea Hawk*'s deck stopped talking and stared. Captain Crazy started wailing at full volume, the soundtrack for the funeral pyre of the boat they'd sailed from their island nation. The ship that would begin their journey home was picking up speed, en route to *Reliance*. As we sailed away, the bright flames receded into the distance and the inferno seemed to be floating in air. The night was too dark to tell where the sea met the sky.

Four hours later the cold front hit with a vengeance. The winds rose and the seas devolved into a jumble of white caps and rolling breakers. Twenty-five of the migrants were still either on the aft deck for medical treatment or else in the time-out pen—we now had seven troublemakers segregated—but the other two hundred forty persons were neatly crammed onto *Sea Hawk*'s bow, twelve tons of humanity sitting quietly in orderly rows, wrapped in blankets, huddling together and sharing food and drink. Sanders and his team had exercised their creative skills and tied a tarpaulin across the breadth of the bow, providing a shallow, tent-like structure that deflected some of the wind that was blowing across the deck. As the storm front passed through we had to slow to clutch speed to prevent spray from soaking our passengers, delaying the rendezvous with *Reliance*. The last thing we needed was dozens of hypothermia victims.

The downsized Red Crew worked nonstop, all hands on deck for twenty-four hours, no time for sleep, just a catnap, when one of us became dangerously exhausted. Two people stood bridge watch, another in the engine room. Stoltz had full-time help in making and delivering the food. The EMTs provided continuous care. Four security watchstanders monitored the crowd, looking for any sign of medical distress or trouble, one watching from the bridge and the others guarding the main deck. A fifth shipmate kept an eye on the instigators held aft, flashlight and pepper spray at the ready.

This group of Haitians was far more unruly than those from *Sainte Bernadette*. The security watchstanders had to break up small gangs that were trying to rile up their compatriots, and a fight broke out when a middle-aged man began stealing food from his neighbors. Three women beat on him, and a dozen others pushed and shoved—a maritime mosh-pit. Two of our crew waded into the crowd, pinned the thief to the deck, and returned the stolen food before hauling him away.

Our EMTs treated thirty-five Haitians, most of them for dehydration and one old woman for seizures. Thankfully, we faced no health calamities. There were more than a dozen small children in the group, the youngest a newborn, and we gave his mother a special hideaway aft of the superstructure, swaddled in blankets and covered by an awning, protected from the elements. Tom Stoltz cooked nonstop, filling and refilling a huge metal pot with rice and beans. He'd learned a lot from our previous Haitian rescue and was doling out the food in paper cups, along with smaller cups of water, making sure that every person was fed. Once breakfast had been served he immediately set to whipping up a midafternoon meal—more rice and beans. No one objected to the monotonous menu.

Our visiting chief petty officer from Group Key West worked at a fever pitch, a great team player, clearly glad to be helping in such a tough situation. He never took a break. Afterward, red-eyed and barely able to stand, he told me in a cracking voice that it was the most important thing he'd done in his Coast Guard career.

Just before 1400 we came alongside *Reliance*, which was drifting in the lee of Andros Island, rolling briskly, a moving target in a wind-whipped sea. *Reliance*'s crew tossed us a four-inch line to use as a sea painter, and we cut our engines, settling with a thud along her port side. Having learned our lesson from the *Sainte Bernadette* transfer, we'd doubled the number of fenders, this time suffering no scrapes or bent rails. Our security detail began walking the Haitians from the bow to *Sea Hawk*'s aft deck. I stood at an opening at the rail, where the Haitians would climb three steps up a Jacob's ladder into *Reliance*'s air castle.

The first person approached, a twenty-something woman who was holding a little boy by the hand. He was six or seven years old, very thin but healthy and alert—a poster-child for cute. I pointed to the Jacob's ladder, and she stepped toward it, then hesitated. *Uh-oh*, I thought. She looked at me, unflinching, her large brown eyes watering, her voice trembling. "Thank you," was all she said, bowing humbly. Floored, I mumbled back, "Uh, sure, of course, you're welcome." I bent down toward the boy to say goodbye and check his life jacket. In a flash he reached up with both arms, hugging me around the neck, snuggling tight.

The emotion hit like a wrecking-ball. This innocent boy, this beautiful child, had survived death's call. Now he would live, and breathe, and, God willing, grow tall and strong. I stood up, deeply moved, eyes blurred with tears, heart bursting with joy that these people had been saved, and held the woman's arm as she took three steps up the ladder, not letting go until a *Reliance* crewmember had grabbed her by the front of the life jacket. She stepped on board, safe. Her son followed, scampering up the ladder, eyes focused on his mom, my hand clamped onto his life jacket in a vise grip. Two people down, 263 to go.

The transfer was long and tedious. We had to recycle the life jackets, tossing them back from *Reliance* onto our main deck, as we only had enough for half the population. I remained at the rail and guided each person up the ladder, giving the saddest ones a smile, staring down the instigators, and receiving many more thank-yous as the Haitians left our cutter. I felt responsible for making sure that every person embarked *Reliance* safely.

Then we were done. Sanders cast off the sea painter, and *Reliance* steamed away, spray flying as her bow cut into a larger wave. None of Red Crew watched for long. We set a three-person watch, two on the bridge and one making engineering rounds, and everyone else got busy cleaning the ship.

The mess was amazing. The deck was littered with discarded clothes, paper cups, garbage, and mounds of blankets. I stood on the bridge wing next to the lookout, Gloria Denton, watching Sanders comb through the trash on the bow. He bent over, picked up a toothbrush from the clutter, looked at it quizzically, and pretended to brush his teeth with it. He was a good actor. Was he really sticking the brush in his mouth? It sure looked that way. Denton didn't think he was joking and ran to the starboard rail, gagging. The rest of the deck force howled with laughter—a needed tonic.

It took three hours for the crew to scrub the topside surfaces and stow the migrant rescue gear. Then we all hit the rack.

Over dinner Lieutenant Justice and I debriefed the operation. We recognized a simple truth: *Sea Hawk* herself had been a key element of our success. The aft step deck, solid stability, and wide open spaces had allowed Red Crew to take on board a record crowd of people and care for their basic needs for more than a day. There was no other type of patrol boat in the Coast Guard with such a capability. *Sea Hawk*'s unorthodox, boxy, barge-like hull had helped save the day.

We also realized that these Haitians had been lucky. Their sailboat had been so grossly overloaded that the weight of the bodies crammed into the bilge provided a form of human ballast, maintaining the boat's stability. But they had no life rafts, life jackets, or other floatation. Had we not pulled them from the coral reef, the boat would have been pummeled into splinters by the cold front's strong winds and heavy seas. There was absolutely no doubt that *Sea Hawk*'s crew had just saved 265 persons from a watery grave.

Red Crew had worked to the point of physical and emotional exhaustion. The misery of the Haitians was tragic on its face, and magnified since we knew to where they were being returned. We were sending them back to the poorest nation in the Western Hemisphere, and all they'd wanted was freedom and a better life. That ate at our consciences and begged the question: was it better to be alive in a hellhole or floating dead at the bottom of the sea? It may have seemed stark, but that was the choice.

I thought of the little boy, and the unexpected hug, and how deeply I'd been touched by his embrace. He'd felt warm, alive, a symbol of hope. To me, the answer was simple. We'd given 265 people a second chance at living, the most precious gift possible. For that we should be proud.

9

Promise Fulfilled

January 1985

The year ended quietly. Red Crew transferred ashore, earning a much-needed two-week break and time to travel home for Christmas. When we returned in early January, the crew was rested and eager to get back under way. It took only a week or two away from operations for the underway itch to strike. Red Crew wanted more action.

In late January we were steaming south from Miami in the worst weather I'd seen as XO Red. The seas were running eighteen feet, steep and breaking, with thirty-five-knot winds from the northeast pushing against the northbound Gulf Stream. The National Weather Service had issued a gale warning earlier in the day, advising boaters to seek shelter.

Shearwater was making turns for twelve knots, headed for a lee at Elbow Cay. District Seven wanted us there to respond to intelligence reports of a drug transfer. We'd departed Miami at 2200 and hoped to get into sheltered waters west of Cay Sal by first light. In the Gulf Stream the ship was barely making eight knots over ground.

I had the midwatch and spent the first hour maneuvering *Shearwater* to dodge a stream of containerships headed north near Biscayne Bay. The quartering seas generated a twisting, thrashing motion that kept most of Red Crew awake. The captain had parked himself in the pilothouse, keeping a close eye on the merchant traffic.

Suddenly I saw a light flash in the water nearby, close aboard, and ran to the port bridge wing, yelling, "What the hell was that?" I turned to Seaman Buttermore, the quartermaster, and ordered, "All stop, lift to zero, rudder amidships." She jumped to the helm, disengaged the autopilot, and pulled back the throttles. *Shearwater* shuddered to a stop. Captain Justice joined me at the port rail. "Something flashed, right over there," I told him. "Maybe 100, 150 yards out. It was a bright light, just for a second." We scanned the murky darkness, the seas cresting and falling, the waves crashing and the wind howling. The lookout, Seaman Denton, picked up the night-vision scope and began to scan the waters off *Shearwater*'s port side. The four of us waited, eyes straining, seeing nothing, one, two minutes passing by, the cutter bobbing awkwardly in the heavy waves.

"There!" Captain Justice had seen another flash and was pointing due east. "Looked like a handheld light, it came on and then went dark," he said. An instant later, the light flashed a third time, then repeated five times in succession. Someone was signaling to us—in the Gulf Stream, in terrible weather, in the middle of the night, thirty miles from shore. My mind raced, thinking that we'd found a disabled boat or a load of migrants, already wondering about the best way to get people on board the cutter in the treacherous conditions.

"Buttermore, energize the searchlight and aim off the port beam, two-eight-zero relative, about a hundred yards out," the captain ordered. She flipped the switch and reached up to swivel the searchlight, the light's white-hot beam tracing across the top of the waves. Then she slowly moved the beam back and forth. At first it only illuminated breaking seas, dark and angry, marching relentlessly toward the southwest. Then came a glint. Something had reflected in the spotlight's beam, then fallen behind a passing wave. "Hold it steady—you got something," the captain shouted. We waited, with Buttermore trying to keep the light on target as *Shearwater* rocked and rolled beneath her. As the wave passed, an object came into view, off-white, wet and glistening in the intense light. It was a boat.

"What the . . ." The captain's voice trailed off. A hundred yards off our port beam, rolling crazily in the churning seas, was a fifteen-foot outboard, seemingly in good shape, a single man standing at the console, wearing a yellow foul-weather jacket and holding a large flashlight. The boat was dwarfed by the waves. The vessel had no cabin or superstructure and just a single upright console in the middle of an open deck. It had, at most, two feet of freeboard.

Captain Justice found his voice. "What the hell is he doing out here in this mess? That's goddam insane!" He paused, rubbing his hands together. "He's gotta be waiting for an air drop. There's no other reason to be out here. This is madness." I stared at the boat through binoculars, focusing on the man. He was tall and lean, middle-aged, with dark hair matted from salt spray. Along with the yellow rain slicker, he was wearing long khaki pants and, incredibly, what looked like dress shoes. "XO, get us over next to this guy," Justice said. The captain was seething. "I need to have a little talk with him," he added.

I maneuvered *Shearwater* to port and closed the gap to fifty feet, waving at the man to come alongside. At that distance, the angle was too steep to train the searchlight beam down on the boat, so Buttermore grabbed a smaller, handheld light and handed it to Denton. She aimed it right at the man, watching as the outboard surged upward on a crest and then fell into the deep trough between two waves. The man was jockeying the boat in a tight circle. There was a small electronic device attached to the console, a LORAN unit, and he probably was using it to keep station at a rendezvous point.

Lieutenant Justice picked up a megaphone, making eye contact with the operator across the expanse of foam and water.

"Sir, this is the U.S. Coast Guard. Can you hear me?" The man nodded yes.

"Sir, where are you from?" The man cupped his ear. The captain repeated the question, more slowly this time. The man nodded and mouthed "Miami." It was hard to hear him over the maelstrom, his voice distant and weak, fading in and out with the gusts of wind.

"What's the purpose of your voyage?" The man paused, considering the question. He hunched his shoulders, tilting his head, as if to say, "I really don't have a good answer for that."

"Sir, why are you out here?" Justice's voice was firm, flashing a hint of anger, his cheeks turning red. This time the man answered, cupping his hands as he yelled back. Through the shriek of wind, it sounded like he said, "Waiting for friends coming back from the Bahamas . . ."

The captain slammed his hand on the railing. The man saw his reaction and flinched. Justice turned to me, growling. "This guy's a doper, there's no other way he'd be out here. If we could, I'd board him in a second and drag him back to Miami. I just can't imagine we can get over there without getting someone killed." He stopped talking to think. "Better yet, maybe we'll just leave his ass out here to fend for himself. Un-goddam-believable."

Captain Justice stared at the white boat, gears turning in his head. Then his face perked up, like a light bulb switched on. He raised the megaphone again, speaking in a deeper tone.

"Sir, this is the captain speaking. We know why you're here. You're waiting for a drug delivery. We have the registration number of your boat and are going to stay nearby until you return to port. You may not be able to see us, but we will be here. Head for shore now, before your boat sinks and before you break any laws. That is your only hope." The man in the yellow slicker stared at us, dumbfounded, not sure how to respond.

Justice turned to me again. "XO, get us the hell out of here. We've gotta get down to Elbow Cay. Just turn off our nav lights first." Denton switched off the handheld spotlight and Buttermore secured the running lights, making *Shearwater* virtually invisible in the storm. I ordered the ship ahead at twelve knots, course 190 degrees true, leaving the man in the open boat to continue his endless circles, awaiting the air drop, but—if Captain Justice's ruse worked—thinking that the Coast Guard was hovering nearby. The captain was confident. "Trust me, XO, that guy'll head home now," he said. "We've blown his cover. I don't think anyone could find him in this crap, anyway. Send Group his registration number so they can put him on the lookout list. Let's chalk this one up as 'air-drop interrupted.'" With that, Justice stepped below to the mess deck to grab a snack and commiserate with his sleepless crew.

As *Shearwater* steamed away I energized the night-vision scope and aimed it toward the spot where the small boat had been circling. At first there was nothing to see—just the froth of an occasional breaking wave. Then there was a glimpse of the outboard, her bow pointed to the northwest and steaming on a steady course, picking her way through the mammoth waves, a white shimmering wake trailing behind it. Sure enough, the man was headed to shore.

———

For the second half of the patrol *Shearwater* took part in a naval exercise in the Gulf of Mexico, one hundred miles west of Tampa. *Shearwater*'s job was to act as an enemy missile boat and try to sneak up on a U.S. Navy battle group, with the goal of sinking the gray-hulls. The rules of the war game were simple. We had to get within visual range of a target in order to launch our "missiles," which actually were a set of white flares. I thought it was a waste of time, plowing through the misty seas and playing kids' games when we could have been chasing real-life criminals, but if there was anything I'd learned over the past two years, it was that orders were orders.

The exercise lasted three days, with Pat George and his engineers battling irksome engine problems. *Shearwater* would head far to the west of the battle group during daylight and then try to sneak toward the Navy task force at night, modifying our deck and running lights to look like different types of boats. It didn't work. The Navy combatants were equipped with sensors that could identify a specific vessel by the electronic signature of its radar. Once they'd acquired our signal, the data was locked into their computers, and they could always tell when *Shearwater* was nearby. In that sense it was an unfair fight.

If nothing else, however, the Coast Guard breeds officers who are adaptive, and on the third night, as we approached the area where we thought the battle group might be steaming, Captain Justice ordered us to shut off our radar. We looped to the north, running at half-speed, to approach from a different direction than expected, and sneaked up on our "enemy" amid a clump of shrimp trawlers that were transiting from the Louisiana coast to the Keys. *Shearwater* was able to sneak into the battle group and launch a half-dozen missiles—just as the Navy ships blew us to pieces with their guns, as indicated by their own green flares. It wasn't clear who'd won the mock battle, but it felt good to have gotten so close to the more capable Navy warships.

In the morning *Shearwater* met up with the 210-foot cutter *Courageous* (WMEC 622), which also had been playing in the war game. There were two commanders on board *Courageous* who needed a ride to shore, and we were directed to take them into St. Pete. Both of the officers were prospective captains of other 210s, and had spent time in *Courageous* on a familiarization cruise. The commanders came on board by small boat, and our captain welcomed them on the main deck. After a cup of coffee, the entourage headed to *Shearwater*'s bridge. Neither of the commanders had seen an SES before, and they were eager to learn more about our ship.

Shearwater was twenty miles west of Tampa Bay, inbound at full speed, when the fire broke out. A heat sensor above the starboard main engine showed an extreme temperature, and oily black smoke began spilling out of the air vents on deck. Senior Chief grabbed the 1MC, his voice blasting out of speakers throughout the ship: "*Fire, fire, fire!* There is a report of fire in the starboard engine room. All hands man your emergency stations. This is not a drill. Fire in the starboard engine room. All hands man your emergency stations." One of the commanders, a stocky, well-manicured officer, had looked sleepy up to that point. Now he was alert, his eyes darting left and right as he watched the frenetic action on deck.

Senior Chief brought *Shearwater* to all stop just before the engineers shut down both main diesels and energized the ship's fire pumps. The pumps were reliable, but some of the fire hoses were old and weather-worn, and one of them burst as it was pressurized. Two of the fire main valves on the main deck began leaking, sending blankets of spray into the air. Members of the fire team assembled on the main deck, donned their firefighting gear, and then entered the hull through the superstructure, winding their way below deck to confront the fire.

Pat George beat them to the punch. He'd been on watch monitoring the lift engines when the fire broke out and grabbed a handheld extinguisher and charged into the engine space to battle the flames. The fire had started when an oil line on a turbocharger had broken free, spraying oil onto the hot surface, which ignited instantly. George put out the fire, but we didn't know that right away, since he had no way to communicate with us.

The captain and I stayed on the bridge, monitoring the firefighting effort and describing to our two distinguished visitors the characteristics of the SESs that made a fire even more dangerous than on a typical cutter. "You see, our entire hull is made of aluminum," I explained, "and once the temperature reaches about 1,200 degrees, the decks will melt and we'll lose structural integrity. At that point we'll have to abandon ship, assuming we can get to the life rafts." I pointed to the rafts, which sat aft of the engine rooms. "If we can't get to them, we'll just have to go for a swim. Fortunately the water's pretty warm around here, at least most of the time." It was a gray, soggy day, cold and clammy, with a heavy overcast, and the air temperature was in the upper fifties. The commanders looked at each other, the stocky one clearly uncomfortable, both undoubtedly thinking we must be crazy to sail a ship like this.

George stomped up to the bridge, his face and hands covered in black soot and his uniform soaked with sweat and salt water. His hair was matted and soiled and stuck out cartoonishly in all directions, as if he'd been shocked. He ignored the commanders and spoke to the captain.

"I've got good news and bad news," he said, pausing. Justice waited for the verdict. "The good news is that the fire's out. It wasn't that big—I'm pretty sure an oil line let go. The bad news is that we're flooding. Something melted or cracked near the bilges, and now there's a hole in the hull. I put a plug in it but it's still leaking pretty bad. The boys are trying to patch it up. I think we can fix it, but if not we're going to flood the entire starboard bilge. Either way it's going take some serious welding to make it right." The stocky commander looked like he was going to pass out.

By that time Hartsock had restarted the port main engine, and *Shearwater* began limping into Tampa Bay. Group St. Petersburg sent a 41-foot utility boat to escort us to shore, while our engineers jammed wedges and plugs into the crack in the hull. The repair team was able to reduce the flooding to a trickle and used the bilge pumps to empty the floodwater from underneath the engine, while George replaced the broken oil line. After a four-hour transit *Shearwater* made it safely to shore, putting the starboard engine on line as we approached the Coast Guard pier. The hole turned out to be easily repaired, and by early afternoon a local welder had put a temporary patch over it. *Shearwater* was ready to return to sea.

Our VIPs left in a hurry as soon as we moored, gesturing and whispering to each other as they walked down the pier, clearly relieved to have survived their eight-hour voyage on the Coast Guard's newest but most temperamental drug-fighting cutter.

———————

The Coast Guard–Navy rivalry stretches back two centuries, since the founding of the Republic. Each branch is confident that it is America's premier maritime service. The Navy is fifteen years older, formed as the Continental Navy in 1775, but was disbanded in 1786 and then reestablished eleven years later. The predecessor of the Coast Guard, the Revenue Cutter Service, was established in 1790 and has been in existence ever since, without interruption, lending truth to the motto that the Coast Guard is the nation's oldest continuing seagoing service.

The Navy, about ten times the size of the smaller branch, brags of its heft, weaponry, ships, and worldwide deployments. The Coast Guard boasts of being the hard nucleus about which the Navy forms in time of war. Navy personnel belittle their brethren by calling Coasties puddle pirates, mud ducks, or shallow-water sailors. Sometimes a brazen Coastie will offer a cruder reply. And so the rivalry goes.

In reality, I'd seen the Navy and Coast Guard work side by side in dozens of operations, never once with animosity, much less outright hostility. Each service has its range of missions, with some overlap between them, drug interdiction a prime example. Both services are manned by dedicated, loyal, and highly professional men and women. Both get the job done.

In November 1984 the SES Division was joined by a Navy cousin. *SES 200* was a research vessel under control of the Naval Sea Systems Command. The ship had bounced between commercial industry and the two services since her launch in 1978. She was built by Bell Halter and known to the company as *BH-110*. In 1981 the Coast Guard leased and commissioned her as USCGC *Dorado* (WSES 1), for a fifteen-month operational evaluation. Tests complete, she returned to the builder and then was transferred to Navy control. In 1982 the 110-foot ship was sawed in half, a new section of hull was inserted, and the pieces were welded back together, extending her length to 160 feet, her hull now painted Navy gray. The moniker *SES 200* reflected the ship's two-hundred-ton displacement. At the time, she was the largest surface effect ship in the world.

SES 200 was older, not as rigorously maintained, and manned by a smaller crew, but had distinct operational advantages over the three Coast Guard SESs. First, her massive aft deck was large enough to land a small, lightweight helicopter, or, for migrant interdiction, could hold three or four hundred persons with ease. Second, the longer hull yielded a better ride. With a superior length-to-beam ratio, *SES 200* sliced smoothly over the tops of the same eight- to ten-foot seas that caused debilitating slamming in the 110-foot cutters. Finally, the Navy ship was even faster than the thirty-knot *Seabird*-class cutters, propelled by similar main diesels but using four lift fans, reaching speeds in the low thirties.

The two services decided to conduct a side-by-side comparison, and the Navy sent *SES 200* to Key West for four months to work alongside her Coast Guard doppelgangers. The intent was to judge *SES 200*'s operational parameters—speed, seakeeping, and endurance—against those of the 110-foot cutters to determine whether the longer hull would be a viable option for the Coast Guard fleet. A five-person law-enforcement detachment was assigned to *SES 200* so that it could conduct boardings during the ship's time in the Seventh District.

As much as we wanted to razz the *SES 200* sailors—as the rivalry required—it was hard not to like them. They did their best to maintain their ship, even with limited funding and too few people in their crew. *SES 200* arrived in Key West with barely any damage-control equipment, and I rounded up spare fire hoses, portable extinguishers, and plugging and patching kits so that they could tend to at-sea emergencies. The Navy ship also suffered from many of the engineering problems that had plagued *Sea Hawk*, *Shearwater*, and *Petrel* over the years, and her crew—augmented by division personnel—spent much of their time working on a cascade of minor but annoying casualties.

As an experimental craft, *SES 200* was not technically in commission and therefore didn't have a commanding officer. Instead, she had an "officer-in-charge"—Lt. Maureen Farren. Lieutenant Farren was a solid officer, humble and decent. She knew the sea, made good decisions, and didn't take any guff from the Coasties. We adopted her as an honorary SES Division sailor. Later in her career, to no one's surprise, she became the first woman to command a full-fledged Navy combatant.

In February the three Coast Guard cutters and *SES 200* set sail for the Florida Straits. There, the nation's four military surface effect ships steamed in formation, skimming across the waves at thirty knots, a Coast Guard photojournalist in a helicopter above taking aerial portraits of the unique fleet. It was the only time that the four ships sailed together. The cutters and *SES 200* weaved back and forth, casting wide, frothy wakes, turning in tandem at the direction of the photographer hovering above, enjoying the light winds, clear skies, and deep-blue sea.

The day provided a much-needed point of reference for the SES Division. Over the past two years the engineers from the division and the Red, Green, Blue, and Gold crews, with support from the naval engineers in Miami, had improved the cutters by an order of magnitude, converting them into better ships—still with many problems but more capable nonetheless. The SES team had tackled the early hull-cracking problems, improved the lift systems, installed more powerful radars and radios, renovated the galleys, added far-more-capable RHIBs and boat-launching systems, and installed vertical stacks. Now, steaming alongside our Navy colleagues, we realized how far we'd come. *SES 200* was where the Coast Guard SESs had been when they were commissioned—saddled by civilian constructions standards and hard pressed to face a grueling operational schedule. *SES 200* was longer, faster, and more stable than our three cutters, but knowing her other limitations, not one of us would have traded places with our Navy counterparts.

A month later, *Shearwater,* with Green Crew on board, began a three-week maintenance period. The engineers would overhaul the main engines, replace the turbochargers, and install more reliable control systems to cut down on the recurring breakdowns. This left the Green Crew captain and XO with little to do. Red Crew, assigned to *Sea Hawk,* was heading out on a ten-day Bahamas patrol but was short on qualified crew. Wayne Justice invited Jerry Lober and Mike Cosenza to sail with us.

Both said yes without hesitation. The patrol would allow them the luxury of serving in an SES without the responsibilities of command.

They'd help out with bridge watches, augment our boarding parties, and, if we were lucky, Lober, the intrepid fisherman, would haul up some fresh dinner. Although it went unsaid, the real payoff was allowing four officers—friends and colleagues—the rare opportunity to work, commiserate, and maybe even chase some dopers together. It was as close as we could get to a working vacation.

Following this patrol Red Crew would rotate ashore for two weeks, and after that we ourselves would become stranded, assigned to *Petrel* for her upcoming engine overhaul. I realized as we steamed south from Key West that, despite having three months left at the division, this was one of my few remaining chances for another drug bust. Red Crew had seized ten dopers, still holding the unique status of nailing three vessels at once, but it sure would feel nice to add one more marijuana leaf to the growing collection of drug bust stickers displayed on the sides of *Sea Hawk*'s deckhouse.

The first week under way was as enjoyable a time as I'd ever experienced at sea. Adding two highly skilled officers to the mix gave every watch, every training exercise, and every boarding a different feel. We bonded like beat cops on patrol, sharing notes, experiences, methods, and ideas. Bridge watches became a contest as to who could navigate the most precisely, spout off the most arcane Rules of the Road, or be first to detect a vessel breaking over the horizon. Lober and Justice had their own special competition, each trying to outdo the other in snagging the largest mahi-mahi.

On March 8, Captain Justice directed the cutter onto the flats of the Great Bahama Bank. Our officer-heavy crew was making the rounds of all the old stomping grounds, and now it was time to swing past the fabled X-spot for a night. *SES 200* was patrolling 150 miles farther to the southeast, in the Old Bahama Channel, with her LEDET embarked.

A new piece of communications gear allowed us to keep in close contact with our Navy brethren. All four SESs had received a black teletype console hooked up to an encrypted high-frequency radio, which allowed us to pass short typewritten notes among ourselves without having to talk in the open. It was a 1980s version of texting—primitive but effective. The Coast Guard wasn't sure it wanted to invest in the equipment fleetwide, so we were trying it out.

Around dinnertime the OOD on *SES 200* sent a teletype message advising that the ship had intercepted a cabin cruiser and that their LEDET was preparing to board it. The boat, named *Tranquil*, was headed to the northwest, bound for Miami. *SES 200* had found the thirty-five-foot cabin cruiser ten miles north of the shipping channel, in relatively shallow water, close to the track that *Macabi* had followed.

After the evening meal the captain rang me on the ship's telephone and, with his voice buzzing with excitement, asked that I come up to the bridge, pronto. I found him huddled around the black teletype with Jerry Lober and Mike Cosenza. They were scanning the screen, and Lober was typing a reply to *SES 200*'s latest message.

Justice looked up and waved me over, pointing to the display. "What do you think, XO?" His voice had an eagerness to it, like a teenager about to buy his first car. "Do you think they've found something?"

I looked at the teletype display, the dim white letters floating on the glossy black background, scanning the most recent messages.

"1947R. FM: Shark 200. Boarding complete. No suspicions. Full at-sea space accountability. Released Tranquil. Orig headed SE, resuming patrol."

"1950R. FM: Shark 2. Did master state purpose of voyage?"

"1952R. FM: Shark 200. Mstr said vsl on trip to Raccoon Cay and return. Sport fish gear on board."

"1954R. FM: Shark 2. Anything unusual?"

"1956R. FM: Shark 200. No. Crew coop. Papers good. Only after boarding, sweep-team member found white paint on coveralls. Not sure where from."

The captain was pointing at that last line. "See that, XO—white paint," he said. "How in the world did the LEDET guy get white paint on his uniform? It couldn't have come from *SES 200*, because even if they were doing touch-ups it'd be Navy gray. It had to come from *Tranquil*. Plus, this boat's coming from Raccoon Cay. That's down by Ragged Island—the same place as one of the last guys we nailed."

Jerry Lober chimed in. "The only time I've seen fresh paint on a cabin cruiser is when they were trying to paint over something they didn't want us to see," he said. I agreed, thinking back to the wet paint on *Mabelu*'s deck.

Mike Cosenza made it unanimous. "Yep, wet paint means trouble," he said. "Something's going on. The LEDET needs to go back and take a closer look."

Wayne Justice was silent for a moment and then turned to us. "Look, I've got an idea," he said. Justice explained that *SES 200* had headed south after the boarding and was probably a few hours from being able to intercept *Tranquil* again. Since their LEDET hadn't found anything the first time, it probably wouldn't spot anything the second time—especially in the middle of the night. He pointed out that the LEDET was new to South Florida and had limited experience with secret compartments.

The captain's eyes narrowed. "I think the best bet is, we intercept the cruiser and give it a lookover with a second set of eyes," he said. "I checked the chart, and we're near the track from *Tranquil*'s last-known position to Miami. They're coming straight to us and should get here around break- fast. What do you say, guys?" We all nodded, enthused.

Justice teletyped *SES 200*, proposing that *Sea Hawk* reboard *Tranquil* in the morning. Neither Lieutenant Farren nor the LEDET officer-in- charge had an objection, but the LEDET officer wagered we wouldn't find anything, since they'd given the boat a good scrub.

We swapped more teletype messages with the LEDET's boarding party. They relayed that *Tranquil* had two people on board, both from Fort Lauderdale, and that the men were cooperative and had provided a solid story. The boarding party found the boat neat and clean and hadn't seen any wet paint, so couldn't pinpoint where it came from. The sweep leader mentioned that he'd crawled around the engine room and assumed that's where the tacky paint had been but said he just hadn't noticed it during the boarding.

I typed back, asking how long the sweep team had spent in the engine room. He replied "about five minutes" and added that the weather had been choppy, making it hard to inspect the space. Another clue. Cosenza read the reply and cocked an eyebrow, thinking the same thing that I was. Five minutes wasn't a lot of time to give the engine room a thorough lookover, and the bumpy seas might have impeded the LEDET. Mike and I headed below to catch some mid-rats and then get some rest before the next day's rush.

March 9 dawned clear and calm, a soft wind casting ripples across the turquoise sea. *Sea Hawk* was tracking a northbound contact, ten miles away. After learning that we were going to reboard *Tranquil*, *SES 200* diverted from her southeasterly jaunt and covertly reacquired the vessel, keeping her under long-distance radar surveillance through the night and enabling us to position ourselves for the morning intercept. At 0730 *Sea Hawk* picked up speed and headed directly for the cabin cruiser, pulling alongside twenty minutes later, taking station off her port quarter.

Tranquil was a handsome vessel, her name written in gold letters across a creamy-white transom. She appeared to be in great shape, clean and bright, with a white canvas canopy stretched over her flying bridge. Like most cabin cruisers, she had a sleek bow, an enclosed cabin, and an open deck aft, about fifteen feet square, with two fishing chairs positioned near the stern. A thin metal ladder on the back face of the superstructure led to the flying bridge, on top of the cabin.

From *Sea Hawk's* bridge wing we could see two men, one steering the boat from the flying bridge, the other relaxing in a fishing chair on the aft deck, beer in hand—the breakfast of champions. Next to the man in the chair were two long fishing poles standing upright in brackets, one trailing a line that skittered across the water. Jerry Lober peered at the boat through the "big eyes." He whistled. "Those are some nice poles," he said. "Looks like these guys have been doing some serious fishing."

Captain Justice queried *Tranquil* by VHF radio, asking the standard questions. The master sounded unsettled and said that he'd been boarded twelve hours earlier. Justice told him that we needed to verify some information from the previous boarding. He then directed *Tranquil* to heave to. The master put the throttles into neutral and the cabin cruiser glided to a stop, her momentum slowly overcome by the resistance from the crystal-blue water.

Our boarding party gathered on the bridge wing for a prebrief with the captain. We'd really stacked the deck. I'd serve as boarding officer with Mike Cosenza as the assistant; Jerry Lober and Seaman Malcolm Smith, new to the crew, would fill out the rest of the team. Three officers and one non-rate. Top-heavy and experienced. Cosenza quipped that considering all our horsepower, we'd better come back with something.

We reviewed the facts. EPIC had no intelligence on either the vessel or the two men on board, but our suspicions were raised by the route of the cabin cruiser as well as the presence of the white paint. Other than that there was nothing to go on. Our goal was to find the source of the wet paint and conduct as thorough an inspection at sea as the law allowed.

We checked each other's equipment, donned our life jackets, and headed for the boat deck. Danny Motley was the coxswain, and Sanders oversaw the launch. The boarding team scrambled down the Jacob's ladder, and Motley whisked us alongside *Tranquil*. At 0809 our team climbed on board, the sun already beating down, the light air barely moving and the heat starting to build. It was going to be one of those hot and sweaty boardings.

I introduced myself to the master, Reymundo Ramirez, and again ran through the litany of preboarding questions. Ramirez was in his mid-forties, skin dark from the sun, one of 125,000 Cubans who'd come to the States during the Mariel boatlift five years earlier. He certainly had done well for himself, sailing the Caribbean in a hundred-thousand-dollar pleasure boat. His description of their voyage was a bit vague, and he couldn't, or wouldn't, identify any particular spot where they'd been fishing. He said there was no catch on board, and when he saw my interest in that nugget he gave a rambling explanation, something about trading the fish for fuel. His obtuse reply piqued my interest.

I asked Ramirez what he did for a living, and he gave a slippery nonanswer: "A little of this, a little of that." His English was passable, but the passenger, also a forty-something resident alien, spoke only Spanish. I explained that we'd be conducting a security sweep of the vessel and asked that they move to the bow, where they'd be safe and out of the way. Ramirez hesitated a second as if he were going to protest, but then turned and walked forward, quietly mumbling in Spanish to his shipmate. They sat on the forward deck, and Seaman Smith slid into the shade of the cabin to keep an eye on them.

Lober, Cosenza, and I huddled. Jerry thought the master's body language showed evasion, and Mike was more blunt: "The guy was making it up as he went along," he said. "His story's a crock." I thumbed through the boat's paperwork while Lober and Cosenza conducted the security sweep, looking through the berthing area under the bow and the other compartments beneath the main deck. They came back empty, saying the boat was clean. The interior design was relatively open and functional, with little of the fancy trim found on more opulent pleasure boats, making it easy to identify any hiding areas for bale- or even kilo-sized stashes. There were a few cabinets in the cabin that we'd need to access later for full space accountability, but Cosenza said that if there was any bulk contraband on the boat it had to be in the hole.

The engine room extended from just underneath the cabin to the stern, eighteen feet long and spanning the width of the boat. There was a large wooden hatch in the middle of the aft deck leading down into the space. Lober and Cosenza had popped the hatch during the security sweep and after taking a quick look into the engine room had propped it open for ventilation. I climbed down, followed by Cosenza. We both knew that if there was dope on board, the fuel tanks were the likely hiding place, but we needed to keep our minds open to other possibilities. The key could be finding the wet paint.

It was one more trip into the mangroves. The engine room was tight, crammed with two diesel engines forward, modest fuel tanks behind them to port and starboard, a small emergency generator, and a jungle of thick bracing and exhaust runs. There was a two-foot gap separating the aft ends of the fuel tanks from the transom. The room was deeper along the centerline than on the sides, the deck slopping downward at a shallow angle from the tanks, creating a V-shaped cross-section: at its tallest point the overhead was five feet above the bilge. Thick longitudinal stringers, about a foot high, sat on deck inboard of each fuel tank, holding them in place, augmented by vertical wooden braces made from two-by-six-inch timbers.

All of the wood and fiberglass surfaces—the bulkheads, the bilges, the braces, the overhead—were gleaming white, unsoiled by oil or grease. That augured a long search to find the wet paint. The exhaust runs were ten-inch-diameter pipes, suspended from the overhead with brackets, running the length of the engine room to the exhaust ports on the transom.

I crawled along the centerline to the forward bulkhead, measuring by eye the contours of the space, while Cosenza squatted aft, examining the bilge. I was thinking in 3-D, asking myself where a smuggler could hide a load of pot. There was no place except the fuel tanks.

The tanks looked normal, not like *Macabi*'s oversized units, and were flush against the port and starboard sides of the engine room, with a six-inch gap to the deck above. It was easy to examine the tank tops and see they were smooth and undisturbed, confirming that there weren't any top-loaded secret compartments. The inboard, forward, and aft surfaces of both tanks also looked original and unblemished. No hidden access points there. That left only the outboard sides and the bottoms of the tanks as possible entry points for a secret compartment, and those sides were completely inaccessible. My initial conclusion was a letdown: there was no dope here.

We began a more thorough inspection. Cosenza and I inched our way through the engine room, starting forward and working aft, seeking wet paint, searching for clues. We used our flashlights to probe the dark corners, twisting and bending around obstructions, grabbing the vertical braces, tapping the tanks walls and bilge for signs of a hidden opening, groping and touching every white surface, like blind men in a maze. After twenty minutes we'd worked back to the transom. Cosenza hunched low, contorting himself to crawl under the exhaust tube into the space aft of the port fuel tank. He leaned forward and put his hand on top of the longitudinal deck stringer holding the tank in place.

"Goddam, here's your wet paint!" he exclaimed. He held out his hand, a smudge of white staining his fingers.

We crouched down to inspect the longitudinal stringer. It was five inches thick and twelve inches high, made of sturdy, cross-meshed fiberglass, a solid structural member rising from the bilge. The stringer ran from the forward bulkhead of the engine room all the way to the transom. There was tacky paint, nearly dry, in a few patches along a fifteen-inch stretch on the top and outboard side of the stringer, near the aft end of the tank. We examined the rest of the longitudinal and found it bone dry and fully intact, with no signs of alterations. Cosenza rapped the fiberglass with his flashlight: it resonated with a solid thud. It was a puzzle—a few dabs of tacky paint in an innocuous, nearly inaccessible spot. Neither of us could come up with a reason for it to be there.

Perspiration from Mike's face dripped into the bilge. The humidity of the day was enhanced by the heat from the idling engines, and I was sweating like a linebacker in the bulky boarding outfit, damning the bulletproof vest. We'd have to shut the engines down to continue the inspection. "Mike, let's get out of here and talk with Jerry," I said. "I'm dying and need some air." We climbed back on deck, where the sea breeze felt like Siberia compared to the sauna below, and told Lober what we'd found.

Jerry wanted to see the wet paint for himself and slid through the hatch, returning quickly, exclaiming, "Damn, it's toasty down there." He wiped his face. "That paint doesn't make sense; that spot's not connected to anything important," he said. "Maybe it's a red herring. Maybe there's something underneath the hull leading up into the tanks. We need to get the telescope and check the keel." Lober wanted to see if there was any sign of an access point on the exterior of the boat's hull.

The telescope was an extendable tube with a mirror on one end and an eyepiece on the other, and in the clear Bahamian waters it could be used to inspect the underside of a vessel for parasitic attachments, hidden hatches, or unusual modifications. Motley zipped back to *Sea Hawk* to retrieve the 'scope and I leaned over *Tranquil*'s port side, seeing that the exterior skin of the boat was flawless, with no imperfections or signs of tampering. Then I walked forward with Cosenza and talked with the master. I told Ramirez we'd be securing the boat's engines and asked if we could have his permission to search the cabinets in the berthing area and cabin. His face twitched and then he said sure, go ahead, look anywhere you want, we've got nothing to hide. For the first time his tone and body language telegraphed he was lying outright.

Motley came back with McCurry, and pulled the RHIB along *Tranquil*'s port side. McCurry inspected the exterior of the hull from different angles, feeling it with his hands, knocking on the fiberglass with his knuckles, seeking a hidden access into the tank. I helped from *Tranquil*'s deck while Lober and Cosenza searched the interior cabinets. We didn't detect anything unusual on either side of the hull. McCurry pulled the telescope out of its plastic carrying case, extended it to its full eight-foot length, and stuck the mirrored end under the boat. He peered through the eyepiece, seeking and searching, slowly dragging the telescope the entire length of the hull, repeating the process twice, finally rendering his verdict: "Clean as a whistle."

We'd been on *Tranquil* more than an hour. Lober and Cosenza finished looking through the cabinets and said they were crammed with cases of beer, piles of fishing gear, two plastic bins full of tools, and a dozen extra life jackets. They'd found nothing suspicious—just typical boating paraphernalia—and had seen no sign of contraband.

It all came back to the fuel tanks. Jerry and Mike broke out the sounding tape to see how much diesel was in them, and I climbed down into the engine room, sitting in the bilge and staring at the tanks, the vertical supports, the longitudinal stringers, and the exhaust tubes, thinking through the situation, reviewing the facts.

Our visual inspection found no entry points into the tanks on the inboard, top, forward, or aft faces. Only the bottom and outboard sides remained unseen, but they were totally unreachable, and there were no alterations to the boat's exterior hull. There was absolutely no way the tanks could be lifted inside the engine room to give access from the bottom. Likewise, the outboard sides couldn't be reached since the tanks were locked in place by the vertical braces, the exhaust tubes, and the thick longitudinal deck stringers.

But what of the wet paint? Why was it on the port longitudinal? None of this made sense. Maybe *Tranquil* was on a legitimate voyage after all, and the paint was from a recent repair.

But the master's fuzzy story, along with his nonverbals, were screaming that something was wrong. I looked at the port longitudinal and began working my flashlight in a lazy circle. The light shone on the bilge, then the dull aluminum wall of the fuel tank, then a vertical brace holding the tank in place. The brace was secured to the overhead with three bolts, the middle one higher than the others, sparkling in the flashlight beam. I stared at the bolts, mesmerized, losing focus in the heat, the bolts morphing into a triangle of fuzzy stars. My mind relaxed. I didn't move, processing, staring, time ticking by, my thoughts hazy, instinctively knowing that something wasn't right, that we'd uncovered a hidden clue, but unable to pin it down.

Then it hit. It was the bolts. They were shiny—*too* shiny. They looked brand new, freshly installed. I crab-walked to the nearest vertical brace and squatted on my haunches, looking up at the three retaining bolts. They were stainless steel, with no sign of oxidation or salt accretion. The wood surrounding the bolts was lightly scratched, and the scratches looked fresh—as if the bolts had been turned.

I called up through the hatch, trying not to let the two men on the bow hear me. "Hey Mike, hand me an adjustable wrench. Need to try something." Cosenza rooted through the boarding kit and passed down the wrench. I held it up to the bolt, adjusting it for size and giving it a twist. The bolt moved under light pressure. "Mike, how about a pair of pliers," I said. Holding the head of the bolt with the pliers, I put the crescent wrench on the nut, again twisting, lefty-loosey. The nut broke free and a dozen turns later was sitting in my hand. I pushed the end of the bolt and it popped out of the hole in the brace. That was way too easy.

Cosenza climbed back down with another wrench, a socket set, and some screwdrivers. He said he'd borrowed the extra wrench from the tool bins that he and Lober had found in *Tranquil*'s cabinets. There were three vertical braces on each side, one near the aft end of each fuel tank, one in the middle, and one near the front. We began testing all of the bolts holding the braces in place. All of the nuts were easy to turn.

Attached to the vertical braces on the port side, near the overhead, was a cable run, with twist ties holding a dozen wires in a bundle, held to the braces by screws. Those screws, too, loosened with only a modest effort. Cosenza and I moved to the exhaust piping, which was suspended from brackets that were bolted to the overhead. We weren't surprised to find that these bolts also looked new, and excessive force wasn't needed to loosen them. This meant that just about every interference in the engine room was removable. Cosenza climbed back onto the main deck to give Lober and Smith an update on what we'd found.

I sat down again, thinking hard. What could explain the new hardware? On an expensive boat like *Tranquil* it wasn't unusual for the engines to be overhauled every few years, and maybe the work had included replenishing the bracing and exhaust ports. That made sense. Or maybe there was a more nefarious explanation. A foggy idea had been drifting through my mind, unclear, unformed, and like a bolt of lightning it snapped into crisp focus. The engine room was arranged for disassembly, so that the crew could move the fuel tanks away from the outer bulkheads. That meant that access into the tanks was on their unseen, outboard sides. You'd have to take down the vertical braces, the exhaust piping, and the wire runs to shift the tanks, but it now seemed possible, maybe even probable, that the tanks would slide inboard. My stomach did a flip as though I'd stumbled across buried treasure.

Except—the deck longitudinals were still in the way. There was no way that either tank could slide inboard over the top of a foot-high stringer. Damn. The excitement ballooning inside my chest drained away, an emotional high to a deep low in a nanosecond. I leaned forward on hands and knees, peering at the port longitudinal. Could it be possible? Were the stringers not an integral part of the boat's hull, but somehow removable? I looked closer, inspecting the juncture where the fiberglass met the bilge, whacking the top of the longitudinal with the flashlight, skittering forward, reinspecting the stringer end to end. As before, it felt rock solid. I shifted to the starboard side and found the same.

The clues were nagging. A few dabs of wet paint in an out-of-the-way spot. An engine room that was scrubbed clean—maybe too clean. Support structures that were easily disassembled, with scratch marks indicating they might recently have been taken apart. Fuel tanks that could be movable, except for the damned longitudinals.

That led to a brainstorm. If the engine room *was* rigged for disassembly, then that was what we'd do. We'd unbolt everything we could. Maybe we'd discover an anomaly, a thin access port or a hidden seam behind one of the vertical braces, or a clue above the exhaust tubes, or an unseen connection to the tacky paint, or some other way to move the tanks.

I called Wayne Justice on the secure headset and gave him an update. The boarding team had been on *Tranquil* for ninety minutes, and I expected him to be impatient, eager for results, but found him just the opposite. We talked deliberately, carefully reviewing the facts, the captain asking about the structure of the tanks, the layout of the engine room, where we'd found the wet paint, and the demeanor of the master. I stated my intent to take apart the supports and hardware that appeared recently installed, and see where that led. We'd either find evidence of a crime or an obstacle that we couldn't overcome, in which case we'd have to put it all back together. He liked the plan and approved the search.

Ramirez was getting antsy and trying to monitor our progress through the forward cabin window. We asked if he was thirsty, and he said yes, so Smith passed him a jug of water and two beach towels from the cabin, so the men could shield themselves from the sun. *Tranquil*'s second crewman had been sleeping on deck but then got up, relieved himself over the side, and went back to sleep on the towel. Ramirez paced back and forth for a few minutes, then sat down heavily on the deck, tapping his foot, clearly unhappy. If he knew what we were doing to his engine room, he'd have been unhappier still.

Smith remained in the cabin, watching over the two men and looking increasingly bored. Jerry Lober would alternate between helping out on deck and in the engine room. Mike and I climbed back into the hole, a large bag of tools with us. Then we began taking *Tranquil*'s engine room apart.

"Let's get the wiring run first," Cosenza said. We'd decided to disassemble the port side, following the sticky paint, and Mike pointed to the tight bunch of wires, noting there was plenty of sag to allow the bundle to be moved inboard, out of the way. The wiring run was held to each vertical brace with two wood screws. Out they came. Cosenza pulled the wires across the centerline and used a set of flexible handcuffs to lash the bundle to an exhaust bracket on the starboard side.

Disassembling the port exhaust tube was next. It was meatier work, with thick bolts holding the brackets to the overhead. The tube was heavy enough that it took two people to hold it up. Lober joined us in the engine room, occasionally peeking out of the hatch to check on Smith, and used a screwdriver to disconnect the exhaust tube from the fitting that secured it to the transom. Once the end of the tube was loose, Cosenza and I scooted along the brackets, unbolting them until the entire tube was free. We manhandled it to the bilge. The tube was made of a stiff rubber compound, thick enough to withstand the high heat of the exhaust. By the time we'd finished with the tube we were ourselves exhausted, the nagging heat of the confined space taking its toll in sweat and energy.

Then we removed the three vertical braces, cranking off the three retaining bolts up top and the two long wood screws at the bottom that secured each brace to the longitudinal deck stringer. My anticipation built, expecting to find a clue behind the braces, some indicator of smuggling.

Twist, turn, pull. Twenty minutes later the braces were lying neatly in the bilge, alongside the exhaust tube. We inspected the tank face that had been hidden by the wood.

Damn. There was nothing behind the vertical braces—just a surface of unblemished metal. No signs of tampering, no entryway into the tank, nothing unusual. I leaned back, deflated. The port side of the engine room was naked, with only the thick, fiberglass longitudinal holding the tank in place. I gave the longitudinal a kick. It was solid as cement. Double damn.

We crawled back on deck for a breather, now at the end of our rope. The excitement of finding the wet paint and the loose bolts had grown as we'd taken down the wires, the exhaust, and the braces. Now that we'd spent an hour taking things apart, we'd run into a brick wall. The fuel tank wasn't moving.

Lober was stoic. "Hey, we did our best, and for the life of me I can't see a way that they've got dope inside that tank," he said. "Unless that stringer is Velcroed to the deck, we're gonna have to start putting things back together." We agreed to rest another minute, make a final inspection of the tank, and then start rebuilding *Tranquil*'s engine space. Mike said he wanted to take one more look at the tools in the cabinet.

Cosenza walked forward into the cabin, pulled out the two plastic bins, and began riffling through them. He surveyed the contents: more wrenches and screwdrivers, a crowbar, two hammers, a set of jumper cables. Suddenly, he flinched, startled, and dumped everything from one of the bins onto the deck, picking up and cradling a slender object. He quick-walked to us and held out his find.

It was a come-along, a tool designed to winch heavy objects, made from a length of sturdy wire rope attached to a ratchet, with silver hooks at both ends of the wire. Come-alongs were used for lifting engines from cars, or freeing trucks that were stuck in the mud, or yanking out stubborn tree stumps—or, just perhaps, for moving a heavy fuel tank across the engine room of a cabin cruiser.

Cosenza and I stared at each other, minds racing, and then I said, "Let's go." We scrambled down into the hole, far livelier than when we'd crawled out a few minutes earlier. For the first time the heat felt good, rewarding, welcoming. We looked up. There—on the top, aft face of the port fuel tank, lurking in the shadows and previously hidden by the wire run—was an innocuous semicircular flange with a hole punched through it, the perfect size for attaching the hook at the end of a chain. Turning, we saw a similar flange on the starboard tank. I leaned closer, examining the port flange from a few inches away, and saw light scratches in the metal. They looked fresh.

That meant that the tanks had been moved. And that meant that the longitudinals *had* to be removable. Inspired, I got on hands and knees and began poking the wet section of the port stringer with a screwdriver, stabbing repeatedly, like a sculptor carving ice. No luck—the longitudinal was hard as stone. More stabbing. Then, at the edge of the tacky paint, the tip of the screwdriver slid into a gap, an eighth of an inch across and two inches side to side, artfully hidden with putty topped by several layers of paint. I used the screwdriver to scrape off the paint and found a paper-thin seam extending across the top of the longitudinal and down both sides to the bilge. Eureka! It looked like the stringer was segmented, and this was where the two pieces came together.

The eighth-of-an-inch gap was just big enough to insert the angled end of a crowbar. Lober grabbed one from the boarding kit and passed it down. Cosenza wedged it into the slot, the shaft of the crowbar sticking up toward the transom at a 45-degree angle. He pulled down on the upper end. Mike was strong but not heavy. Nothing moved. I grabbed the top of the crowbar, my hands over his, and we leaned into it with all our strength.

A lot happened at once. The engine room echoed with an ear-shattering screech, something akin to pulling a long rusty nail out of weathered wood. The longitudinal popped up, explosively, four inches off the deck, as the handle of the crowbar, now under the full weight of the two of us, crashed into the bilge. Mike and I tumbled down, the crowbar no longer supporting us. His elbow drove into my ribs. My forehead cracked on the fiberglass. Lying in a heap, we both turned and looked forward, trying to comprehend what we were seeing, neither of us speaking.

It was ingenious. Absolutely goddam ingenious. A large section of the longitudinal deck stringer—about ten feet long, extending a few inches past each end of the fuel tank—was fake. The original stringer had been cut away, flush with the deck of the bilge, and a thick fiberglass cap put in its place, disguised to look exactly like the original stringer. From all outward appearances, the stringer was an integral part of the boat's structure. In reality, the false cap, cemented to the bilge and to the nubs of the original longitudinal, could be removed, allowing the tank to slide inboard. The slight gap between the real and phony stringers had been so expertly camouflaged with putty and paint that we'd missed it in our visual exams.

Now things were making sense. Cosenza scrambled forward, using the crowbar to pry up the fake stringer until it was completely free of the bilge, and then wrestled it to the starboard side of the engine room. I sat back down underneath the hatch leading topside, staring at the port fuel tank, now held in place by nothing but its own weight.

Lober was already climbing down, the come-along in hand, muttering, "My turn, boys." Jerry and his toys. He attached the hooked ends of the wire to the flanges and began ratcheting the lever, taking out the slack. The come-along came under strain, the wire rope taut, stretched across the engine room between the port and starboard tanks. In theory, as he tightened the wire, with the starboard tank securely in place, the port tank should slide inboard. Lober pulled the lever hard, straining, beads of sweat popping out on his forehead.

"Moment of truth, boys, moment of truth," Lober said. He was clearly enjoying himself. He took a deep breath and leaned harder into the come-along, muscling down the ratchet lever. The port fuel tank shifted. It jerked inboard an inch, stopped by weight and friction. Lober squeezed the ratchet again, and the tank slid another two inches toward us.

Son of a bitch, was all I could think. We were in the bowels of a ritzy cabin cruiser, had taken apart its engine room like a life-sized jigsaw puzzle, and were dragging a two-thousand-pound fuel tank across the bilge, inch by painful inch. In the middle of the ocean, in a slowly swaying boat, in 110-degree heat. And, I was convinced, once we crawled around the back side of that fuel tank, we'd find it full of pot and then would throw cuffs on the two men trying to smuggle the dope into Miami.

We'd been on *Tranquil* for more than two hours, each of us pounds lighter from water loss, our faces flushed, our uniforms soaked through, backs and legs burning from hunching and squatting, arms and hands worn out. There was no better place in the world to be.

A dozen tugs later, the aft end of the fuel tank had moved a foot from the outer hull. The front of the tank hadn't slid down as far, putting it at a slight angle to the centerline of the boat. Cosenza, smallest among us, crawled around the back of the tank and shined his flashlight forward into the gap between the tank and the boat's hull, looking for the access hatch that would lead us to the dope. "I see it!" he called out. "There's a metal cover about a third of the way up, pretty small. Move the tank out some more and I can get to it." Lober continued working the come-along, and the tank slid another six inches toward the centerline, then hung up and wouldn't move any farther. "I think that's it," he said. "Mike, can you squeeze back there?"

Cosenza could. He crawled forward into the eighteen-inch gap, slithering on his left side. It was a tight fit, with the gap narrowing the further he moved forward. Once Cosenza reached the access plate he told us there were a dozen stainless steel bolts, with what looked like half-inch heads, holding it in place. From the center of the engine room all we could see were Mike's feet sticking out from behind the tank. I passed him a half-inch socket-wrench. It fit the bolts, and he got to work removing the foot-square cover.

Crammed into the tight space, Cosenza had little room to maneuver and found it difficult to get leverage on the bolts. The first bolt seemed to take forever. Hands slick with sweat, he dropped the flashlight and then the wrench, feeling around in the dark to retrieve them, helped along by some sharp curses. I crouched behind him, shining my flashlight into the gap to give him some extra light. Mike got into a rhythm, removing a bolt and sliding it into the chest pocket on his coveralls, then another, and ten minutes later all twelve were out, the small access cover still stuck in place. He pulled a flathead screwdriver from his pocket and jammed it into one of the now-empty bolt-holes, twisting. The cover popped off. From my viewpoint, four feet behind the access cover and at a steep angle, I couldn't see into the hole. Cosenza shined his light into the tank opening, then told us what he saw.

"It's empty," he said.

Lober and I stopped breathing. We were speechless.

"I said, it's empty," Mike repeated. "Completely goddam empty. As in, nothing there. Crap. I need air." He crawled backward, out of the gap, sitting up, his face bright red from heat and exertion, and took some deep breaths. "It's a tiny compartment, maybe two feet deep, three feet side-to-side, but there's not a damn thing in it," he reported. "These guys are running dry."

The three of us climbed out of the engine room and stood on deck, stretching, unbuttoning the front of our coveralls, swigging water and pouring it on our wrists to cool our blood. I called *Sea Hawk* and told Captain Justice what we'd found—or rather, hadn't found. He was flummoxed, convinced that such an elaborate secret compartment would've been packed with dope. "Okay, go ahead and button things up the best you can, then come on back," he said. His voice was somber, defeated. "I'll call District and see if they want us to bring this guy in for outfitting for smuggling. Not sure they will. Unless you've got something else, I guess you're done over there, right?"

It would've been natural to say yes, to wrap up and head back to the cutter, to strip off the weapons belt and coveralls and bulletproof vest and change into a uniform that wasn't glued to my body with sweat. But there was still work to do. It was a long-shot, but we weren't done looking for drugs. "Uh, no sir," I replied. "We'll put things back, but we need to see if there's a compartment in the starboard tank. It'll take a while, but I don't want to leave without checking it out. Do we have another hour or two?"

Justice didn't hesitate. "If you're up to it, absolutely—go for it," he said. "But do you really think there'd be dope in one tank if the other's empty?"

"No. I really don't," I confessed. "The starboard side's probably empty, too. But we have to find out. I'll let you know if we need more manpower over here, but for now we're good to go."

"Okay, XO, sounds like a plan," he said. "We'll be standing by." *Sea Hawk* was drifting only fifty yards away, and the captain was standing on the bridge wing, staring at us, shoulders drooped, the disappointment clear even from a distance. I gave him a lazy half-wave, half-salute, too tired for protocol. Beyond the cutter, three miles out, was the silhouette of another ship, light gray and low to the water. It was *SES 200*, hovering nearby to see if we'd find anything. So far we'd done some good investigating, and we'd proven our worth as construction workers, but without any dope it was hard to call the boarding a smash success.

We went back into the engine room. The short break had recharged our batteries, and Cosenza, Lober, and I set to work jacking the port tank back into place. Whoever had designed the sliding tank had done quality work. There was a small eyebolt in the overhead, on the outboard side of the compartment, just above the tank. Lober rerouted the hook through the eye-bolt and was able to pull the tank toward the outer hull with the come-along, while Mike and I leaned into the tank with our shoulders. It crammed back into position after fifteen minutes of pushing and wheezing. Next, we reassembled the phony longitudinal stringer, attached the vertical braces, and reinstalled the exhaust piping and wire runs. Forty-five minutes later, *Tranquil*'s engine room was good as new, minus the scrapes and gouges that we'd put in the white paint.

Then we disassembled the starboard side of the engine room, repeating the process, more quickly this time with experience, no wire run to deal with, exhaust tube first, vertical braces next, then finding the hidden gap and levering free the longitudinal. This one was harder to remove, and it took a few minutes to wedge the longitudinal from the bilge. We probably should have taken a heat break; instead, we rushed to finish the job.

The invigorating tingle of anticipation that I'd felt disassembling the port side was gone, replaced by a dull sense of duty. We were going through the motions just to check a box. Hook up the come-along—check. Heave around and pull the tank away from the starboard hull—check. My turn this time. I crawled forward into the dark gap, found a foot-square hatch identical to the one on the port fuel tank, this one also secured by a dozen bolts, and began ratcheting them off.

The air was stifling hot, almost painful to breath, and I thanked the Big Man upstairs for not making me claustrophobic. The easterly winds had picked up to fifteen knots and had begun to churn the shallow water. *Tranquil* was slopping side to side as she wallowed in the waves. I realized with a start that if the tank slid back toward the outer hull due to the wave action, it would crush me. "Hey, Mike, make sure that come-along stays tight—okay?" I said. "I don't want to get squashed in here." Even more reason to finish the job and get back to *Sea Hawk*. I kept working on the bolts, daydreaming about an icy shower.

Ten bolts out, eleven, twelve. Finally, done. As I reached for a screwdriver to pry free the hatch cover, it fell off on its own, onto my hand on the deck. Damn, that stung, the sharp edge of the metal cover breaking skin. I pivoted the flashlight beam toward the opening, to confirm that it, too, was empty, expecting to see the dull sheen of a vacant compartment's far wall. The beam lit up a glossy reflection, something black and shiny, only inches from my face. At the same moment, the smell hit home. Marijuana.

My eyes refocused on the reflection. There, a fist-width away from my nose, was a package, the size of a large brick, wrapped in a chunk of black plastic trash bag. It was wedged into the secret compartment, mashed in tightly with other packages, some in light brown wrapping, others white. We'd found a stash of pot.

I didn't say a word but pried the black package free of the compartment and backed out of the gap between the hull and the tank. Still silent, I pointed at Cosenza, made eye contact, and tossed the black brick to him. He caught it and stared at the package, feeling its heft, then smiled and began to laugh. Lober had been standing up with his head through the hatch, checking on Smith, and when he bent down and saw what was happening his face lit up with a look of incredulity, and then he asked: "Why the hell didn't we go after the starboard tank in the first place?"

The three of us climbed on deck to test the drugs. I walked up to Smith and whispered in his ear that we'd be arresting *Tranquil*'s crew as soon as we had a positive test. He'd been watching the two men for almost three hours and had seemed long ready for the boarding to be over, but instantly he was spazzing with energy, eyes wide open and jaw unhinged. "Damn, XO, this is my first drug bust!" he whispered back. "I can't believe you guys found something down there. Son of a bitch! Man, it was worth the wait!"

I walked back to the transom. Cosenza held the package as I cut it open, ready to scoop out a sample of green leafy material to test for THC. White powder spilled out. It was cocaine.

Clumsily, I let my hand slip and my index finger brushed against the powder. The skin instantly turned numb. It was cocaine, all right. I hoped not to be subject to random drug-testing anytime soon. Cosenza pawed through the boarding kit, looking for the cocaine drug test. We'd never had to use one on actual contraband before.

The test was positive. I alerted *Sea Hawk* about our find. We heard a familiar "Hot damn" echo across the water and could see Wayne Justice shoulder-punch Dan Sanders. Maybe my eyes were failing from the heat, but it looked like Senior Chief was dancing a jig. Cosenza and I walked around the cabin to the bow, Mike approaching on the port side, me on starboard. Ramirez and his passenger had been lounging on deck and sat up as we walked toward them.

I said: "You're under arrest for suspicion of smuggling cocaine into the United States. Both of you, lean forward and lie flat on the deck, face down, and place your hands behind your back." Ramirez did as he was told, his shipmate following. We knelt alongside their prone bodies, snapping on the handcuffs and then helping them back to their knees. Cosenza conducted quick body frisks as I read them their Miranda rights, in English and Spanish. Ramirez looked at me and said the most honest thing he'd said all day. "I knew we were screwed when you guys took that come-along down below." It was the hardest, most complex drug seizure that Red Crew had made. And it was by far the most rewarding.

By late afternoon *Tranquil* was cruising toward Key West. Jerry Lober and I were serving as custody crew, and we had the throttles mashed forward, turning for twenty-four knots. The weather was gorgeous. The modest breeze on our stern and the three-foot chop in the deeper water of the Santaren Channel made for a pleasant ride. As soon as we'd gotten under way Jerry and I had stripped down to bathing suits and sunglasses; it wasn't every day we had the chance to sail in a fancy cabin cruiser, and we were going to enjoy every minute of it. The ride got even better when Jerry discovered a cooler full of premium beer, still iced down.

The Navy ship's patrol was complete, so *SES 200* would escort us to shore. Wayne Justice was a proud and happy captain; we'd given him the ultimate present, bragging rights as skipper of the first Key West–based crew to snag a cocaine smuggler. After arresting Ramirez and his partner, our boarding team remained on *Tranquil* to unload the secret compartment, inventory the drugs and evidence, and prep the boat for the 150-mile trip to port. Cosenza emptied the packages from the fuel tank, handing them back over his shoulder to me, and I passed them up to Lober. Mike pulled out a total of seventy packages, most kilo-sized, but a few lumpier and irregularly shaped. Several of the mini-bales were filled with high-grade marijuana, tightly compressed, some oozing a dark, viscous liquid. The grand total was seventy-six pounds of pot and eighty-six pounds of 100-percent pure, uncut cocaine.

We marveled at the hidden compartments, clearly the product of skilled craftsmen, well constructed and highly innovative. Each compartment was only three feet wide, eighteen inches deep, and two feet high, and, like the tanks on *Macabi*, was totally surrounded by fuel except on the side where the hatch was located. In *Macabi*'s case that had been on the overhead, and on *Tranquil*, even more ingeniously, it was on the inaccessible outboard side that butted up against the hull. Without disassembling the engine room and sliding the fuel tank inboard, it would have been impossible to find the drugs.

We didn't bother pushing the starboard tank all the way back into place; we moved it only as far as was necessary to reassemble the exhaust tubing. Lober secured the tank in place using the come-along. Then we took photos and made sketches for the evidence package and headed back to *Sea Hawk* to write our witness statements. The two prisoners refused to talk, making for a short interrogation. After getting cleaned up, Jerry and I returned to *Tranquil* for our victory lap, the cruise back to Key West.

We'd gone about fifty miles and were passing near Dog Rocks when *Tranquil* broke down. Jerry was at the helm on the flying bridge, and I was stretched out in the cabin, enjoying a cold brew. The port engine began to sputter and then died, a plume of black smoke roiling from the exhaust port. Uh-oh. Rather than our trying to fix it, *SES 200* volunteered to tow us in.

With nothing much to do except guard the dope, Jerry and I spent the evening talking about our careers, our aspirations, and the longer-term future for ship-drivers like us. He'd soon be departing Key West, having received a great set of orders to command the Tactical Law Enforcement

Team in Miami. He'd oversee a dozen LEDETs and would supervise the most highly trained law enforcement ninjas in the Coast Guard. I'd be at the District Seven OPCEN, across town, so we figured we'd be seeing a lot of each other over the next few years. Jerry had been an ideal captain and intended to go back afloat after the TACLET assignment. I said it'd be an honor to sail with him again. He returned the compliment.

The next morning, after an uneventful trip across the Gulf Stream, *SES 200* and the seized vessel moored at Station Key West. A gaggle of Coast Guard, Customs, and DEA officials were waiting for *Tranquil* and swarmed the boat to look at the unique arrangement of the sliding fuel tanks and the built-in compartments. After a few minutes below deck, the senior agent from Customs climbed out of the engine room, mopping his brow, and spoke to his colleagues clustered on the pier. "That's the most sophisticated tank arrangement I've ever seen in a boat like this," he said. "It's almost impossible to find at sea. We need to let everyone know what we're up against, and the indicators that led to this seizure. Believe me, guys, these smugglers were good, and this is some really serious shit."

At the SES Division, there were congratulations all around. Commander Council was so thrilled about one of his cutters having made a cocaine bust that he wrote a letter of commendation to Red Crew—something he hadn't done for any of our earlier exploits. Captain Justice made sure that copies of the commendation were put in the service records of the entire crew, noting that it took a full team effort to find, board, inspect, and seize the smugglers. Red Crew was beaming when we pasted the first blue snowflake sticker on the side of *Sea Hawk*'s deckhouse, a perfect complement to the nineteen marijuana stickers lined up in neat rows.

It was important to keep the seizure in perspective, though. The division had been established less than three years earlier, and the four SES crews had seized more than fifty different vessels, accounting for more than one-tenth of all drug interdictions Coast Guard–wide. *Tranquil* was just one in a long line of busted dopers. Despite their engine casualties, hull failures, torn bow fingers, and cracked water tanks, the surface effect ships had proven to be a smart investment for the Coast Guard, bridging the gap until the new and improved class of monohull patrol boats entered service.

And that day was right around the corner. Congress had again become impatient and instead of waiting for the 125-footers to come online, had approved money for the Coast Guard to build patrol boats using an existing design. With that funding, headquarters chose a well-established 110-foot British hull, contracted with a shipbuilder, and announced that it soon would be commissioning sixteen of the newly dubbed *Island*-class cutters. From all indications the new ships would be fast, sleek, and sexy. USCGC *Farallon* (WPB 1301), the first 110-footer, had already been launched and would be placed in commission in July.

The *Island*-class ships were the best-looking patrol boats on the planet, and, as I'd told Jerry Lober during our cruise home on *Tranquil*, it was my stated desire to command one of them—good luck and Coast Guard headquarters willing—after finishing my three-year tour at OPCEN Miami.

———

It took a few days for the intoxicating buzz of the *Tranquil* seizure to begin wearing off. I'd spent the time thinking about how the drug war had changed and how much we'd all learned in our quest to discover carefully hidden secrets on vessels large and small, fast and slow, most often far at sea. Now, a different buzz was taking over—the excitement of a new assignment and a new tradecraft. Soon, in Miami, I'd be planning and overseeing large-scale searches, directing cutters and aircraft on missions across a diverse operating area, sometimes coordinating with the coast guards and navies of other countries. Lives would depend on my judgment, expertise, and knowledge. It was essential work, and there was an immense amount to learn, making me excited and anxious at the same time.

The week after we seized *Tranquil* there was another surprise, this one from the assignment officer who wrote orders for shore duty. OPCEN Miami was out. OPCEN Boston was in. There'd been a reshuffling of assignments, and somehow I'd won the lottery, getting my first choice, moving back to the rougher waters, heavier weather, and cooler climes of New England. Better yet, my Gold Crew counterpart, Mark Hoesten, who'd been expecting orders to the West Coast, also was headed for Boston. I'd been worried about the high cost of living in Beantown and now could afford a decent place, with a roommate ready to split the rent.

As much as I loved sailing the SESs and would miss the wind in my face, the smell of salt spray, the thrill of the hunt, and the incredible shipmates that made up Red Crew, OPCEN Boston promised a fresh and important new world.

It was then, for the first time since seeing *Shearwater* two years earlier—a visage fascinating and unique, offering the promise of excitement and adventure—that I knew it was time to move on. The SES promise had been amply fulfilled.

Epilogue

Reflections

May 1985

omeone was banging on the door to my stateroom in the middle of the night, and it was really pissing me off.

Thump, thump, thump. Whap! "Jim, wake up," a voice said. "Get out here—I need your help. You're not gonna believe what's going on. Hey, get up, now! We just made a coke bust—and I mean a *lot* of cocaine!"

My mind was foggy, confused. The voice sounded like Jerry Lober's, but how could that be? I was on board *Petrel,* and we were moored at Base Miami Beach, getting under way in just a few hours for a two-week stint at a local shipyard. Lober was the commanding officer of the Tactical Law Enforcement Team stationed at Air Station Miami, miles away. It was three o'clock in the morning. What the hell was he doing on our ship? What sort of weird dream was this?

I sat up just as Lober slammed open the door, bursting into my stateroom. No dream here. "Come on, Howe, get dressed!" he shouted. "We just caught a guy driving a go-fast that was completely loaded with coke!

I mean completely loaded! There's bales everywhere, big ones, I think we may have a ton of the stuff!"

Those are words that will shake the sleepiest drug warrior instantly awake. I yanked on pants and a shirt, stammering. "Where—where'd you catch the guy?" I asked. Lober reverted to our old relationship. "Damn, XO, we caught the guy screaming in through Baker's Haulover Cut." The Cut, as the inlet was known informally, was a man-made inlet about nine miles north of Base Miami Beach, in the pricier part of town, home to a forest of expensive high rises and condos. It connected the twists and turns of northern Biscayne Bay to the Atlantic Ocean.

Lober continued, talking rapidly, like a kid babbling about his Christmas booty. "It was right out of the movies," he said. "A helo had spotted them coming in from the east, no lights, and was on their tail, maybe thirty-five, forty feet up. The go-fast was moving, probably making fifty knots. But it wasn't going outrun that helo—hell, no! We were in one of the new seven-meter RHIBs, the really fast ones, patrolling in the Cut. So in comes this go-fast, blasting into Biscayne Bay, with a helo right on top of him. There were people in the condos looking down at the top of the helo, it was so damned low. Can you imagine? So we chased the go-fast all the way through the Bay, for half an hour, in our RHIB. It was crazy! I mean, really crazy! They tried everything, weaving, quick turns, going under bridges, but they couldn't shake us. When they got down by Venetian Causeway the go-fast slowed near shore and all the guys jumped overboard and swam for it. There were three of them, but we only caught one—a scrawny little guy, hiding in the bushes." He paused for breath. "Want to meet him?"

I threw on shoes, and we scurried down the pier toward Station Miami Beach. Tied up along the seawall, behind a pair of 41-foot utility boats with their blue lights flashing, was a twin-engine go-fast, a 29-foot Mirage, a sleek, high-speed vessel. She was piled with bales wrapped in red, white, and blue plastic, some stuffed into cardboard boxes. A small army of federal agents was hovering around—DEA, FBI, Coast Guard, Customs. Two agents with guns that looked like Uzis were watching the pier, glaring as we sauntered past. No one was getting near that boat without their say-so.

Lober's eyes were sparkling as he told more about the chase. "At one point these guys just about sideswiped a big yacht, missed it by a few feet, scared the hell out of everybody. They were trying everything they could to shake us. But they sure as hell weren't going to get away from someone who was Red Crew–trained." He looked at me, his face laced with pride.

We walked into the station, and in a side room a pair of Customs agents was interrogating the lone captured smuggler. The man was middle-aged and rail-thin, shivering in his wet clothes and staring down at his feet. One of the TACLET members offered the prisoner a blanket, and he wrapped himself in it. Once his teeth stopped chattering, Lober and the others peppered him with questions, in English and Spanish. Where'd they get the coke? Where were they taking it? Who were the other guys in the boat? The man clammed up, saying nothing, and the interrogation quickly turned into a staring contest. Lober and I left.

It was May 9, 1985. The cocaine haul was the largest ever made by the Coast Guard—1,909 pounds, 100-percent uncut, enough coke to feed the drug habits of a middle-sized city. Only two months earlier Red Crew had done backflips over finding a cache of coke one-twentieth as big. Now we knew that the traffickers were moving immense loads, a ton at a time, and maybe they'd been doing it for months, or even years. As if to prove the point, later the same morning a patrol officer in Florida City stopped a Winnebago for a simple traffic violation as it traveled up Route 1 from the Keys. Inside the motor home the officer found dozens of duffel bags filled with coke, also a load of 1,900 pounds. One night, two seizures, almost two tons of cocaine. The cartels were flooding the country. The drug war was continuing to evolve, and quickly.

My final month as XO Red was anticlimactic. All three SESs were experiencing a new and more serious set of structural problems, brought on, it was thought, from the extra weight of the vertical smokestacks. Cracks were forming in the wet deck, allowing air and water to blow into the engineering spaces when the ships were on lift. Not good. At the same time, the new and improved propellers that had been installed during the previous year's shipyard periods had begun to fail, each throwing blades and incapacitating the cutter. Not good at all. Both types of casualties led to emergency shipyard repairs and cut way back on patrol hours. During the spring and summer of 1985, the three SESs spent far too little time at sea.

In May I spent three days house-hunting in Boston and then returned to Key West, just in time for another emergency drydocking in Fort Lauderdale. There, on June 14, I met my relief, Lt. (jg) Kevin Quigley, a sharp-witted, savvy, and earnest officer who'd spent the past two years on the 378-foot cutter *Chase* (WHEC 718). He was a quick study and had done his homework, understanding the strengths and weaknesses of our unique cutters. We spent the week together, inspecting the ship, talking with the crew, inventorying classified materials, and walking through emergency drills, all to give Quigley a sense of what he'd gotten himself into.

Then came the hardest part—saying goodbye. I wandered the decks, talking one-on-one with my shipmates, not knowing whether I'd see them again. We'd plowed through heavy seas, navigated shallows, chased smugglers, and saved lives together, all part of a cohesive team, as much a family as we were a crew. Most of the original group had moved on, with Dan Sanders, Bill Hartsock, Chuck Meisner, and Senior Chief the only remaining plank-owners. We swapped sea stories, had some laughs, and wished each other well. Senior Chief said I was the best damned XO he'd ever sailed with. I replied that as far as senior chiefs went, he was king of the hill. He gave me a bear hug, almost popping my spine.

Outside I was steel, the consummate professional headed to a new assignment, but inside I'd become mush, emotions swirling, cast off from a band of brothers. Damn, I'd miss these guys.

The transition week ended. On June 18, 1985, Kevin Quigley and I signed a letter of relief, addressed to Commanding Officer, U.S. Coast Guard SES Division Red Crew. There were no discrepancies and no facts in dispute. Quigley assumed the title of XO Red, and I headed north.

———

The structural failures that plagued the SESs in 1985 led to a reevaluation of the multi-crewing concept. The Coast Guard decision makers in Miami and Washington looked at the data from the first three years of operations and came to the conclusion—a simple conclusion, really—that the civilian ships just couldn't stand up to a grueling pace of 240 days under way each year. In October 1985 the Coast Guard formally ended multi-crewing of the SESs, assigning members of the Red, Blue, and Green crews to individual cutters and divvying up Gold Crew among the three ships. Kevin Quigley, for a short time XO Red, was now *Shearwater*'s full-time executive officer. Red Crew was no more.

And then, a few months later, the SESs bounced back from their latest round of casualties. The Coast Guard's engineers had systematically diagnosed and eliminated the structural weaknesses, leading to a renaissance for the ships. In 1986 and for the next eight years, the Surface Effect Ship Division set a torrid pace at sea, accumulating more patrol hours per hull than any other class of cutter: more than the new 110-foot *Island*-class patrol boats, more than the service's 210- and 270-foot medium-endurance cutters, and, almost unbelievably, more than the largest high-endurance cutters and icebreakers.

With those hours at sea the operational successes continued to flow. Migrant interdiction, search-and-rescue operations, drug seizures, and the occasional foray into fisheries enforcement dominated their world. *Petrel* rescued the disabled vessel *Tampawitha* in twenty-two-foot seas off the Cuban coast; *Sea Hawk* nailed a Haitian freighter named *Lucelia* with 2,055 pounds of cocaine hidden on board; *Petrel* seized 730 pounds of shrimp from a vessel violating federal conservation laws; *Shearwater* found 5 tons of pot on the 51-foot lobster boat *Billy D*. In 1989 alone, the three Coast Guard surface effect ships made four of the nation's top six maritime cocaine seizures.

But as the ships matured they grew tired, and the cost of repairing them rose sharply—an increasing disadvantage in a budget-constrained world. The fleet of new *Island*-class cutters had continued to expand, and it became increasingly difficult to justify the added expense of keeping the three highly capable but exotic SESs in service. So the decision makers pulled the plug. After more than a decade of work, *Sea Hawk*, *Shearwater*, and *Petrel* were decommissioned en masse on January 28, 1994.

Throughout their relatively short lives, the surface effect ships were the most prolific drug-hunters in the Coast Guard fleet. In less than a

dozen years, SES crews arrested 340 suspected smugglers and seized 107
vessels, their haul totaling more than 480,000 pounds of marijuana, 12,000
pounds—6 tons—of pure cocaine, and $312,000 in cash. Not counted
in these totals were the thousands of pounds of drugs found floating at
sea after disrupted air drops and surface transfers or the contributions
made in multi-unit seizures, where an SES would chase a fleeing doper
into the arms of another cutter, the Royal Bahamian Defense Force, U.S.
Customs, or shoreside law enforcement authorities.

Most proudly, the only SES built specifically for the Coast Guard,
Petrel, led the way. *Petrel*'s crews seized forty-three smuggling vessels,
at the time more than any other patrol boat in commissioned service.
Petrel had come a long way since the first Captain Red and a handful
of shipmates had whisked the ship into Tampa Bay in the dark of night,
flying through the channel at thirty-five knots. Apparently, we'd readied
the cutter for a fast but fruitful life.

The decision to decommission the SES fleet was made with little
warning, surprising their captains and crews, who were given only a
few weeks to prepare the ships to leave active service. It was sold as a
budget-driven decision, with the Clinton administration inexplicably
tightening the noose on funds flowing to the Coast Guard. At the time, I
was assigned to the Seventh District office in Miami, and the staff there
was flummoxed by the decommissioning order. Migrant operations were
intensifying, with increasingly large numbers of people fleeing toward
the United States in unseaworthy vessels, and the district's leadership was
concerned about having enough hulls to handle the flow. And they were
right. Political conditions in Haiti and Cuba deteriorated, and there were
mass migrations from both countries later that year. The ample deck space
and quick sprint abilities of the SESs were sorely missed as cutters from all
across the country surged to the Windward Passage and Straits of Florida
in order to rescue 60,000 desperate souls.

———

The four-hour drive from Miami to the decommissioning ceremony in
Key West permitted time for reflection. Now a lieutenant commander,
I realized that the SES experience had been pivotal to my career,
providing the leadership and life lessons that allowed success in follow-on

assignments. After the stint as XO Red, I'd spent a productive three years at the Boston Operations Center and then commanded a brand-new *Island*-class cutter, based in the best small city in the world, where our crew had faced down and overcome terrible challenges. Now I had a high-profile job on the District Seven staff, part of a vibrant team that oversaw all Coast Guard activities over 6 million square miles of ocean. It was exciting, demanding, and important work, and I treasured every bit of it.

One thing was certain: none of these successes would have happened without the encouragement, guidance, and mentoring of the two Red Crew captains, Jerry Lober and Wayne Justice, or the insights and judgment gleaned from Senior Chief Quartermaster Ivan B. Aiken, navigator extraordinaire, or the high spirits, dedication, and work ethic shown every day by an elite enlisted team, from Dan Sanders and Walt Goodrum to Bill Hartsock and Carrie Corson, and every other sailor who'd served as a member of the Red Crew. They were all solid shipmates and loyal professionals, and working with them had made me a better officer—and a better man. Because of them, Red Crew had served with distinction and made the Coast Guard proud.

The decommissioning ceremony was both melancholy and uplifting. The crews on board *Sea Hawk*, *Shearwater*, and *Petrel* had taken remarkably good care of the cutters, their decks brightly shined and hulls gleaming, looking almost better than new. It was hard to believe that these impressive ships, all in pristine condition, were being ripped from the fleet, a bitter end to their distinguished careers. The Seventh District Commander, Rear Adm. Bill Leahy, presided over the ceremony, and in his gravelly Massachusetts growl spoke movingly of the contributions of the three cutters and the great works of their crews, not just in the drugs seized and the smugglers arrested, but also in the lives saved. The men and women of the SES crews lined the ships' rails, resplendent in their dress uniforms, not unlike a dozen years earlier when fellow cuttermen, the plank-owners, had placed the one-of-a-kind vessels into the service of the nation.

Toward the end of the ceremony, the three SES commanding officers read their orders, reporting in the finest naval tradition that the ships' galley fires were doused and the crews' rations commuted; that all was secure about the decks, the cannonballs removed and the cannons spiked; that the shafts were locked and rudders placed amidships; and that the running lights were extinguished and the chronometers run down. With more than a tinge of emotion, the three captains reported that the SES fleet, "El Tiburon," was prepared to leave active service. Then, slowly, the quartermasters, misty-eyed and somber, hauled down the ships' commissioning pennants. It was over.

The ceremony left me heavy-hearted, witnessing these special cutters torn from active duty, never again to ply Caribbean waters, with no future of high-speed chases or drug busts or migrant rescues or exotic ports-of-call. Our best days in Red Crew flashed by: the triple seizure of *Moses* and her two companions, just after midnight on Friday the 13th; nabbing a go-fast and chasing down another in the shallows of the Great Bahama Bank; plucking 265 Haitians from a becalmed sailboat and housing them on *Sea Hawk*'s forward deck, saved from certain disaster; and towing *Gulf Express* and her bulky propane barge, staving off collision and grounding, in grinding, stormy seas. In all of these cases the speed, breadth, and stability of the cutter had been vital elements of success. The decommissionings would leave a void in the fleet, taking away unique patrol boat capabilities that hadn't existed before and that wouldn't be matched again.

Yet the glum visage was countered by a grander realization. Yes, the cutters were special, but none of the operational triumphs would have happened without a superb crop of sailors, a cohesive, inventive, never-say-die team—the members of Red Crew and all of their SES Division compatriots, dedicated to their profession and devoted to their country. They truly made the difference.

The bottom line was as clear as the waters of Blossom Channel. If Coast Guard men and women could take these temperamental, thin-hulled, civilian ships and turn them into hard-charging, record-setting, life-saving cutters, they could do almost anything. America was lucky, indeed blessed, to have such a force at the ready.

Walking back from the decommissioning ceremony, I couldn't hide a smile, proud to the bursting point to have served as XO Red, and uplifted by the energy and the commitment of the Coast Guard team, great Americans all, the finely crafted words from the decommissioning pamphlet echoing in my mind:

> It is often said that a ship consists primarily of people. The spectacular career and outstanding materiel condition of the WSESs serve as testimony to the high caliber of the Coast Guard men and women who sailed in, and cared for these incredible ships. *Viva El Tiburon!*

Index

About the Author

Capt. Jim Howe, USCG (Ret.), served twenty-seven years in the U.S. Coast Guard, eleven at sea and five in command. A graduate of the U.S. Coast Guard Academy, he has earned master's degrees in government, strategic studies, and space studies. He works in the nuclear-power industry.

The Naval Institute Press is the book-publishing arm of the U.S. Naval Institute, a private, nonprofit, membership society for sea service professionals and others who share an interest in naval and maritime affairs. Established in 1873 at the U.S. Naval Academy in Annapolis, Maryland, where its offices remain today, the Naval Institute has members worldwide.

Members of the Naval Institute support the education programs of the society and receive the influential monthly magazine *Proceedings* or the colorful bimonthly magazine *Naval History* and discounts on fine nautical prints and on ship and aircraft photos. They also have access to the transcripts of the Institute's Oral History Program and get discounted admission to any of the Institute-sponsored seminars offered around the country.

The Naval Institute's book-publishing program, begun in 1898 with basic guides to naval practices, has broadened its scope to include books of more general interest. Now the Naval Institute Press publishes about seventy titles each year, ranging from how-to books on boating and navigation to battle histories, biographies, ship and aircraft guides, and novels. Institute members receive significant discounts on the Press' more than eight hundred books in print.

Full-time students are eligible for special half-price membership rates. Life memberships are also available.

For a free catalog describing Naval Institute Press books currently available, and for further information about joining the U.S. Naval Institute, please write to:

Member Services
U.S. Naval Institute
291 Wood Road
Annapolis, MD 21402-5034
Telephone: (800) 233-8764
Fax: (410) 571-1703
Web address: www.usni.org